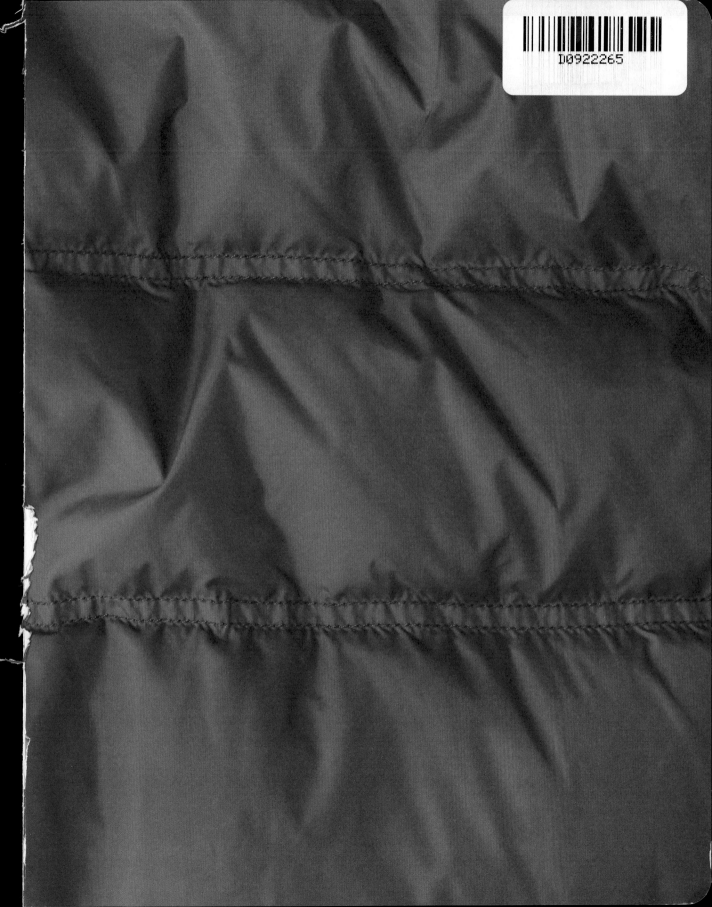

FIELD & STREAM

THE TOTAL CAMPING MANUAL

FIELD&
STREAM

THE TOTAL
CAMPING
MANUAL

T. Edward Nickens

weldonowen

WHERE TO GO

GEARING UP

ESSENTIAL SKILLS

AROUND THE CAMPFIRE

COOKING

FAMILY CAMPING

OUT THERE

AUTHOR'S NOTE

My wife and I knew we'd done at least one thing right when our daughter hollered down from her upstairs bedroom: "Mom! Am I going to potty outside or inside?" She was maybe 8 years old, and we were all packing our clothes and personal gear for a weekend away. And she needed to know: Was she sleeping in a tent, or in a hotel room? When nature called, would she trudge to a certain tree, or have access to a real toilet and even the luxury of running water in a modern, indoor bathroom? She could handle either option.

"In the woods, sweetie!" Julie sang out. "Pack for camping."

Our eyes met and we grinned. "That's just good parenting," I said.

In fact, Markie and her younger brother Jack have as much to do with this book as does my own lifelong passion for camping. the fact that they grew up loving to camp as much as Julie and I meant that our family slept under the stars frequently on summer vacations, spring breaks, and long holiday weekends. Camping is woven into our family identity. We share memories from campfires that flickered from Florida Keys beaches to Rocky Mountain lakeshores to sequestered campsites in the rainforests of the Pacific Northwest. Markie and Jack never complained when their friends went to Disney World while we flew to the middle of nowhere to drive even deeper into the back of beyond, for the pleasure of sleeping on the ground and waking to a wild world unfurling just beyond the tent door. They loved an apple pancake eaten on a plastic plate in front of a campfire. I hope they'll agree with me about the most wonderful aroma in the world: Pajamas that smell like wood smoke.

Through my work with *Field & Stream* and other magazines, I've pitched tents from the Arctic to equatorial Central America. I camp on fishing trips, hunting trips, canoeing trips, and just for the heck of camping itself.

I think there's great value in learning to be comfortable in the cold, to go a few days without an honest shower, to know how to cook a meal on a fire of your own making, to rig a tarp and tie a trucker's hitch... and to potty in the woods, if there's no bathhouse nearby.

Which is what this book is about. More and more people are discovering the astonishing possibilities that await those willing to pitch a tent, a hammock, a pop-up camper, or even an RV with satellite television and air conditioning. Public lands are a portal to some of the most inspiring landscapes on the planet, which are yours for free, or rarely more than twenty bucks a night. Private campgrounds help you tailor your experience to your level of comfort off the beaten track. Even your own backyard can host a night of unplugged adventure that just might whet your appetite for more.

Out there, you might not get turned-down sheets and a mint on your pillow. But you'll warm yourself in your own personal beam of sunshine coming through the treetops, and season each meal with views of woods and streams and mountains. And laughter.

Sound good? I sure think so. Let's start packing.

T. Edward Nickens
Editor-at-Large, *Field & Stream*

WHERE TO GO

This Land Is Your Land
Our public lands handbook

Got Your Ticket?
Reserve a campsite anywhere

Go Glam
User's guide to glamping

Where in the World?
Nail down an international campsite

Private Campgrounds
Find your perfect spot

Gotta Go
A guide to camping potties

PITCH PERFECT

It's really quite complicated. We pull up to the campground and I can sense my family shaking its collective head. Not this again. Please, Dad, don't make this a big deal. We creep along the loop road—it seems to be a rule that all campgrounds are laid out along loop roads—peering at the empty sites. Picnic tables beckon. Smoke rises from recently extinguished campfires. Tension builds, until some brave soul says, meekly: "That spot looks kind of nice. What about that one?"

I gaze out the window and smolder. Can they not see that the ground slopes just enough to roll you off your sleeping pad? Do they not realize that around the next bend might be the campsite of dreams?

This ground looks a little too rocky. This picnic table is a little too close to the tent. That tent site is at the base of a hill. If there's a flash flood, the water will pour down that gully and swamp us all.

Please, Dad.

What if the next spot has a better view? What if there's a more private campsite where late-arriving guests won't sweep our tent with their headlights? What if there's a better place to hang a clothesline? What if we just keep looking for another few minutes? And yes, I know it's almost dark.

Complicating the matter is the game-show approach to scoring the best campsite. You scout out a suitable spot—say, Loop C, #27— and place a cooler or camp chair on the picnic table to stake your claim while you drive back to the campground office to register your find. Meanwhile, everyone else is on the hunt, too, circling the campground loops with lean and hungry looks. It's a little like early pioneers racing for the good land in the old homesteading days: You have to move fast, make a quick decision, and stick to your guns.

None of which suit my style: I poke around from site to site, driving the loops time and again, mulling over the merits of C-27 versus B-13. Even when I make a decision and plant my cooler on a picnic table like the Nickens national flag, I second-guess myself. What's the rush? Let's take another loop around the campground. I'm like a dog turning around three times trying to find a place to sleep.

My wife, my kids, my pals—whoever is unlucky enough to share my company at the time—wail in anxious desperation.

Please, man, could you just choose a spot?

If only it were that simple.

001 KNOW YOUR NATIONAL PUBLIC LANDS

This land is your land–national forests, national parks, and other treasures that comprise the 640 million acres of federal land ownership in America. Camping on public lands is an American birthright. It's inexpensive and often free. It's your gateway to the wildest corners of the country as well as fun activities for even the youngest kids. If you have a tent or RV, a camp stove, a sleeping bag, and a cushy pillow, you're ready to stake your claim to a little piece of public land. And at least for a night or two, act like you own it.

BY THE NUMBERS

36.6 MILLION (14.8 MILLION HECTARES)
Number of acres of wilderness in National Forests

9,100 Miles (14,500km) of Scenic Byways in National Forests

277,000 Number of heritage sites on National Forests

13.2 MILLION ACRES (526,000 HECTARE/HA)
Largest national park–Wrangall-St. Elias National Park & Preserve in Alaska

.35 ACRE (0.14 HA) Smallest national monument–African Burial Ground National Monument in New York City

4 MILLION Average annual number of visitors at Yosemite National Park in California.

100 Average annual number of visitors at Aniakchak National Monument, Alaska

6,000 Miles (10,000 km) of National Scenic and Historic Trails on Bureau of Land Management lands

13,500 Total miles (21,600 km) of the 226 rivers in the National Wild and Scenic Rivers system

NATIONAL PARKS

There are more than 85 million (34 million ha) acres in the U.S. National Park Service system, and more than 120 units that offer camping. These locations can be as far flung as Haleakala National Park on the Hawaiian island of Maui and Alaska's Kobuk Valley National Park. Camping in a national park is a formative experience for many, kicking off a lifelong quest for adventure. The variety of camping experiences is as varied as the landscapes. Offerings vary from park to park, but national parks typically offer a mix of tent sites, RV sites, and backcountry options. For kids, ranger-led activities and tons of access to nature trails and visitor centers are a hit. And the costs for camping in national parks can be lower than many private campgrounds.

WHY CAMP HERE The fun stuff! While the wilderness experience of national parks is a huge draw, most also offer nature and history activities for every age group.

NATIONAL FORESTS

U.S. National Forests make up the biggest backyard of all: 193 million acres (78 million ha), most of which is open to camping. National forests are managed for "multiple use," so activities such as timber harvest, hunting, and off-road vehicle use are allowed on some units. While there are designated campgrounds in many national forests, many of the system's 4,300 campgrounds are dispersed through the forest unit, offering an opportunity for self-sufficiency. You won't find staffing and activities as you would at a national park. But you can find yourself in blissful solitude–and in most national forests, you won't have to pay a dime.

WHY CAMP HERE A major draw of national forests is the ability to pitch a tent outside of an established campground–along old forest roads and in primitive campsites tucked into the woods.

HALEAKALA NATIONAL PARK, HAWAII

CHUGACH NATIONAL FOREST, ALASKA

ST. MARKS WILDLIFE REFUGE, FLORIDA

CRATERS OF THE MOON NATIONAL MONUMENT, IDAHO

NATIONAL SEASHORES & LAKESHORES

If long, gorgeous, and often empty beaches sound attractive, then head for one of the 13 U.S. national seashores and lakeshores. Think of these as national parks on a beach vacation. National seashores preserve some of the wildest, most wildlife-rich coastlines in the country, so there are plenty of opportunities to watch migrating hawks and waterfowl, fish for dinner, swim, and watch the sun set–or rise–from your campsite. Run by the National Park Service, national seashores and lakeshores offer some ranger-led activities, but the main draw is to be out there where the water meets the sky.

WHY CAMP HERE In a word, the beach. Whether it's a sandy stretch of the Atlantic or a sandstone cliff towering above Lake Superior, waking up as close to the water as possible is the goal.

NATIONAL MONUMENTS

While national parks are created by the U.S. Congress, national monuments can be created by the president to preserve important natural and cultural sites. In fact, many beloved national parks started out as national monuments, including Grand Canyon National Park and Olympic National Park. National monuments can be managed by the U.S. Forest Service, U.S. Fish and Wildlife Service, or U.S. Bureau of Land Management, among others, so you'll need to check with each agency for camping opportunities and regulations.

WHY CAMP HERE Some of these national monuments are gigantic. If you want to lose yourself in empty landscapes, check out large national monuments such as Craters of the Moon in Idaho.

BLM LANDS

Many people who don't live in the American West have never heard of the U.S. Bureau of Land Management, but this federal agency manages 245 million acres (99 million ha) of mostly western U.S. public lands for outdoor recreation, livestock grazing, mineral development, and energy production. That's almost as much land as there is in national parks and national forests combined. There are lots of developed campgrounds on BLM land, so there's opportunity for RVers and tent campers alike. But the biggest draw to most BLM properties is the chance to strike out into the middle of the American West and make camp far from the nearest human.

WHY CAMP HERE Dispersed camping on most BLM properties is free of charge.

NATIONAL WILDLIFE REFUGES

These pristine lands are set aside by the U.S. Fish and Wildlife Service for their value to wildlife and native fish, so camping opportunities can be limited. If you're a serious birder or wildlife watcher, though, scoring a campsite at a refuge is definitely worth the research.

WHY CAMP HERE Possibly your best chance for solitude on public lands. At St. Marks National Wildlife Refuge in Florida, primitive campsites are 8 miles (13km) apart. At Montana's Red Rocks Lakes National Wildlife Refuge, there are only two primitive campgrounds on the entire 65,810 acres (26,600 ha).

NATIONAL WILD & SCENIC RIVERS

Created in 1968, the National Wild and Scenic Rivers System preserves free-flowing rivers with outstanding natural, cultural, and recreational values. The public lands and waters are administered most often by the U.S. National Park Service or the Bureau of Land Management, but some wild and scenic rivers have been absorbed into state park systems.

WHY CAMP HERE Some of the best guided river trips in the country take place on National Wild and Scenic Rivers, so book a trip with an outfitter for a stress-free camping experience.

002 FACTOR IN STATE PARKS

On June 30, 1864, President Abraham Lincoln signed the Yosemite Valley Grant Act, which gave the state of California the Yosemite Valley and nearby Mariposa Big Tree Grove. Lincoln gave the land to the state "upon the express conditions that the premises shall be held for public use, resort, and recreation." State parks have opened the door to nature and the joys of camping to countless millions since.

Don't overlook state parks when settling in on a camping site. There are more than 6,700 state park units in the U.S., and with more than 800 million visitors they actually see more use than national parks.

FUN FACTOR Many state parks offer far more amenities and services than national parks. If you're looking for swimming pools, golf courses, or even services such as laundromats, a state park might be the answer.

EASY ACCESS While national parks and national forests tend to be off the beaten path, you can find many state parks near major transportation routes. State parks can be fabulous destinations for longer stays, but they're often also a great choice for a quick overnight while you're headed elsewhere.

LOW COST Many state parks offer free entry, and for those that do charge for access, the fee is typically very low. You'll still likely have to pay for a campsite, but state parks are often a less expensive option than national parks.

003 GO LOCAL

Many counties, towns, cities, and other municipal entities offer great camping options. At James Island County Park, near Charleston, South Carolina, for example there are 159 campsites–plus freshwater lakes, fishing piers, and even places where you can catch crabs and cast for dinner in gorgeous tidal creeks. At Guajome County Park near Oceanside, California, there are tons of hiking trails and the campground is just an hour-and-a-half drive to Disneyland. St. Croix Bluffs Regional Park in Minnesota sprawls across more than a half-mile of shoreline. To find a great local public campground, search for the parks and recreation departments of any county or city. And don't forget state forests and wildlife management areas.

004 LOCK DOWN YOUR CAMPSITE

Two online reservation systems cover the vast majority of public lands campsites in the United States, be they operated by the federal government, states, counties, or cities. They differ by the types of campgrounds they include and the tools they offer users. It's best to familiarize yourself with both.

FEDERAL ISSUE Most federal lands campsites, including those in national parks and national forests, are reserved through the website recreation.gov or its associated app. You can search for sites based on location and time, but also narrow your options based on activities. Want to flyfish for trout? Plan an overnight hunting trip? Go on an awesome ranger-led canoe float? Recreation.gov has the tools.

STATES AND LOCALS For the vast majority of campsites at state parks and local government properties, go to reserveamerica.com or the ReserveAmerica app. It's a well-designed experience. You can plug in search values such as location, dates, and site type—tent or RV, full hookups, and other amenities. And future planning is even easier if you create an account so you can save favorite campsites while you search. You'll search, reserve, and pay at one single online site.

005 KNOW WHEN TO GO PRIVATE

Large chain campgrounds such as KOA (Kampgrounds of America) and Yogi Bear's Jellystone Park can be found in many popular camping areas. They range widely in amenities and amount of privacy. Private campgrounds might not offer quick access to wild country, but here are three times when a private campground could be a perfect fit.

THE FUN STUFF For families with younger children–or campers who need a break from wild places–private campgrounds can offer far more amenities and activities than public-land campgrounds. Playgrounds, swimming pools, mini-golf, laundry facilities, and even hot tubs and spas can be found at some private campgrounds. Do your research.

HITTING THE TOWN Most public campgrounds are located far from cities and towns. If you're looking for access to shopping, in-town dining, and other more urban activities, a private campground is likely your best bet.

ON THE ROAD Many private campgrounds are located fairly close to highways and roads. That makes them a great option for when you simply need a place to crash for the night while you're on a road trip.

006 NAVIGATE ONLINE RESERVATIONS

Camping's growing popularity can make it tough to land a campsite at popular campgrounds and destinations, and online reservation systems only increase the competition. But if you know how to work the system, you'll improve your chances of landing a primo site.

MAKE A DATE Campgrounds vary widely in terms of how far ahead you can make a reservation. Some allow reservations a year in advance, others six months out, and others considerably less. Once you zero in on a campground of choice and the dates you want to go, make a note on your personal calendar to remind you to make the reservation. And bear in mind that you might have only minutes– or seconds!–to seal the deal.

SITE BY SITE It's amazing how much information is available online about campgrounds and even specific campsites. You can find photographs of individual sites and even camper reviews on the pros and cons of many campgrounds and campsites. Have a prioritized list ready to go.

GO TEAM GO Enlist a pal to work together, and go online at the same time, with a shared list of your top campsite picks. It's also helpful to have a third–or fourth–companion call in on the reservation phone line to increase your chances.

WORK THE WEB A half-hour before your campground will open for reservations, have your preferred campsite ready on your browser. Open multiple tabs for individual campsites, and have them all lined up for the final countdown.

DON'T DESPAIR If you don't score your desired campground, keep checking for cancellations, which are common. Check back in on the last day possible to cancel without penalty, as lots of sites could open that day.

007 SCORE A PRIVATE-LANDS CAMPSITE

A growing number of websites and mobile apps help connect travelers to private landowners and allow users to research and book campsites on privately owned farms, ranches, forest tracts, and more. Their community-based vibe encourages information sharing, and they've opened up tens of thousands of new campsites in just a few short years.

HIPCAMP (hipcamp.com) Think of Hipcamp as the Airbnb of camping. While the website lists nearly a half-million campsites on U.S. public lands, more than 60 percent of the U.S. land base is privately owned, and Hipcamp partners with private landowners for a new twist on camping. Campsites might be as basic as a flat place to pitch a tent on a private farm or as memorable as a shady spot in a vineyard grove. There are also glamping-style treehouses and retro trailers, plus add-on activities such as foraging trips and pick-your-own fruit harvests.

TENTRR (tentrr.com) This private network of campsites offers a couple of options. Tentrr Signature campsites are sleek, accessible, ready-to-go experiences that include all the gear you need–tents on wooden platforms, beds and bedding, outdoor furniture, and even sun showers. Tentrr BackCountry sites offer access to more remote private lands in which the camper brings all equipment and supplies.

THE DYRT (thedyrt.com) Its founder describes the Dyrt as the Yelp of camping. It lists nearly 50,000 public and private campgrounds, including RV campgrounds. Its best features are the user reviews–more than a million of them–and photographs. It's a great website to use when you're headed to an unknown area or want to spread your wings locally and try a new spot.

HOMECAMPER (homecamper.com) An international take on the phenomenon, HomeCamper lists more than 30,000 privately owned campsites in 42 countries. Catering to campers, bikepackers, backpackers, and travelers in vans and RVs, HomeCamper accents affordable stays around the world.

008 CATCH A HAWK MIGRATION

Most birds migrate under cover of darkness, but hawks, falcons, and eagles put on a daytime show. These birds of prey rely on rising air to carry them high above the earth, then they lock their wings and glide as far as they can before hitching another ride skyward. Each autumn, broad-winged hawks pour down from the north, using centuries-old migration corridors that skirt the Atlantic, Pacific, and Gulf coasts, and along the Rocky Mountains and Appalachians. They're followed by Swainson's hawks and golden eagles, kestrels, merlins, falcons, and kites. On some days in the Blue Ridge Mountains of Virginia, several hundred migrating raptors can be seen. In the Goshute Mountains of Nevada, or along the Texas Gulf coast, the figures run into the tens of thousands. At Veracruz, Mexico, the famed "River of Raptors" flows through a pinch-point of mountains and sea. In an average year, volunteer "hawkwatch" counters tally 3 million raptors migrating through the region.

Across the country there are some 400 established "hawkwatch" sites where scientists and volunteers regularly count the skies for migrating hawks. Check out the Hawk Migration Association of America, and plan a camping trip near a hawkwatch site. Or set up along any ridge or promontory, dial in binoculars, wait for the sun to heat up the air, and watch the show.

009 KNOW THE LINGO: GLAMPING

Don't want to make your own fire? Don't want to sleep on the ground? Don't want to poop in a latrine? Don't want to give up your wine-and-cheese approach to leisure? With glamping, you don't have to. A portmanteau mashup of the words "glamour" and "camping," glamping has taken the outdoor recreation world by a pillow-top storm. It's an approach to camping that dials up the luxury of accommodations, cuisine, and activities. Glamping operators offer luxury options such as African safari-style tents, rustic cabins, massage therapists, white-linen dinners, and nearly white-glove service. You can choose a yurt, treehouse, tipi–even a night in a cave. But even glamping's deep-fried luxury isn't a one-size-fits-all experience. Here are three things to consider when choosing a glamping vacation.

BASICS VS BONKERS For many, glamping is simply a way of getting off the ground–dialing up the comfort of camping but still staying connected and involved in the experiences of fire building, campfire cooking, and nature appreciation. When booking a glamping trip, make sure you understand how involved–or not–you'll be in the authentic aspects of camp chores and skills.

LEVEL OF INTIMACY The popularity of glamping has led many operators to serve up increasingly intimate experiences. Some destinations have only a handful of luxury tents and leave you to find your own adventure, while others offer concierge-level services and over-the-top amenities.

GLAMPER BEWARE Lots of operators are jumping on the glamping bandwagon, so watch out for companies that try to pass off a gussied-up RV or a makeshift cabin as a true glamping experience. There are tons of websites where online reviews help identify less-than-ideal experiences. Do your research.

LOG ON FOR LUXURY Finding and reserving glamping locations and travel operators has spawned a robust industry of websites through which you can search for and reserve campsites, amenities, and full-blown vacation experiences. Here are some of the leading online companies:

GLAMPING.COM This website lists nearly 1,000 locations around the world, including everything from wild, open spaces to private rooftop terraces in Chicago, Beverly Hills, and Denver.

GLAMPINGHUB.COM With offices in Denver and Seville, Spain, (the company started in Spain) this luxury camping website is a great resource for both U.S. and international travel. Lodging options include things like boutique hotels, though, so be careful to weed out the non-camping options if that's not what you're looking for.

UNDERCANVAS.COM Gorgeous safari-inspired tents in stunning natural locations–often near national parks–are on the menu at UnderCanvas. Each community of tents can include amenities such as café-style kitchens, yoga classes, and daily housekeeping.

AUTOCAMP.COM The company might have a limited number of locations–Yosemite and the Russian River Valley in California, and Cape Cod, Massachusetts–but it makes up for that with the incredible curated experiences it offers. Sailing on historic schooners, flyfishing, culinary tours, and more, all while lodging in Airstream travel trailers or classic wall tents.

READYCAMP.CO.UK ReadyCamp is Britain's largest glamping network, with nearly 50 locations scattered from southwestern England to Scotland. The floored safari tents include beds with mattresses, dining tables and full kitchens. Many ReadyCamp locations are near top zoos and family attractions.

010 GLAMP ON EVERY CONTINENT

The glamping phenomenon is world-wide. In fact, some of the oldest and most respected glamping destinations are in some of the world's most far-flung places.

NORTH AMERICA

SÉPAQ READY-TO-CAMP Sépaq administers recreation across a vast swath of wild Quebec, where its French-inspired Huttopia tents are a hit. You'll get a high-ceilinged canvas tent on a wooden platform with beds, lighting, a small refrigerator, and stove. And it's all located near national parks, stunning fjords, remote rivers, and wild coastlines.

EUROPE

HIDDEN VALLEY ANDALUCÍA Traditional bell tents are scattered through an olive grove near the Caminito del Rey walking path and the wild landscapes of Málaga, Spain. The glamping resort is only 45 minutes from the international airport in Málaga and even closer to the train station in Alora.

ASIA

4 RIVERS FLOATING LODGE Talk about an immersive experience: These luxury tents are each sited on a floating pontoon in Cambodia's Tatai River. Surrounded by the rainforested Cardamon Mountains, you'll relax in furniture handmade from local water hyacinth and listen to monkeys and birds as you try to talk yourself into swapping a hammock for a kayak.

AFRICA

SINGITA GRUMETI Custom-designed tented suites can follow the Great Migration of a million wildebeest across the 350,000-acre (142,000 million ha) Serengeti Mara ecosystem. Open-fire cooking and billowy canvas help retain the feel of a wilderness safari, while a full staff—private field guides, chef, and host—ensure the pamper meter stays in the red zone.

SOUTH AMERICA

GALAPAGOS SAFARI CAMP On the edge of the Galapagos National Park, this tented resort follows a credo of "appropriate luxury." Given the region's fragile nature, rainwater is collected and tents are powered mostly by the sun. The camp is nestled in the forested rim of an ancient volcano, a place so carefully developed that the island's signature giant tortoises ramble by for a visit.

ANTARCTICA

WHITE DESERT Jet to the bottom of the world in a private Gulfstream—all carbon offset with accredited projects—and bunk down in heated sleeping pods with access to other reception, lounge, library, and dining areas. Cocktails and gourmet meals will compete with expeditions to see emperor penguins and notch a visit to the South Pole. Heads up: Start saving your pennies now.

AUSTRALIA

PAPERBARK CAMP If roughing it with bamboo-cotton linens, solar lighting, and a treetop restaurant sounds like your idea of getting back to nature, put Australia's pioneering Paperbark Camp on Jarvis Bay on the bucket list. You'll snooze in elevated canvas safari tents nestled under eucalyptus and paperbark trees and watch for kangaroos from the private showers. Stunning white sand beaches, coastal bush wilderness, and quick and easy access to three national parks seal the deal.

CAMINITO DEL REY, SPAIN

SINGITA GRUMETI, TANZANIA

KNOW THE LINGO: CAMPING STYLES

There's more than one way to fall asleep beneath the stars. Here are the four basic approaches for putting some wild in your life.

CAR CAMPING

MODUS OPERANDI: You pull your vehicle to within steps of your home away from home and pull out everything you could possibly need for maximum happiness. Living out of your car never felt so good.

WHY IT'S AWESOME: If it fits in your vehicle, bring it.

WHY IT'S MEH: Unpacking all that junk.

CAN'T LIVE WITHOUT: Seriously comfy camp chair.

BACKPACKING

MODUS OPERANDI: It's all going with you–every step of the way. Whether you're on the trail for a quick overnighter or three months at a stretch, backpacking requires a minimalist approach.

WHY IT'S AWESOME: An exhilarating sense of self-sufficiency.

WHY IT'S MEH: The novelty of freeze-dried food wears off after 1.5 meals.

CAN'T LIVE WITHOUT: Trekking poles.

RV CAMPING

MODUS OPERANDI: Whether it's a small pop-up camper for four or a tricked-out megabus suitable for a rock star's concert tour, recreational vehicles can be packed with all the comforts of home.

WHY IT'S AWESOME: Meeting tons of other happy campers.

WHY IT'S MEH: The sound of generators running all night long.

CAN'T LIVE WITHOUT: Flamingo string lights.

DISPERSED CAMPING

MODUS OPERANDI: Car camping on public lands but away from designated campgrounds dials up the solitude and the access to adventure. It's like backpacking–with your vehicle trunk.

WHY IT'S AWESOME: Quick access to fishing spots and hiking trails.

WHY IT'S MEH: Pooping in the woods.

CAN'T LIVE WITHOUT: The fattest sleeping pad money can buy.

012 CALCULATE YOUR HIKING PACE

Day hiking just may be the top camping activity, whether the route is an easy stroll along a nature trail or an arduous loop along a high-elevation ridgeline. Either way, the question is always, "How long will this hike take?" The Scottish mountaineer William W. Naismith came up with the accepted formula–called "Naismith's Rule"–in 1892.

Allow one hour for every 3 miles (5 km) of forward movement, plus one more hour for every 2,000 feet (600 m) of ascent. Add 10 minutes of time for every 1,000 feet (300 m) of steep downhill and subtract 10 minutes for every 1,000 feet (300 m) of gentle descent.

This is for a hiker in average physical condition moving at a moderate pace on fairly level ground. If you're traveling in a group, you'll need to calculate the time required based on the slowest person on the trail.

013 GET OUTTA TOWN FAST

One of the most common complaints among campers is how much time and energy it takes to pack up for even a short trip, but organization wins the day. Buy several large plastic storage bins and designate them for the different categories of gear. In one or two bins, store all sleeping bags and pads, tents, and tarps. In others, pack up stoves and kitchen gear, lanterns, hatchets, and other camp tools. Store the bins in your basement or garage so that all you have to do is load them into your vehicle when it's time to go. At camp, the empty bins serve as great dirty laundry hampers and dry storage for firewood until it's time to pack up and head home.

114 KNOW BEFORE YOU GO

You've got your gear and the car's packed, but before you hit the road, whether you're off to a state park an hour away or embarking on a two-week camping road trip, get the answers to these 5 questions.

WHAT IS PROVIDED AT THE CAMPSITE?   At developed campgrounds, you might find everything from hot showers to Wi-Fi. At others, you might not have a picnic table, fire ring, or tent pad.

CAN I BUILD A FIRE?   If so, find out if a fire permit is required, and if you have to build a fire in an established firepit. You'll also want to know about the availability of firewood and any regulations on bringing firewood from another location.

IS THERE POTABLE WATER AVAILABLE?   Most developed campsites have easy access to water, although you might have to haul it several hundred feet from the nearest source.

WHAT ARE THE ROAD CONDITIONS?   Camping often takes place far from a paved road, so make sure you know about road closures due to fires and floods, and any rough roads that would require a high clearance or four-wheel-drive vehicle.

SHOULD I BRING MY PET?   It's a two-part question. First, are pets allowed at your destination? And second, are you prepared to take care of your pooch 24/7 in the tent, on the trail, and everywhere in between?

015 PRACTICE FOR PERFECTION

Got your campsite reserved? Totally stoked for your first camping experience? Then it's time for a practice session. You don't want to learn how to put up your tent when the sun is going down and the mosquitoes are coming. And everyone will be happier if you figured out how to work the camp stove and lantern before it's time to start dinner. A backyard trial run–or two–will pay big dividends.

HOME SWEET TENT At a minimum you'll want to set up and break down your tent a couple times before you're actually in the woods. Tent pole arrangements can be confusing, and there's nothing more embarrassing than having to untangle poles and guylines while being read the instructions by impatient family members.

GET YOUR GRUB ON Cook a few meals on your cook stove to familiarize yourself with the mechanics. Some models simmer like a high-end restaurant range, while others flicker out when you try to dial down the heat. And nearly all camp stoves have smaller burners than your home stove, so you'll need practice to avoid hotspots.

OVERNIGHT SUCCESS If you plan on bringing younger kids or pets on their first camping trip, you'll definitely want to spend a night or two with them in the backyard. That will help children get used to a tent's dark interiors and all the normal sounds of the outdoors at night. Many pets need a little time to feel comfortable bunking down in a tent or camper, too.

016 PICK YOUR POTTY

You might not be able to choose *when* you go, but *where* you go is a different matter. Here are the most common camping options when nature calls–in that special way.

BATHHOUSE A full-service bathhouse with hot showers, flush toilets, and running water in the sinks is a luxury most commonly found in large public and private campgrounds.

COMPOSTING TOILETS You do your business and then add a double handful of leaves to jump-start the natural decomposition process. It's a bit of a pungent affair, but you know you're doing your part to protect the ecosystem.

PORTA–POTTIES A common solution in some larger campgrounds, the Johnny-on-the-spot shows up in more pristine areas where human waste has to be collected and carted away.

PORTABLE CAMP TOILETS Often made of plastic, a portable camp commode can be as basic as a 5-gallon (19-L) bucket with a seat or as elaborate as a fully enclosed, freestanding loo.

WAG BAGS Basically a doggie bag for humans, these lightweight, puncture-resistant (cross your fingers), resealable bags often contain a powder that solidifies your business for easy transport.

GROOVER A toilet used on many river trips, the groover holds all the goods and can be moved from campsite to campsite. The beloved groover can be a 20mm ammo can, a.k.a. "rocket box," or a manufactured–and more user-friendly–modern version.

BUMPER DUMPER Hitch your pooping comfort to the receiver of a vehicle trailer hitch with these sturdy enclosed portable toilets.

COMPOSTING TOILET

GROOVER

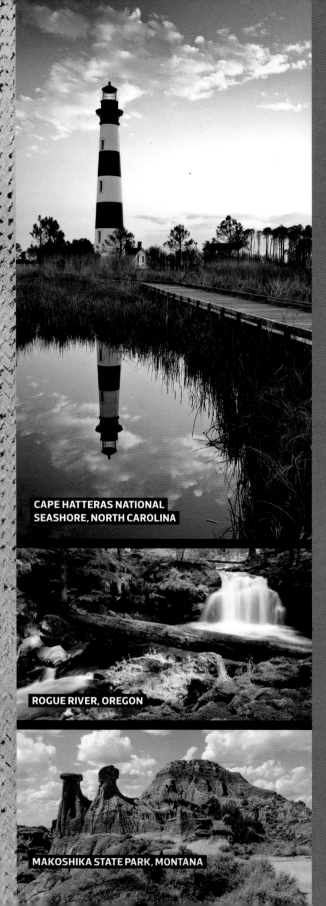

CAPE HATTERAS NATIONAL SEASHORE, NORTH CAROLINA

ROGUE RIVER, OREGON

MAKOSHIKA STATE PARK, MONTANA

017 FAMILY CAMPING

1 CAPE HATTERAS NATIONAL SEASHORE, NORTH CAROLINA Along the famed Outer Banks you are literally on the edge of the continent. It's wild beach, but there are just enough ice cream shacks and surf shops in the smattering of small villages such as Hatteras, Buxton, and Avon.

2 ROGUE RIVER, OREGON One of the greatest river-rafting destinations for families, the Rogue features thrills aplenty, but not the kind of crazy whitewater that will keep you up at night. You can leap from tall cliffs, feast on wild blueberries, and snooze on sweet sandy beaches. Tons of reputable whitewater outfitters work the water.

3 MAKOSHIKA STATE PARK, MONTANA Big Sky Country's largest state park features gorgeous badlands studded with pine and juniper, plus tons of displays on dinosaurs, fossils, and geology.

4 RATCLIFF LAKE RECREATION AREA, TEXAS If your family is looking for a break from Texas heat, this oasis in Davy Crockett National Forest has a pine-shaded lake for great swimming and camping. Much of the area's visitor facilities were built in the 1930s by the Civilian Conservation Corps, which makes for a great side helping of history for young campers.

5 BANFF NATIONAL PARK, ALBERTA One of the crown jewels of Parks Canada, Banff is a mashup wonderland–incredible wildlife viewing opportunities are minutes away from an Alps-like mountain village, plus glacial lakes, world-class family-friendly biking, and 14 different campgrounds.

018 TOP 5 PICKS FOR SOLITUDE

1 ARCTIC NATIONAL WILDLIFE REFUGE, ALASKA
Alaska's Coastal Plain is a vast sweep of tundra, glacial rivers, jagged mountains, and exquisite remoteness. Its nearly 20 million acres (8.1 million ha) contain the largest designated wilderness system in the U.S. Travel to, and through, ANWR is difficult...and unforgettable.

2 BAXTER STATE PARK, MAINE Talk about big woods. The park's 200,000 acres (81,000 ha) are trellised with 220 miles (354 km) of foot trails and uncountable mountain coves, creeks, and summits you can have all to yourself. That is, if you don't mind sharing them with moose, bear, huge white-tailed deer, gorgeous lynx, and 857 species of plants.

3 CARSON NATIONAL FOREST, NEW MEXICO A lush, forested swath of canyons and mountains—including the soaring 13,000-foot (3,900 m) Wheeler Peak—this 1.5-million-acre (0.61 million ha) getaway rarely sees the crowds associated with other western landscapes.

4 VOYAGEURS NATIONAL PARK, MINNESOTA If you'd rather share your wilderness view with a loon than a crowd of campers, this less-visited gem is for you. Its more than 220 campsites are mostly limited to water access, so with a paddle and a few days of adventure you might stake a temporary claim to your very own island.

5 ABSAROKA–BEARTOOTH WILDERNESS, MONTANA Not for the faint of heart or the weak of knee, this 944,000-acre (382,000 ha) wilderness touches Yellowstone National Park and three national forests, and overlaps two different mountain ranges. There are no vehicles allowed, so gaining access to solitude comes compliments of Pat and Charlie.

ARCTIC NATIONAL WILDLIFE REFUGE, ALASKA

BAXTER STATE PARK, MAINE

VOYAGEURS NATIONAL PARK, MINNESOTA

ABSAROKA–BEARTOOTH WILDERNESS, MONTANA

TOP 5 PICKS FOR
019 A WATERFRONT VIEW

1 ACADIA NATIONAL PARK, MAINE With two campgrounds on Mount Desert Island, one on the Schoodic Peninsula, and five lean-to shelters on Isle au Haut, you can pick your level of relative comfort. But there are lots of private campgrounds nearby, so don't get discouraged if online reservation systems block you out of the park proper.

2 HARRIS BEACH STATE PARK, OREGON No other place on the planet can outdo the Pacific Northwest for jaw-dropping coastal scenery, and this state park in southern Oregon has everything from smooth sandy beaches to rocky headlands sparkling with tidal pools.

3 CAYO COSTA STATE PARK, FLORIDA With no automobile access, you'll have to boat–or hitch a helicopter ride–to this pristine oasis amidst the hubbub of Captiva Island. Plan early–there are only 30 very popular tent sites for overnight campers.

4 PETOSKEY STATE PARK, MICHIGAN If you like your waterfront view to be framed with the bow of a canoe or kayak, this paddler's paradise is the spot. There is plenty of easy flatwater paddling on Round Lake and Little Traverse Bay, and you can dial up the adrenaline on the nearby whitewater runs of Bear River.

5 SAN ELIJO STATE BEACH, CALIFORNIA You might think twice if you're afraid of heights. Otherwise, put this towering blufftop campground on your list. Nearly 160 campsites cling to rocky cliffs or nestle near sandy beaches about 40 miles (64 km) north of San Diego. Bring your surfboard.

ACADIA NATIONAL PARK, MAINE

BOUNDARY WATERS CANOE AREA WILDERNESS, MINNESOTA

EVERGLADES NATIONAL PARK, FLORIDA

020 TOP 5 PICKS FOR FISHING

1 SIERRA NEVADA MOUNTAINS, CALIFORNIA Four national forests blanket several million acres of Northern California, and there's a wealth of lakeside campgrounds and more remote roadside pullovers for car camping. You'll find brown, golden, rainbow, and brook trout, plus kokanee salmon, steelhead, and even good catfish populations.

2 BOUNDARY WATERS CANOE AREA WILDERNESS, MINNESOTA The million-acre Boundary Waters may be America's best-known wilderness paddling region, but there's plenty of hoofing it for non-paddlers. Plenty of walleye and pike for a trail dinner on the routes around Snowbank Lake or the Angleworm Trail.

3 EVERGLADES NATIONAL PARK, FLORIDA This waterworld of mangrove forests, salty bays, and miles of roadside canals has enough to make both beginner and expert anglers happy. There are peacock bass in the quieter waters, snook and redfish in the mangroves, and world-class tarpon all around.

4 BULL SHOALS–WHITE RIVER STATE PARK, ARKANSAS With easy access to one of the most famous trout streams in the U.S., the recently expanded campground is a hit for families with powerboats or canoes. The marina at Bull Shoals Lake also offers boat rentals and fishing guides.

5 GEORGE WASHINGTON & JEFFERSON NATIONAL FORESTS, VIRGINIA Eight major rivers are born in this picturesque region, which includes the crest of the Appalachian Mountains for nearly the entire length of Virginia. Trout fishing is sublime, with more than 60 percent of the state's native brook trout populations here.

021

TOP 5 PICKS FOR

HIP CAMPING TOWNS

1 **CANYON RIMS RECREATION AREA, UTAH** It might be that more people come to this dramatic part of the country to hang out in Moab than visit Canyon Rims and the nearby Arches and Canyonlands national parks, but a mountain biker and off-roader vibe infuse the popular jumping-off spot.

2 **PISGAH NATIONAL FOREST, NORTH CAROLINA** The highest peaks east of the Rocky Mountains lie at the feet of uber-cool Asheville. The sprawling downtown is chockful of breweries, local artisans in stores and out on the street, and fabulous restaurants. The stunning Biltmore House mansion is a short drive away.

3 **PEDERNALES FALLS STATE PARK, TEXAS** Just 42 miles (67 km) west of Austin, this giant 5,200-acre (2,100 ha) park includes 5 miles (8 km) of the the Pedernales River, plus tons of both developed and backcountry campsites.

4 **ADIRONDACK PARK, NEW YORK** The massive 6.1-million-acre (2.5-million-ha) park is larger than Yellowstone and Yosemite combined, and actually encompasses more than 100 towns and villages, from the Olympics-worthy Lake Placid to the historic Ticonderoga.

5 **FRED HENNE TERRITORIAL PARK, NORTHWEST TERRITORIES** One of the world's great destinations for viewing northern lights, this Far North Canada park is also close to the territorial capital of Yellowknife. On the shore of Great Slave Lake, there are museums, historic cafes and bars, and opportunities to charter bush and float planes for flights to distant campsites.

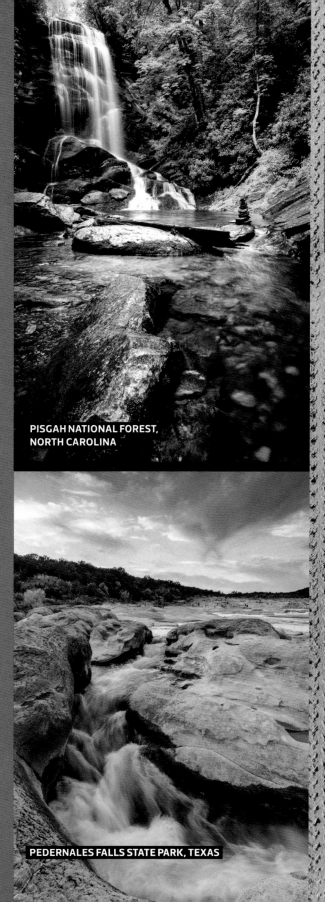

PISGAH NATIONAL FOREST, NORTH CAROLINA

PEDERNALES FALLS STATE PARK, TEXAS

022 NOD OFF AT A DREAMY ISLAND CAMPSITE

No roads, no cars, no t-shirt shops, no hot dog stands, no tacky souvenir shacks. And if you're really lucky, no cellphone service. The best island campsites are a respite from all the hullabaloo that lies somewhere beyond the water's edge. You've left it all behind, paddle stroke by paddle stroke, to be voluntarily marooned. Your piece of paradise could be in a lake or river, deep in the North Woods, or tucked into a saltwater marsh where the sounds of surf lull you to sleep at night. Watch the stars move through treetops. Listen to water. Follow a deer's tracks by the shore. Camping on an island doesn't feel like being stuck in the middle of nowhere. It feels like you've cut yourself free from the ties that bind the camper's spirit.

023 HEAD FOR THESE
SOUTHEASTERN GEMS

The highest mountains in eastern America, the wildest beaches, the biggest swamps–the Southeast has it all when it comes to family camping. Surf rods or trout rods? Canoe or kayak or bass boat? You want alpine views or beach sunsets? Just pick a spot and start packing.

SPRING FLING Florida boasts of more than two dozen first-order freshwater springs that bubble to the surface to form fabulous swimming holes and clearwater rivers. Many anchor state or federal parks with great family camping, and many are close enough to attractions like Orlando and the Florida beaches for a do-it-all vacation. A family favorite is Alexander Springs in the Ocala National Forest, with large wooded campsites, a sweet sand beach by the spring, and great access to easy canoeing along a wildlife-rich river.

HIGH VISTAS It's a little bit of Switzerland in the high country of Virginia. At Grayson Highlands State Park, expansive rolling alpine meadows crown some of the tallest peaks in the state. These are the "balds" of the Southern Appalachians–ancient grasslands where you can see for miles, hike among wild ponies, and do your best not to hum "The Sound of Music" for days on end. The state park campground provides easy access in a gorgeous forested setting.

WATER WORLD It doesn't get much more Southern than the scenery along the Santee Lakes of South Carolina. Two major lakes on the Santee and Cooper Rivers–Marion and Moultrie–have more than 450 miles (720 km) of shoreline studded with cypress trees and are blanketed with wide, sandy beaches. Tons of family campers show up with boats in tow.

GATOR COUNTRY At Georgia's Stephen C. Foster State Park, you actually camp inside the Okefenokee National Wildlife Refuge, which sprawls across 400,000 acres (162,000 ha) of cypress swamp and freshwater ponds, plus miles of the famed Suwannee River. This is a wildlife lover's dream–a remote wilderness park with alligators, wood storks, black bears, and endangered woodpeckers.

ALEXANDER SPRINGS, OCALA NATIONAL FOREST, FLORIDA

GRAYSON HIGHLANDS STATE PARK, VIRGINIA

SANTEE LAKES,
SOUTH CAROLINA

OKEFENOKEE NATIONAL
WILDLIFE REFUGE, GEORGIA

024 HEAD FOR THESE DESERT WONDERS

Sand, sky, and more stars than you can count–desert camping definitely has its charms. And while it can certainly be hot, visit in the spring and fall and you'll be surprised at how comfortable–and sometimes cold–a desert night can be. Deserts offer enormous views, deep canyons, and a chance to hike among dinosaur fossils, making them a favorite of both families and adventure seekers.

FOSSIL MANIA At 600,000 (242,000 ha) wild acres, Anza-Borrego Desert State Park is California's largest state park. You'll find more than 110 miles (176 km) of hiking trails that wind through crazy geology, with fossils more than 5 million years old. Kids love the more than 100 giant metal animal sculptures the rise out of earth.

LOOK UP Big Bend Ranch State Park is a massive, 275,000-acre (111,000 ha) chunk of the Chihuahuan Desert in Texas. It's accessed by 238 miles (383 km) of hiking, biking, and horse trails, and another 70 miles (112 km) of four-wheel-drive roads. But the best thing to do at Big Bend State Park is stretch out on your back and revel in the star show. An International Dark Sky Park, Big Bend Ranch offers perhaps the best night views in the country.

GETTING SANDY The famed "singing dunes" of Killpecker Sand Dunes include a 55-mile-long (88-km) living sand dune located in one the most remote regions of Wyoming. Run by the Bureau of Land Management, both developed and primitive campgrounds are nearby.

SPOOKY STONES At Utah's Goblin Valley State Park, soft sandstone has eroded into a landscape studded with towering, surreal shapes. It's a maze-like atmosphere where kids love to explore along the nooks and gnome-like stone formations.

ANCIENT SPACES Studded with petrified trees and home to 2,000-year-old petroglyphs, Nevada's Valley of Fire State Park is an accessible desert destination. There are tons of trails that wind under limestone cliffs, and lots of shady campsites.

VALLEY OF FIRE STATE PARK, NEVADA

GOBLIN VALLEY STATE PARK, UTAH

BIG BEND RANCH STATE PARK, TEXAS

ANZA-BORREGO DESERT
STATE PARK, CALIFORNIA

025 HEAD FOR THESE APPALACHIAN HOTSPOTS

The Appalachian Mountains reach from Alabama all the way to Newfoundland and consist of rolling, weathered mountain ridges up to 480 million years old. There are lonely stretches of vast wilderness and boisterous tourist towns. You can cast to trout in quiet mountain waters or rock-and-roll down breathtaking rapids in kayaks and rafts. One thing remains constant: Sitting by a campfire in these ancient landscapes will take you back to a slower, more relaxing time.

TOUCH THE SKY North Carolina's Black Mountain range is capped by Mount Mitchell, the highest peak east of the Mississippi. Named for the dark cloak of spruce and fir in the high elevations, the Blacks are latticed with some of the finest hiking trails and fishing streams in North Carolina. Mount Mitchell State Park has plenty of amenities for tent campers and RVers alike.

WATERFALL WONDER Situated around the 7,500-acre (3,000-ha) Lake Jocassee, Devils Fork State Park in South Carolina is a surprising mix of soaring mountains, tumbling rivers, and jaw-droppingly gorgeous alpine lakes. Some of its waterfalls and perhaps the best trout fishing in South Carolina are accessible only by boat.

RIDGETOP GLORY You'd be hard-pressed to design a more family-friendly mountain park than Shenandoah National Park, which protects the mountain ridges of a 105-mile-long (168-km) swath of the Appalachians. Skyline Drive is a scenic byway that bisects the park's entire length, making it a snap to strike out for day hikes with only moderate elevation change. The trout fishing here is some of the best in the state.

GOING WILD Tucked into the 830,000-acre Monongahela National Forest, the Dolly Sods region is a weird, treeless, rocky expanse in the otherwise heavily wooded wilderness. Formed when massive clearcutting leveled the forests and the soils dried out and burned, Dolly Sods provides soaring vistas of the Allegheny Mountains. You can backpack in or pitch a tent at local national forest and commercial campgrounds.

RIVER RAMBLING At the Delaware Water Gap in New Jersey and Pennsylvania, you can visit a sprawling mosaic of river valleys, agricultural floodplains, and big wooded mountains, with both historic villages and fabulous wilderness. Each day you get to choose your adventure quotient. A big hike through shady hemlock forests? Knock out a chunk of the Appalachian Trail? Join an interpretive hike through a colonial farm? It's all close by.

FAR NORTH Along the Gaspe Peninsula of Quebec, broad fjords, deep forests, and above-the-treeline alpine scenery await—as does the the northern terminus of the International Appalachian Trail. There are nearly endless camping options, from private campgrounds to a growing number of glamping destinations. For a trifecta of Applachian perfection, hit three national parks on the peninsula: Forillon, Gaspésie, and Percé.

FORILLON PARK, QUEBEC

MOUNT MITCHELL, NORTH CAROLINA

SHENANDOAH NATIONAL PARK, VIRGINIA

MONONGAHELA NATIONAL FOREST, WEST VIRGINIA

026 GREAT SMOKY MOUNTAINS NATIONAL PARK

On my last family camping trip to the Great Smokies, the high-country wonderland of North Carolina and Tennessee, we swam at the base of tumbling waterfalls, hiked through cathedral forests so quiet even the kids were whispering, sang around the campfire, ate burned biscuits, and watched Native Americans demonstrate the fine art of shooting a blowgun. Bunking down in the Great Smokies ticks off just about every iconic family camping experience you can imagine.

Of course, a lot of other people agree. The park is within a day's drive of 60 percent of all Americans, and there are times when it seems like 100 percent of them are in the park. But this is really big country, nearly a million acres of serious forest and rugged terrain, and it only takes a bit of planning and a small expenditure of sweat to have a memorable piece of the Great Smokies all to yourself. Here are three ways to find a little Southern Appalachian solitude in America's finest family camping park.

STAY LATE Sure, the standard line is to hit the trail at dawn, but is your 12-year-old really up for a sunrise hike? Uh-uh. Better to toss a trail dinner in a small daypack and stay in the woods from afternoon till sunset. By late afternoon, many visitors shuffle back to the gateway towns of Gatlinburg, Tennessee, and Cherokee, North Carolina, to beat the crowds to the all-you-can-eat buffets, or head back to the campground while it's still light enough to open a can of beans. That leaves trails void of crowds just as the deer and elk come out to play.

GO DEEP The park's traffic jams are legendary, but the vast majority of visitors never make it farther than a couple hundred yards from their car. Hoof it down one of the park's more than 800 miles of trail and you can leave the crowds behind quickly. And you don't have to pile on the miles. There are tons of designated "Quiet Walkways" that aren't longer than a half-mile, but lead to gorgeous mountain streams shaded with laurel or coves of ancient hardwoods.

HEAD FOR THE CORNERS The towns of Cherokee to the south and Gatlinburg to the north attract the biggest crowds, so campgrounds like Smokemont and Elkmont can get crazy. To flee the masses, head to the eastern and western corners of the park. The quietest campgrounds are Abrams Creek, Cataloochee, and Big Creek.

027 OLYMPIC NATIONAL PARK

Olympic National Park is what you get when you smash all the amazing icons of the Pacific Northwest into a single, accessible, wildly improbable package: Soaring cathedral forests of old-growth fir trees draped in moss. Black sand beaches fanged with rocky cliffs. Snow-capped peaks that top 8,000 feet (2,400 m). You can check out tidal pool starfish in the morning and mountain goats after lunch.

This part of the world is famous for its rain, but later in the summer, big blue skies and tons of sun are more common. Over the years I've probably camped 30 nights in the Olympics, all in the summertime. Maybe I'm just super lucky, but I've not gotten wet more than a half-dozen times, so don't let the Pacific Northwest's reputation for soggy weather turn you away.

Take it all in with a couple of big bites. There are two separate sections to the national park: the big forests and high mountains of the interior and the coastline. My family first bunked down in a lush rainforest valley near the Hoh River and struck out for trout streams, canoe trips, and a hike along Hurricane

Ridge with views into Canada. Mountain meadows in the summer almost hurt our eyes with their kaleidoscopic wildflowers. We took solar showers inside a hollow tree at our campsite and long hikes along Lake Crescent.

Then we headed to the iconic coast. In between is a wide swath of industrial timberlands, so be prepared for a few hours' drive through big timber cuts. But once you're on the other side of the peninsula's midsection, all that awaits is staggering beauty. A 57-mile-long (91-km) strip of cliff-armored coastline edges the Olympic peninsula shore, and the biggest challenge to a beach hike is not tripping over your bugged-out eyeballs. We spent hours and hours exploring Second Beach, Third Beach, and Rialto Beach. We skim-boarded on black sand flats at the foot of towering rock headlands and sea stacks. Massive jumbles of driftwood logs demanded serious climbing and clambering. Decades earlier I'd backpacked the Olympics with a buddy from college, and those beaches seemed just as wild, remote, and unchanged from my memory. That's a national treasure.

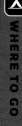

BUCKET LIST

028 BAHIA HONDA STATE PARK

When you close your eyes and imagine what beachfront camping in the famous Florida Keys might be like, this is what you see: A white sandy beach curving nearly out of sight. Blue waters to the horizon. Kids in snorkeling gear. Dads in ridiculous hats. The challenge is to score a campsite: Sites at Bahia Honda can be reserved up to 11 months in advance, and they fill up very, very quickly.

The park stretches across 500 acres (200 ha) of Big Pine Key, right where the Seven Mile Bridge makes landfall in the Middle Keys. It's a fabulous mashup of natural and human history, with a historic old railroad bridge that's now reserved for hikers and some of the best snorkeling, beachcombing, and wade fishing along the entire archipelago. While plenty of day visitors find their way to Bahia Honda–its 2-mile-long (3.2-km) public beach is the longest in the Keys–campers have the market cornered on sunrise and sunset views literally right from the campsite.

There are three separate campgrounds on Bahia Honda, and they differ in ways large and small.

RV NIRVANA At the Buttonwood campground, the gravel sites are the largest in the park, and each one is outfitted with electric and water hookups, plus a picnic table and grill. Buttonwood sites have little shade, however, and many sites don't have a lot of privacy. Still, they afford easy access to the park's beaches, boat charters, camp store, and marina.

SMALL WONDER Lots of folks love the eight sites at Bayside. Since you have to drive under the Bahia Honda Bridge, a vehicle height restriction of 6 feet, 8 inches (1.8 m) keeps out big rigs. Some sites allow hammock camping.

SEE THE SUNRISE Scattered through a hardwood hammock along a gorgeous beach, the 24 Sandspur sites allow mostly tents with a few sites large enough for small pop-up campers. My family has camped at Sandspur for three Spring Breaks over the years, and it's a hands-down favorite. We string up tarps for shade, snorkel for hours, and day-trip from Bahia Honda to Key West, Marathon, and Islamorada.

029 GRAND TETONS' JENNY LAKE CAMPGROUND

I've camped at Jenny Lake Campground in Grand Tetons National Park many times over a span of 30 years, and I'm not sure I've stayed at another national park campground that can top it. It's smack in the middle of the park, nestled in the big pines, on the water, with life-altering views of the Teton Range. There are only 49 sites, and they're all for tents only. That means there's a bit of a dance to score a patch of ground. Sites are full by early in the morning, so grab coffee and muffins and get in line by 7 a.m. Sounds crazy, I know, that you have to approach scoring a campsite like you're camping out for concert tickets, but it's worth it.

From the campground, Jenny Lake Trail circumnavigates one of the prettiest alpine lakes in the country, with a mid-way stopover at Inspiration Point, one of the best views in the park. Another trail heads off to String Lake, a moderate loop with awesome views of 11,000-foot (3350-m) snow-capped peaks and a great chance at spotting moose.

Jenny Lake also puts you in the heart of some of the greatest auto tours in the West. In the hour before sunset, we always take a slow tour along the Jenny Lake Scenic Drive to catch glimpses of grizzly bears moving through the lodgepole pines. Antelope Flats Road is just a few minutes' drive away from the campground, and you can tick off pronghorn antelope and bison there amid a landscape where abandoned farms and barns speak of the Tetons' homesteading days.

Or you can just hang at Jenny Lake Campground and take advantage of having locked down one of the country's greatest tent sites. Some of our fondest family-camping memories at Jenny Lake had more to do with family time than the surrounding wilderness: Taking solar showers in the woods behind the campsite. Washing socks and underwear on the camp stove. Snoozing off mid-morning pancake feasts in hammocks hung from the pines. Sometimes the best thing about being in the middle of the action is kicking back and doing nothing at all

BUCKET LIST

030 CUMBERLAND ISLAND NATIONAL SEASHORE

To camp on a wild island clad in ancient forests and 40-foot (12-m) dunes, and that teems with sea turtles and wild hogs and the occasional 10-foot-long (3-m) prehistoric reptile, you could fly to Indonesia...or you could head to the Georgia coast and hop the short, 15-minute foot ferry to Cumberland Island National Seashore. Nearly 18 miles (29 km) long, this salt marsh-to-seashore national park boasts canopies of live oaks, emerald groves of saw palmettos, miles of easy trails, and backcountry camping areas nestled among its near-wilderness charms. You can pitch a tent, surf fish, swim, ride bikes, or just lay on the beach for hour after blissful hour. And the kids can roam without you worrying about traffic–there are no public vehicles on the island.

Campsites and spots on the ferry can be reserved up to six months in advance, but midweek visitation is much less than on weekends all year long. Getting to the main Sea Camp Campground is little more than a 10-minute stroll from the ferry depot, though you'll have to schlep everything you'll need, from food to beach toys to bug spray (a must for mosquitoes). But once you're at Cumberland, you'll see the wild, unsettled eastern coast like the first

European explorers did. And you'll fall in love with this new world.

NICE AND EASY The Sea Camp Campground and its stunning live oaks are a short walk from the ferry landing, and the park service provides gear carts to make it even easier. Sea Camp has a restroom with cold-water showers, and each campsite has a grill, fire ring, food cage (pesky raccoons!), and a picnic table.

TAKE A HIKE Stafford Campground is 3.5 miles (5.6 km) up the island from the ferry dock and visitor contact center. It's a flat walk, though sandy, so it's great for beginning backpackers. There's a small restroom at Stafford but not much more. From Stafford, the beach is a short quarter-mile (400 m) walk down a good trail, and it is very uncrowded.

AWAY FROM IT ALL There are three backcountry sites in the island's designated wilderness. Hickory Hill is a 5.5-mile (8.8-km) hike from the ferry, Yankee Paradise is 7.5 miles (12 km), and Brickhill Bluff will cost you 10.6 miles (17 km) of sweat from the dock. My favorite is Brickhill, where the marsh sunsets will knock your socks off.

031 HOME IN ON A EUROPEAN CAMP

There are tons of private campgrounds, holiday parks, and farms that allow camping across Europe. Here are four ways to find them online.

INSIDER INFO Camping.info posts descriptions of more than 23,000 campsites across 44 European countries, including reviews and photographs submitted by campers. You can research and book online from anywhere. The service is available as a website, app, and a printed guide with various European editions.

PRIVATE AFFAIRS Eurocamp is a mashup of a travel agency and booking website, with private campground offerings in nine European countries. There are two camping setups: Classic Tents include bed frames and mattresses, a gas grill, a small refrigerator, and an electric light. Safari Tents are perched on a wooden platform with luxury beds, bedding, fully equipped kitchen, sun loungers, and an electric heater. Many destinations include access to swimming pools and are close to tourist villages, so Eurocamp is a great option for traveling families. If you're packing your own camping gear, Eurocamp Independent can handle the details of campsite reservations, ferry and Eurotunnel bookings, and renting a refrigerator, and includes Michelin maps and travel guides to your destination.

JOIN THE CLUB The United Kingdom's Camping and Caravanning Club has roots that reach back to 1913, and may be the oldest camping club in the world. It owns more than 100 club sites, and has access to another 1,600 inspected and certified campsites plus an international travel service. You don't have to be a member to gain some access to the bookings, but members do get discounts.

BUDGET WINNER Pitchup is a London-based online booking service with more than 6,000 campsites listed across Europe and the U.S., and services translated into nearly a dozen languages. It's a great choice for budget-conscious travelers.

032 GO BOONDOCKING

In many European countries, "wild camping" refers to camping away from public parks and private campgrounds, often without express permission, and mostly on private lands or public properties without developed facilities. It's also called "boondocking" or "dry camping." The devil is in the details, however. Some countries allow wild campers to build fires and swim in lakes and rivers, while other countries are more restrictive. Check regulations.

Across Scandinavia, the principle of what the Swedish call *allemannsrätten*, which means "the everyman's right," is a treasured principle. In Norway, campers can pitch a tent on uncultivated land as long as they camp at least 500 feet (150m) away from inhabited houses or cabins, pick up their trash and leave no trace. If you want to stay more than two nights, landowner permission is required. In Sweden, wild campers can stay for up to two nights, and are allowed to build campfires unless local restrictions are in place. Finland and Iceland also allow campers to access private lands.

Wild camping is allowed, in various forms, across much of Northern Europe, including Estonia, Latvia, Lithuania, Austria, Czech Republic, and Switzerland.

033 EXPLORE THE DARK SKY

One of camping's greatest pastimes is to simply marvel at the stars, planets, constellations, meteors, and galaxies overheard. Sadly, the vast majority of people live in areas where light pollution obscures the view of the stars. In fact, one-third of the world's population can't even see the Milky Way. Many camping areas are in great night sky-watching regions, but some locations are head and shoulders above the rest. The International Dark-Sky Association certifies locations that meet criteria for exceptional darkness and sky quality. There are numerous Dark Sky Parks around the world, but just a few top-shelf International Dark Sky Reserves. Put these on your starry wish list for camping.

AUSTRALIA River Murray

ENGLAND Cranborn Chase; Exmoor National Park; Moore's Reserve

FRANCE Alpes Azur Mercantour; Cévennes National Park; Pic du Midi

GERMANY Rhön; Westhavelland Nature Park

IRELAND County Kerry

NAMIBIA NamibRand Nature Reserve

NEW ZEALAND Aoraki Mackenzie

QUEBEC Mont-Mégantic National Park

UNITED STATES Central Idaho

WALES Brecon Beacons National Park; Snowdonia National Park

BANFF NATIONAL PARK, CANADA

034 HEAD FOR THE BORDER

Just north of the U.S. border is a wonderland of camping options in the world's second-largest country by total land (and water) area. Camping in Canada is a storied tradition, from wilderness canoe camping to national park hopping across the Canadian Rockies. And it's easy to search and book a campsite.

FEDERAL WONDERS Canada has 174,000 square miles (450,000 sq km) of national parks, but it's a snap to put your name on a campsite in its 48 national parks and reserves. The official Parks Canada website has extensive search and reserve functions that cover national parks and historic sites, and even urban areas with convenient camping options. You can reserve a standard tent site or RV campsite, backcountry sites, and even sign up for "equipped camping"–simply show up and your tent, stove, lantern, picnic table, and other gear will be waiting. Parks Canada also offers

tipis, yurts, cool suspended teardrop shelters called Óasis, and a combination of a tent and an A-frame cabin called oTENTik.

FEELING PROVINCIAL There are more than a thousand provincial and territorial parks across Canada's 13 provinces and territories, so you'll need to visit the websites of each for details. But many of these parks are more akin to a U.S. national park than a state park, and include vast territories with everything from frontcountry RV camping to some of the most remote backpacking and canoe camping on the continent.

PRIVATE TIME Many private campgrounds in Canada can resemble their European counterparts, –a mashup of campground and theme park. Before you book a site, make sure the facility meets your needs in terms of privacy, relative remoteness, and level of amenities.

GEARING UP

Home Sweet Tent
Sleep like a baby with the right camp crib

Pad Your Palace for All-Night ZZZs

Fixer Upper
Repair hacks for zippers, boots , and more

Assemble a Camp Kitchen

Lights, Canteens, Axes!
Choose all the right gear

035 ANATOMY OF A TENT

A lightweight home away from home should keep you dry, have plenty of room for everyone in your camping party, and allow enough ventilation for a great night's sleep. Four-season tents are built to handle very high winds and heavy rains and can withstand high accumulations of snow. Three-season tents are made for spring, summer, and fall use.

A TENT BODY The inner walls and floor of the tent to which the frame poles are attached. Many tents can be pitched without the rainfly, utilizing the tent body only for warm nights with no rain.

B GUYLINES Cords attached to the tent body or rainfly that are staked out to pull the rainfly away from the tent body and to prevent the tent from moving or collapsing in wind.

C POLES Thin, flexible tubes typically made of fiberglass or aluminum that provide structure and rigidity to the tent. Much of a tent's cost is based on the technology and materials in pole design. Heavier, cheaper fiberglass poles are fine for car camping and weekend use, but for backpacking or camping in rough weather, high-quality aluminum poles are preferred.

D VESTIBULE A roofed section over the door that provides additional dry storage outside of the tent's interior. Most often a part of the rainfly.

E MESH PANELS These improve ventilation and reduce interior condensation. They also allow you to see the stars overhead when not using the fly.

F BATHTUB FLOOR A floor design in which the weatherproof floor fabric extends up the wall sides a few inches.

OTHER FEATURES TO LOOK FOR

RAINFLY Waterproof sheet placed over the tent body and staked to the ground.

FOOTPRINT An extra layer of material that protects the floor of the tent.

GEAR LOFT Lightweight fabric tied or clipped into the tent roof to provide an interior shelf for storing spare clothing and lightweight gear off the floor.

VENTS Small windows at the roof that allow heated interior air to pass out of the tent.

TENT DIVIDER Removable fabric wall panels that allow for a tent to be partitioned for privacy.

POLE HUB A hard plastic central hub that allows for quicker tent pitching and more vertical walls.

036 SPLURGE ON THIS

DOUBLE DOORS Doors on both the front and rear of the tent keep campers from having to climb over each other to enter and exit the tent, particularly during midnight potty breaks.

MESH PANELS Large mesh panels in the walls of the tent body allow for increased circulation, which is critical for camping in warmer weather.

NEAR-VERTICAL WALLS New tent designs with pre-bent poles and pole hub configurations allow for tent walls to be nearly straight up and down. That dramatically increases the usable interior space.

G SEALED SEAMS High-quality tents will have seams that are waterproofed with tape or sealant.

H STAKE LOOPS Fabric loops for the metal or plastic pegs that hold the tent to the ground.

I POLE CLIP Clips or hooks sewn into the tent body that attach to the poles. They're much faster than sleeves and allow for greater air movement and ventilation between the tent body and fly.

037 CHOOSE THE BEST TENT TYPE

There's really no such thing as one tent that does it all, so you'll need to match the tent type with your camping situation. Need a tent with maximum stormproofing? A geodesic dome might be for you. Looking for a spacious and airy home away from home for the entire family? Zero in on a tunnel tent or cabin tent. The good news is that modern tent designers have figured out all the angles, and there's an ideal tent out there for every camping situation.

A-FRAME TENT Pitched over a ridgeline or with poles in an A shape at the front and the back, these are simple, often inexpensive tents.
PRO Steep walls channel rain effectively.
CON Cramped interiors.

POP-UP TENT With flexible poles sewn into the tent body, a pop-up tent goes up in mere seconds. They're great for backyard camping or even a quick shelter at a music festival or family gathering.
PRO Easy set up.
CON Poor weatherproofing.

DOME TENT Built with a rounded, mushroom-cap shape, dome tents are a step up in design from A-frames. Most go up easily with two poles that cross in the center.
PRO Great interior space for the money.
CON Often limited vestibule space.

GEODESIC DOME TENT A dome tent designed with multiple poles, which cross to form triangular shapes.
PRO Can withstand extreme winds, rain, and heavy snow.
CON Often pricey.

TUNNEL TENT Long, roomy tents designed with poles that arch from one side to the other to create a half-moon profile.
PRO Can handle lots of people and gear; great for groups and families.
CON Often quite heavy, so best suited for car camping.

PYRAMID TENT Lots of new tipi-styled tents are available, made with modern materials.
PRO Super roomy, and some can be used with tent stoves.
CON Can be pricey.

CABIN TENT The ultimate family tent, a cabin tent is shaped like a small house and can include multiple rooms.
PRO Tons of space.
CON Bulky and tricky to set up.

WALL TENT A classic vertical-wall structure often used for basecamping in remote areas. Many wall tents can be outfitted with wood-burning stoves and pitched on wooden platforms.
PRO Maximum interior space.
CON Can be very heavy and time-consuming to put up.

038 UPGRADE A TENT'S GUYLINES

Tripping over a tent's guylines is a common camping mishap and can result in a trip-ending injury. It's easy to replace all your tent's standard guylines with reflective tent cord. Use a simple bowline knot to tie the cord to the small fabric loops on the rainfly. If your tent's original guylines came with line tensioners, you can easily remove them and add them to the new reflective lines. Now your guylines will shine in the light of a headlamp or even the glow of your campfire. Want to go the budget route? Simply wrap reflective tape around each guyline in a few places. It's a cheap way to keep you out of the first-aid kit.

039 BEEF UP OLD SHOCK CORDS

In older tents, the elastic cord that holds tent pole sections together can loosen and get overly stretched. If that stretchy cord breaks, you'll have a pick-up-sticks mess of random tent pole sections to deal with. Once your tent pole cords get a little loose, it's time to replace them.

In most cases, elastic bungee cord is threaded through the pole sections and held in place with a stopper knot that jams against a washer or some other stop inside each terminal pole section. A few tent models require a kit if the shock cord goes south, but most can be handled with nothing more than new bungee.

STEP 1 Access the cord by prying off a pole tip. Remove the old cord.

STEP 2 Tie an overhand knot in one end of the new cord. Thread the cord through the poles one section at a time, joining the sections together as you make progress. If the bungee bunches up while being pushed, cut a straight length of coat hanger wire, attach to the end of the bungee, and feed the wire through the poles. When finished, leave some slack in the cord.

STEP 3 Tie another stopper knot, but don't cut off the excess just yet; you may need to experiment with the cord length to get the tension right. You want enough to hold the poles together, but not so much that the cord is stretched too tightly when you decouple the sections.

040 STORMPROOF TENT SEAMS

When it comes to rainproofing a tent, take no chances. Even high-quality tents can use a little extra effort when it comes to staying dry. Don't wait until you have a soggy sleeping bag to seal the seams on your tent.

IDENTIFY THE PROBLEM SPOTS Examine all tent seams. If they look like they have a narrow band of tape sewn inside the seam, those are called "taped seams" and require no additional work. All other seams, especially around the tent floor and anywhere on the rainfly, require sealing.

UPSIDE DOWN PITCH Pitch the tent body and stake it down. Then turn the rainfly upside down and stake it out tautly. It's a cumbersome thing to do, but this step will open up the needle holes in the stitching.

CLEAN THE SEAMS Start with the rainfly. Clean all the seams with a cotton swab and household alcohol first. Next, apply sealant with even strokes. Then crawl inside the tent to work on the seams from the inside so the sealant doesn't abrade off so easily in the field. Clean with the cotton swab and alcohol, then apply the sealant. Let the first layer dry for two hours and then reapply.

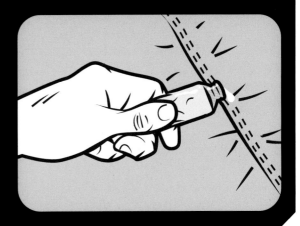

041 CUSTOM-CUT A TENT FOOTPRINT

Once more commonly called a "ground cloth", a footprint helps keep your tent floor from soaking up water, but an improperly fitting footprint is almost worse than none at all: If the waterproof material sticks out beyond the edge of the rainfly, it will catch the rain and channel it right under the tent. Most tents either come with a custom-sized footprint or offer one as an additional purchase. But you can also easily make a custom-cut model for your tent. Set up the tent body without the fly on a waterproof tarp or sheet of Tyvek. Stake it out and then trace the outline of the tent with a marker. Remove the tent and cut the plastic 2 inches (5 cm) smaller than the outline so no material will stick out from the edges to funnel rain under the floor.

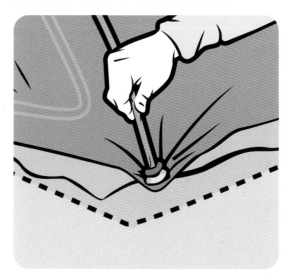

The image shows a camera icon.

042 WHAT'S THAT SOUND?

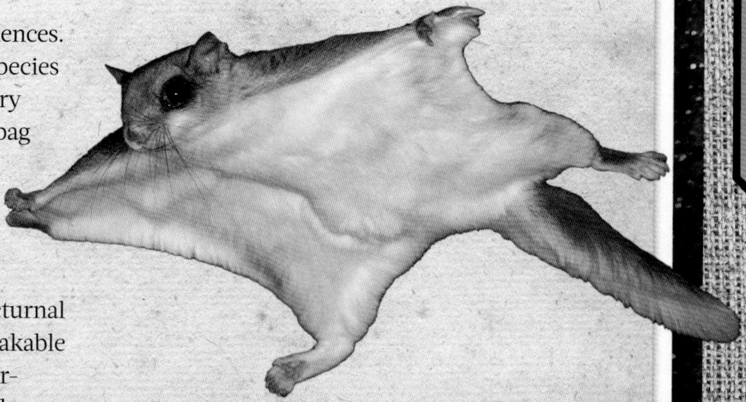

When the sun sets, the wildlife party commences. Deer, elk, and bears are on the move. Bird species migrate. Critters shuffle and skitter across dry leaves. Meanwhile, you lie in your sleeping bag wondering what in the world could be making all that racket. Here are some likely candidates for the fuss beyond the firelight.

BARRED OWL One of the loudest of the nocturnal loudmouths, barred owls hoot in an unmistakable series of short, loud syllables: Who-cooks for-you? Who-cooks-for-you-all? Barred owls also emit great raucous caterwauling sounds called "monkey laughs," with owls all around the woods answering each other.

GREAT HORNED OWL You'd think such a large, royal predator would split the night with its calls, but that's not the case. The great horned owl's nocturnal song is a series of low "hoos" emitted in groups of 4 to 5 syllables: hoo-hoo-to-hoo-hoo.

WHIP-POOR-WILL By day, these seldom-seen birds sleep on the ground. Then they seem to party all night long. The summertime chorus at night can seem endless–the birds chant *whip-poor-will* over and over. It's loud and relentless. One researcher counted a bird that sang its loud, piercing song 1,088 times without missing a beat.

WHITE-TAILED DEER You may not think of deer as noisy creatures, but they make a hair-raising short alarm snort that sounds like a wheezing sneeze coming through a concert amplifier. If you move around the edges of your campsite at night and scare a buck or doe, it will let you know what it thinks of the disturbance.

FLYING SQUIRREL There are some 50 species of flying squirrels worldwide, and they are more common than you might think. Strictly nocturnal, they are rarely seen. But these aerial acrobats have excellent hearing, and at night, they frequently chirp and twitter. If you're camping in the woods, walk quietly down a trail at night without a flashlight. If you hear mouse-like raspy squeaks in the trees, that could be a bit of flying squirrel gossip.

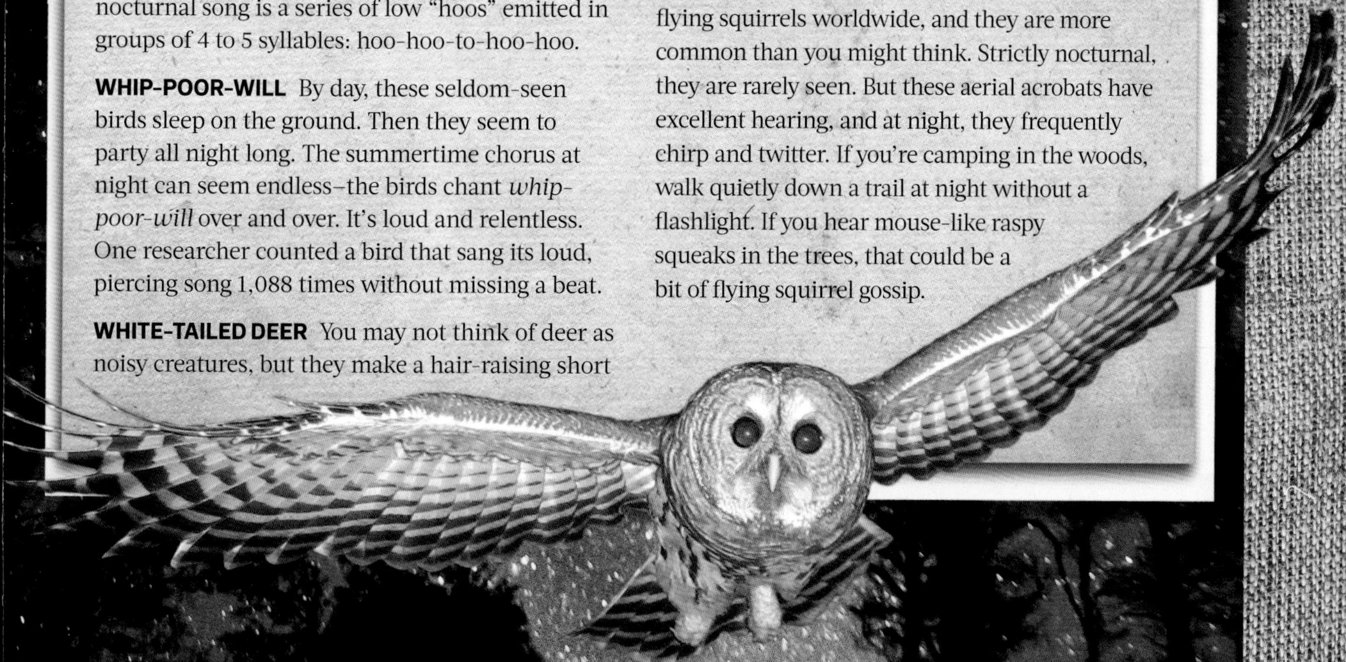

043 HANG OUT FOR THE NIGHT

Proponents of hammock camping enjoy carrying less gear, having a more scenic vantage point, and never having to worry about rocks or roots digging into their backs all night long. Modern hammocks are very lightweight, and new designs with integrated rain covers and bug netting are closing the comfort gap between these swinging shelters and traditional tents. Here's what to think about if you're hankering for a hammock.

SWINGING EASY Forget the tree hooks and heavy ropes. High-tech hammock suspension systems come with everything you need to string up an overnight trapeze, and most use webbing straps and carabiners so you never have to tie a knot. One huge benefit of webbing straps is that the material is much more tree-friendly than ropes and hooks, which can dig into the tree or damage bark.

COMFY CUSHION Add structure and support to a hammock for a better night's sleep. Cut a closed-cell-foam sleeping pad to add cushion and insulation, and help hold the hammock's side walls farther apart during the night. You can also use a partially inflated sleeping pad.

COVER UP It's one thing to watch the sunset from a breezy hammock. It's something else to make it through a rainy, buggy night. Invest in an expedition-style jungle hammock with an integrated bug net and rain fly. Or DIY it with mosquito netting and a tarp strung overhead.

044 HIT THE SACK

A cozy sleeping bag will give you a deep, restful night's sleep, but the wrong choice could make for a freezing cold–or sweltering hot–night on the ground. Sleeping bags come in a variety of shapes designed for very different uses. Here's what to think about when you're ready to catch your zzzzzs.

RECTANGULAR BAG

WHY IT'S GREAT The full, boxy cut lets you stretch out your arms, cross your legs, and roll over without bunching up the sleeping bag. A rectangular bag won't compress down as small as some other styles, but it wins points for deluxe comfort in all but the most frigid conditions.

WHO IT'S FOR Tossers and turners. Sleepers who can't stand to be confined.

SEMI-RECTANGULAR BAG

WHY IT'S GREAT A tapered lower section helps hold in heat, so a semirectangular bag can be warmer than a comparable rectangular bag, plus you still have room to move your arms around for a less confined night's sleep.

WHO IT'S FOR Folks who don't mind a snug feel and are headed out for colder conditions.

MUMMY BAG

WHY IT'S GREAT Cut to fit snugly from top to bottom, a mummy bag is the most thermally efficient option, as there's little wasted space that needs heating. And a mummy bag can stuff down smaller and weigh less than other sleeping bag styles.

WHO IT'S FOR Backpackers, bikepackers, and others who need the smallest, lightest sleeping bag.

DOUBLE BAG

WHY IT'S GREAT Basically a super-sized sleeping bag, built for two. The thermal qualities will be similar to a rectangular bag, but double bags are even warmer since two bodies will be producing heat. They're great for snuggling with a companion, and can double as a monster-sized quilt.

WHO IT'S FOR Couples. Or maybe you and your dog.

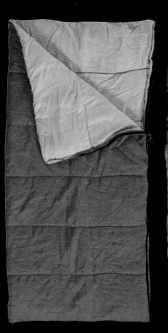
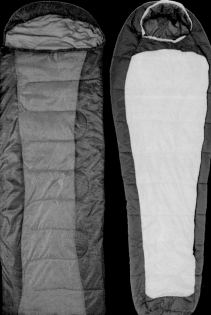

RECTANGULAR BAG   **SEMI-RECTANGULAR BAG**   **MUMMY BAG**   **DOUBLE BAG**

045 RECONSIDER THOSE RATINGS

Temperature ratings for sleeping bags should be taken with a grain of salt...or perhaps a full cup. Overnight comfort is derived from an equation that includes the sleeping bag, the sleeping pad, and whatever the sleeper is wearing. And folks vary widely. Some are hot sleepers and will break a sweat whenever it's more than 60°F (15°C) outside. Others might shiver when the sun goes down in the middle of summer. Consider a bag's comfort zone guidelines as a very general rule of thumb. And bear in mind that sleeping inside a tent will raise the ambient air temperature significantly–as much as 15°F (9°C) or so for two people sleeping in a smaller tent. Most sleeping bags will fit into one of these three categories.

SUMMER BAG Typically good for nights that are 40°F (4°C) and warmer.

3-SEASON BAG Choose a 3-season bag when the nighttime lows are between 20°F (-7°C) and 40°F (4°C).

WINTER BAG If the forecast calls for a night colder than 20°F (-7°C), hunker down in a winter bag.

046 GET DOWN AND TOASTY

Down is the super fluffy underfeathers found close to the body of a duck or goose. Each down feather is made up of hundreds of tiny filaments, and when placed inside a sleeping bag or garment, those tens of thousands of crisscrossing filaments excel at trapping and holding heat. The thermal efficiency of down is rated by its "fill power." To measure fill power, a known quantity of down is placed inside a tube and a light weight compresses it. The fill power relates to how much loft the down retains. The higher the fill power, the less down it will take to provide warmth. There are lots of factors that affect how warm a sleeping bag will be, but the quality of the bag's down is a good starting point for consideration. Lower quality down is rated at 450 to 550 fill. Anything over 800 fill is top quality.

047 GET YOUR FILL

Sleeping bags keep you warm by trapping warm air within the insulation material, called the "fill." There are lots of different fill types, but they can be broken into two broad categories: down and synthetic.

QUACK QUACK DOWN Goose and duck down are the lightest, most compressible fill materials. Pound for pound–or kilogram for kilogram–down fills are warmer than synthetics. But down loses much of its insulating properties when it gets wet. Some modern downs, however, are treated with a water-resistant process that helps keep them from going totally flat when wet.

SUPER SYNTHETICS There are tons of synthetic sleeping bag fill materials. Compared to down, synthetic fills can be heavier, but they weather wet conditions far better. Synthetic bags don't compress as small as down bags, but they are often more affordable. If you're going to be in excessively wet environments, or are pinching your pennies, there are plenty of great synthetic-fill bags for a wide variety of camping situations.

048 ADD A LAYER OF COZY

A sleeping bag liner is a thinner, lightweight bag designed to go inside a sleeping bag. Liners can be made of silk, cotton, fleece, or some other synthetic material, often with a low-profile zipper. They add extra warmth, but also protect a bag's inner lining from being soiled with dirt and body oil. If you need an extra dose of cozy you can also sleep while wearing insulated underwear, or stuff extra clothing made of soft fleece or wool into the empty space inside your sleeping bag. Then you'll have warm clothes first thing in the cold morning.

049 MAKE A SLEEPING BAG LAST (PRACTICALLY) FOREVER

Compressing a sleeping bag for days, weeks, and months while in storage can impair the fill's ability to bounce back and loft up enough to keep you warm– whether the bag is made with down or a synthetic fill. While it's perfectly fine to keep a sleeping bag in its small stuff sack while you're traveling, you don't want to keep it smashed down tightly for longer than you must. For long-term storage, use an inexpensive net laundry bag. They're perfectly sized to keep a sleeping bag in a tidy package without overly compressing the fill.

FIX ✕ THIS

050 UNSTICK A ZIPPER

When it comes to gear failure, temperamental zippers top the list of potential frustrations. Problems with a $5 zipper can turn a $500 sleeping bag or tent into a heap of useless nylon. Broken or stuck zippers are often easy to fix, though, and here's how.

CLEAN THE MACHINE If a zipper is just dirty and so gunked up the pull doesn't want to slide, scrub with hot water and a toothbrush. If you're in the field, lubricate a zipper with a few strokes of a graphite pencil, bar soap, or a smear of lip balm. You'll want to clean thoroughly once at home.

DIY PULL TABS Replace broken or missing zipper pulls with a short loop of reflective tent guyline cord or old flyline. Use a double fisherman's knot to provide a smooth, grippy connection.

FIX SLIDER SLIPPAGE A loose slider fails to stitch a zipper's teeth together. Fix with needle-nose pliers. Crimp each side of the slider very slightly, alternating between sides, and check after each round of crimping so you don't overdo it.

PREVENT TOOTH DECAY Sometimes an individual zipper tooth goes out of whack. Gently squeeze it back into formation with pliers.

CLEAR THE PATH If you've wedged a wad of fabric between the slider and the teeth, you'll need to either tug the fabric gently from the slider's jaws or move the slider past the point where the fabric bunches up. A squirt of window cleaner can help. Test a small swatch of the fabric first to make sure the window cleaner doesn't stain, then soak the slider and fabric with the solution. It acts as a cleaner and lubricant that will make removing the fabric wad much easier.

051 CHOOSE THE RIGHT PAD

A sleeping pad has as much to do with a good night's sleep as a sleeping bag, so choose wisely to snooze well. Smartly designed pads incorporate different kinds of foam, air channels, and insulation types, so thicker is not necessarily more comfortable. Think about where and how you'll be camping, and narrow down your pad choices with this chart.

SLEEPING PAD TYPE	HOW IT WORKS	BEST FOR...	THE DOWNSIDE
AIR MATTRESS	Basically, a full-size twin, double, or queen mattress, inflated with a battery- or foot-powered pump.	Car campers with large tents or sleeping areas. Can convince the timid to give camping a try.	Big, heavy, bulky, and cold in the winter. And no way you can blow it up without a pump.
CLOSED-CELL FOAM PAD	A simple cushioning and insulating layer of dense foam made of closed air cells.	Backpackers who place a premium on thrift and durability, since there's nothing to puncture.	The least cushioning of all the options.
INFLATABLE PAD	You blow it up using your own lung power or a small pump. Inflatable pads can be thin or thick, and made with multiple channels for comfort.	A great choice for all campers, since they come in a wide variety of thicknesses and sizes.	Can be punctured in the field, though easily patched. Basic uninsulated models can be cold in bitter conditions.
SELF-INFLATING PAD	Layers of foam sandwich an air chamber. Open the valve and they magically inflate.	Car campers and weekend backpackers who don't need a super-compact pad.	Can be heavier than other options.

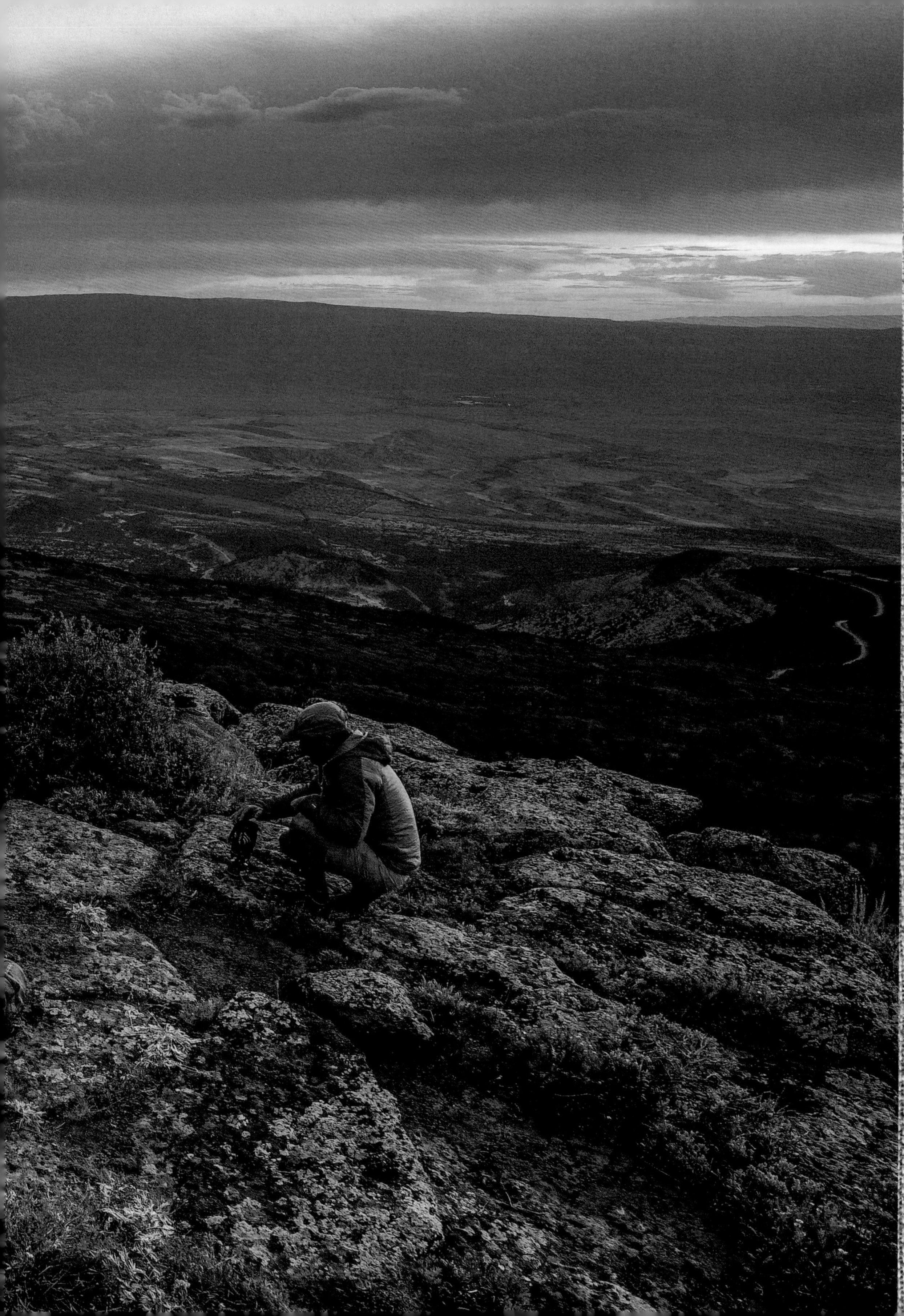

052 UP THE R-VALUE

A sleeping pad does more than cushion your tush. It also insulates you from the cold ground. If you use a thick, uninsulated inflatable sleeping pad, the air inside will chill as the nighttime temperatures fall, leaving you tossing and turning on a slab of frigid air. If you're headed out in the fall, winter, or early spring, choose a sleeping pad with a high R-value. The "R" stands for "resists," and refers to how well the pad will turn away the cold. Pads with high R-values are filled with insulation or feature heat-reflective materials. The higher the R-value, the better the insulating properties. If you'll be snoozing in temperatures below 20°F (-7°C), look for sleeping pads with an R-value of 4 or higher.

053 CONSIDER A COT

Can't abide sleeping on the ground? You're not alone. Great cots abound, and most are much more comfortable than the old "army cots" of yore. And older campers might appreciate how easy it is to get in and out of a cot versus crawling out of a sleeping bag on the ground.

MAXIMIZE SPACE If you're in a larger tent, a full-size cot can boost the usable interior space since there's room underneath for duffel bags and gear. Look for models with storage pockets and even integrated side tables.

PACK IT IN A cot that fits in your backpack? You bet. There's a growing number of modern cots that are lightweight and packable. They're a great choice for warm-weather camping since they maintain airflow underneath the sleeper.

054 GO ULTRA-COMFY-DELUXE

A new crop of crazy-comfortable sleeping pads has emerged from the road-tripping, glamping, and "van life" worlds. They're relatively large and heavy, but you'll never have a princess-and-the-pea night. While these new pads don't have a Google-worthy category name to help you in shopping, look for pads that are at least 3 inches (7 cm) thick, with bottom layers made of heavy-duty materials for maximum puncture-proofness and an emphasis on comfort rather than weight. Most utilize heavy-duty sidewalls to keep the pads from collapsing, with inches and inches of open-cell foam for comfort. Others stack a memory foam mattress on top of an inflatable layer for otherworldly comfort. If you're not backpacking and want the absolute best night's sleep possible under the stars, check out the new frontier of sleeping pads.

055 ANATOMY OF A HIKING BOOT

A great hiking boot makes the loads seem lighter and the hills less steep. That's a bonus on an ordinary hike, but when you add a daypack or backpack, it's even more important to take care of your feet and joints. With each level step, a force of 3 to 6 times your body weight is exerted on your knee. Carry a 10-pound (4.5 kg) daypack, and that's an extra 30 to 60 pounds (14 to 28 kg) of additional weight on your joints. If you plan on stacking up the miles, or just striking out for a half-day hike, investing in good boots pays off. Here are the terms you need to know when shopping for this essential piece of gear.

HOW HIGH? The "cut length" of a boot relates to how tall it is. A low-cut boot is about as high as a running shoe. A mid-high boot measures approximately 6 inches (15 cm) from the bottom of the sole to the top of the collar. It's a great compromise between support, comfort, and weight. A high-top boot measures approximately 8 inches (20 cm) from the bottom of the sole to the top of the collar. It provides increased ankle support, additional stability when carrying a heavy load, protection of shins, and some additional weatherproofing due to the increased height. But high-top boots can be heavy.

A TONGUE A hiking boot's tongue is often padded to allow laces to be tightly cinched.

B COLLAR The rim around the upper is often padded for comfort.

C LACING HOOKS, EYELETS & D-RINGS There are several approaches to lacing systems. Round metal eyelets are an inexpensive approach. Lacing D-rings reduce friction and hotspots to the top of the foot by moving the lace so it doesn't run under the lacing hem. Metal or hard plastic lacing hooks, or "speed lacing," make lacing much quicker on tall boots, and allow for a quick, custom fit by reducing friction.

D TOE BOX The part of the boot that encloses the toes.

E TOE CAP A hard rubber or reinforced plate that protects toes from being smashed and pinched.

F LUGS The protruding rubber studding that provides traction. Deep, aggressive lugs provide traction and support in boots designed for backpacking. But even dayhikers need good grip. Lugs spaced widely apart can self-clean themselves of caked-on mud.

G OUTSOLE A harder outsole will be more durable, but has less traction on wet rocks and logs.

J UPPER Everything above the sole. Leather uppers are most traditional. Leather stretches for comfort but retains its shape for durability. Synthetic or fabric uppers are lighter and more breathable, but often require lots of seams that can fail under long-term heavy use.

WEATHER REPORT A primary consideration is whether to purchase waterproof boots. Most waterproof boots are built with a breathable, waterproof liner, but they will still cause your foot to sweat in anything but cool temperatures. If you tend to hike only on trails and rarely cross streams, consider boots that aren't waterproof and pick up an after-market waterproofing product to boost their creek-shedding potential.

INSIDE THE BOOT

INSOLE The part of the sole that makes contact with your foot. Many hikers invest in custom insoles to provide additional comfort and support.

MIDSOLE The part of the sole between the outsole and insole. A stiff midsole cushions against impact and adds stability to the boot.

INTERIOR HEEL COUNTER Molded to the contour of the boot heel, this counter protects the boot shape and helps keep ankles from rolling.

UPPER PANEL Also called the vamp, this is the material that wraps the foot.

I EXTERIOR HEEL COUNTER A stiff plate protects the heel exterior from abrasion and adds rigidity.

H HEEL BUMPER An added layer of protection over the exterior heel counter to stiffen and protect the heel.

WATERPROOF

Here it comes: Summer's boiling heat. Temperatures that will bake a cooler and melt ice faster than you can drive to the nearest quick-mart for $3-a-bag reinforcements. Whether you're out for a quick overnight at the lake or a week-long expedition to some distant desert oasis, here are six proven ways to keep ice longer, drinks cooler, and meats and veggies safe from spoilage day after day.

PRE-CHILL APPROACH Dump ice into a cooler that's been roasting in a hot car or at a campsite and you might go through a couple of bags just to lower the temperature of the cooler itself. Always store a cooler in a corner of the basement or the shade of a tree at a campsite prior to loading with ice and food. And consider sacrificing a single bag of ice to pre-chill the cooler–just toss it into an empty ice chest, close the lid, and give it a few hours. You can drain off the meltwater and add to the remaining ice.

GO BIG The larger the block of ice, the longer it takes to melt. Splurge for block ice when you can find it, or simply fill washed milk jugs two-thirds full of water and freeze at home.

CUDDLE YOUR COOLER Direct sun will cook the cool right out of the icebox. To blunt the sun, wrap or cover the cooler with some kind of reflective shield. A white towel will work okay. Covering the top with a foil windshield screen works very well. Or wrap the cooler in a lightweight emergency space blanket. The difference is amazing.

DRY ICE BATH Precautions are required for safe handling, but dry ice is so cold–almost minus 110°F (43°C)–that using it is a go-to strategy for folks on long camping trips. It's best used to keep frozen items frozen, as anything stored nearby will freeze like a rock. Mix a 4-to-1 ratio of regular ice to dry ice to make the standard stuff last for days. Just wrap the dry ice in newspaper and place it on the bottom of the cooler. Cover with a layer of standard frozen ice, then the food and drink items. Dry ice is frozen carbon dioxide, and you have to handle it with heavy gloves and vent cooler lids so the sublimating vapor can escape.

CUT A GASKET Seal the top of the cooler with a DIY cooler gasket to prevent cool air from escaping around the lid. Cut a sheet of thin closed-cell foam to the exact dimension of the cooler interior, or recycle an old foam sleeping pad. Simply place this cooler gasket on top of the ice chest's contents. No foam? No problem. Several layers of newspaper will work wonders.

GO TANDEM Keeping hot air out and cold air in is as much a matter of keeping the lid closed as anything else. Cut the number of times people dig through the cooler by packing a separate, smaller cooler dedicated to drinks and snacks.

057 SEASON A BLACK IRON POT

Dutch ovens and cast-iron skillets and pots have a long and beloved history in the annals of camp cooking, from cattle drives to modern backcountry river rafting and hunting. What makes them awesome is the famous black pot patina, which prevents food from sticking to the hot iron. That almost microscopically thin coating also protects the pot or pan, since the surface of cast iron is rough and porous and will rust quickly. Seasoning this classic cookware will give it a nonstick coating that works better the more you use the pot.

DRY IT OUT Preheat a kitchen oven to 450°F (232°C). Wash the cast iron cookware with hot, soapy water and rinse well. Put it in the oven for ten minutes.

BAKE THE FINISH ON Remove the item and let it cool. Turn the oven down to 300°F (149°C). Now, grease the entire pot or pan inside and out, including lids and handles, with a light coating of cooking oil. Place it back in the oven for an hour. Crack a few kitchen windows and turn all smoke detectors off. It's going to smoke and smell like burned metal. That's what you want.

SEASON WITH A SHINE Remove the cookware and let it cool. Wipe away excess grease. Store with a paper towel inside. Newly seasoned cast iron will sport a shiny caramel color that turns black with use, especially if you cook bacon in it the first few times.

058 CLEAN WITH RINGS OF STEEL

Tired of fussing over crusty, crud-covered black iron pots and pans? Try a chain-mail cleaning patch and make your life easier. Made of small stainless-steel rings soldered together like those used in ancient armor, these incredibly useful kitchen tools will scrub off baked-on, burned-on bits of food in no time at all. They won't scratch your pot's seasoning layer, and they're easy to clean in a pot of boiling water or in the dishwasher back home.

059 DIAL IN A DUTCH OVEN'S TEMPERATURE

Camp cooking with a Dutch oven is part science and part art. It's not like you can just crank the stove up to 350°F (175°C) and set a timer. But there's a method to the mystery of setting a Dutch oven's temperature with charcoal briquettes. Experiment at home to fine-tune the numbers, since Dutch ovens and briquette brands vary. But start here and you'll have your pioneer street cred long before you fire up the charcoal chimney.

TO BAKE Use twice the number of briquettes as the number of inches in the diameter of the oven. Place three-quarters of the briquettes on the lid and the remaining under the oven, arranging the briquettes in a ring. For a 10-inch (25-cm) oven, use 20 briquettes with 15 on top and 5 underneath.

TO FRY Frying is a snap: Use the same number of coals as the number of inches in the oven's diameter, and place them all underneath.

TO KEEP IT EVEN The hard part of any Dutch oven meal is keeping the burn at bay. Rotate the entire oven every 10 to 12 minutes by lifting it straight off the coals and turning it a third of a revolution. Set it down, lift only the lid, and rotate it a third of a turn. Most coals will burn at an even heat for 30 minutes or a bit longer, so be prepared with additional briquettes if you need a longer cooking time. Once your buns in the oven are done, whisk away the lid ashes with a small broom or a handful of grasses before cracking the lid on black-iron perfection.

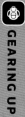

060 DOUBLE UP WITH A 2-BURNER STOVE

Two-burner camp stoves are the workhorses of the outdoor culinary scene. They allow you to fry and boil or sauté and simmer at the same time. You can cook a ton of food for a large group or go gourmet for a smaller one. The possibilities are endless–and the choices seem that way, too. When shopping for a double-barreled camp stove, you'll want to look for a number of features that set the best ones apart.

HEAT OUTPUT While other factors matter, the BTU output of a stove is a good place to start. Modern stoves might rate an anemic 7,000 BTUs or a total rocket-worthy 20,000 BTUs and more. In general, the higher the BTU rate, the quicker the stove will boil water. A stove with burners rated at 10,000 BTUs is a good starting point for consideration.

WINDSCREENS A stove's ability to burn in a moderate to stiff breeze is a huge consideration. Look carefully at windscreens, which block the breeze before it can get to the burner. And consider burner diameter; a large burner can be more affected by wind since more flame area is exposed to the breeze.

SIMMERING ABILITY If all you want to do is boil water for ramen noodles, then a stove's ability to cook on a low simmer doesn't matter much. For others, an easily adjustable flame is critical. Some stoves are total blast furnaces on high, but try to turn them down to a simmer and the flames sputter and die. Test a stove before you buy, or read online reviews about how well it simmers. A stove that will cook well on low means less burned bacon and French toast.

TOUGHNESS AND PACKABILITY If you're a car camper who never ventures far from the picnic table, a tough stove isn't all that important. But if you pack a stove in the family ski boat, canoe, or ATV trailer, look carefully at its construction. Stay away from too many exposed knobs, which can easily be knocked off. And give the stove a good shake to make sure the grills won't rattle around when you're headed over rough terrain.

OVERALL SIZE Think about how you cook and which pots and pans are your favorites when preparing an outdoor meal. Compact stoves are great when it comes to packing, but some stoves place the burners so close together that there's no way a pair of decent-sized frying pans will fit at the same time. Make sure your choice fits your cooking style.

AUTOMATIC IGNITION Do I want to light this stove with finger-scorching matches or the lighter I might have left in the truck, or do I want to push a button? 'Nuff said. But neither do you want to be stuck without a backup lighter or matches, so pack those as well.

EASE OF CLEANING Ah, yes, KP duty. Look for a stove that doesn't require complex partial disassembly to give it a brisk wash. Some stoves have cooking grates that require removal; others come with drip pans that do a great job of catching grease but are a pain to clean.

061 FIGURE ON FUEL

Camping stoves and lanterns are some of the handiest gear items you can purchase, but you'll first need to know a bit about the various fuel sources that fire them up. Here's a rundown on the most common types of camping fuel and how they stack up, no matter the weather.

THE GAS	WHAT IT IS	PROS	CONS
PROPANE	A highly stable gas stored in liquid form. 1-pound canisters are most common, but newer 5-pound canisters are great for car camping.	Burns at a constant rate in cold temperatures, and burns great at high altitudes. Commonly found in gas stations and grocery stores.	Compared to other fuel solutions, propane is heavy due to the bulky canisters.
BUTANE	A liquid gas with a slightly higher boiling point than propane.	Burns at a slightly more efficient rate than propane. Can be stored in lighter containers, and the connectors are easier to use than those of propane.	Does not perform as well as propane in very cold temperatures. More difficult to find than propane.
NAPHTHA	Highly refined liquid gas, also known as white gas. Used for many liquid-burning stoves. The most common brand is Coleman Fuel.	Burns hot and consistently in low temperatures. Is relatively inexpensive. Can be bought in one-gallon cans and transferred to smaller vessels.	When used in a stove, the stove must be primed so it burns as soon as it leaves the canister.
DENATURED ALCOHOL	Alcohol that has been treated with additives to make it smell foul and taste fouler—so you won't drink it.	Burns very clean and does not require a special canister. Lightweight and easy to use in stoves.	Doesn't burn as hot as other fuel options.
HYBRID FUELS	Various mixes of propane, butane, and isopropane.	Performs well in all temperatures and all altitudes. Canisters are generally very compact.	More expensive than other options.
WOOD	If this needs to be explained, you may want to rethink camping!	Widely available, mostly free, and environmentally sustainable. A growing number of highly efficient wood-burning camp stoves are on the market.	Inconsistent temperature, and stoves must be carefully tended to keep them burning hot.

062 ANATOMY OF A TREKKING POLE

More than a mere walking stick, a modern trekking pole is a highly engineered tool that can reduce fatigue, help to blunt knee pain, and make it safer to hike with heavy loads or in difficult terrain. They're beloved by many backpackers, but will also help day hikers go farther, faster, easier, and more safely.

Trekking poles can be as simple as a strong shaft with a comfortable grip, or carefully crafted aids with hidden spring mechanisms to absorb shock. Nifty locking devices allow strong poles to be broken down into easily carried sections and shortened or lengthened on the fly. Here's what you need to know about these invaluable knee-savers.

CROWN The top of the grip often has a slight flare to prevent the pole from slipping out of your hand. Some come with a threaded camera mount affixed to the crown.

GRIP Grips can be plain and smooth or include finger grooves for greater purchase. Materials range from plastic and foam to rubber and cork, which absorbs sweat to help prevent blisters on fingers and palms.

SECONDARY GRIP Some trekking poles include a cushioned grip area below the primary grip to make it easy to choke up on the trekking pole in steep topography.

WRIST STRAP A great wrist strap does more than keep you from losing the pole. Many are made to break free under high stress to help reduce injury.

SHAFT The stiff sections of the poles are often made of aluminum. Carbon fiber is a lighter, stronger, and more expensive choice.

ADJUSTING MECHANISM Look for trekking poles that can be easily adjusted for length. You'll want them slightly longer for downhill trail sections, and slightly shorter when you're headed uphill. Being able to quickly change the length of the trekking pole allows for efficient hiking.

BASKET Changeable baskets help tailor a trekking pole's performance to ground conditions. Larger baskets prevent the tips from sinking deep into snow, while smaller baskets are good for muddy conditions.

TIP A carbide tip is super tough and will last for years, even with hard use in rocky conditions. They also provide some grip on rocks and boulders. For safe transport and use in ecologically sensitive areas, rubber tip covers come in handy.

063 CLEAN A WATER BLADDER GONE FUNKY TOWN

Leave a hydration bladder sitting around, and the stuff that grows inside could kill a vulture. Here's the 3-step process for giving a grimy hydration bladder an at-home spa treatment.

SCRUB AND SOAK Remove any mold, mildew, or unidentifiable funk with a water bottle brush or wadded up paper towels. Next, prepare a sanitizing solution: Mix 1 teaspoon (5 ml) of bleach and 1 teaspoon (5 ml) of baking soda in a half-gallon (1.75 l) of water. Fill the bladder and let stand overnight.

TACKLE THE TUBE Work on the tube and bite valve the next morning. With the cleaning solution inside, hold the bladder upright and pinch the bite valve so some of the cleaning solution runs all the way through the tube. Shut the valve and let the cleaning solution sit in the tube for an hour. Flush the bladder and tube with clean water.

STORAGE WARS The biggest threat to a clean hydration bladder is storage. You can store it in a freezer, but over time, the constant freezing and thawing can damage O-rings and tubes. Instead, try this: Bend a painted or vinyl-covered metal clothes hanger so the two wings are parallel to each other. Thread them into the bladder opening and the wings will hold the bladder sides apart for drying. Or clip off the top wire in one arm of the hanger and thread the long horizontal piece into the bladder. Hang in a warm, dry spot.

064 NEVER LOSE A SCREW

All the bumping and jostling involved in a camping trip–driving over rough roads, packing and unloading gear–can cause bolts and screws to loosen on all kinds of equipment. You don't want to open up a camp stove and find a small bolt rattling around. The solution is to pack a small bottle of medium-strength threadlocker. Smear a small dab on the threads of loose screws stoves, lanterns, camping trailers, and campers, even the pocket clip on your folding knife. Tighten the screw and never again worry about it backing out.

065 KNOW THESE LIGHTING TERMS

How bright is a light? That depends on its power bank, the bulb type, how the beam is directed through the lens, and other technical features. Thankfully, the American National Standards Institute, or ANSI, created easy-to-understand metrics for assessing how well flashlights, headlamps, and lanterns perform. Here are some common ANSI ratings on lights. You'll find these icons and ratings on the packaging of many high-quality products.

 LUMENS A measure of total light output. A light that puts out 20 lumens works well for close-at-hand tasks such as reading in a tent. Lights of 1,000 lumens or more will illuminate an entire area or cut through the night for hundreds of yards.

 BEAM DISTANCE The distance, in meters, at which a light projects a useful beam. Technically, a "useful beam" is 0.25 lux, which is the light emitted from a full moon on a clear night.

 RUN TIME How long a light will run with fresh batteries. Run time is measured from 30 seconds after the light is turned on until light output falls to 10 percent of full strength. A single light can have multiple run times based on different power settings. Battery choice is a factor, too, as lithium batteries provide a longer run time than alkaline batteries in most quality lights.

 PEAK BEAM INTENSITY The brightest point in the overall light beam. Measured in candelas, which replaces the old metric of "candle power."

 WATER RESISTANCE The international rating system for water resistance. An IPX4 rating means the product was tested against water sprayed from all angles. An IPX7 rating means the product passed a submersion test to a 1-meter depth for 30 minutes.

066 MAKE YOUR CAMPSITE SHINE

Having a variety of lights on hand in addition to a hand-held light or headlamp will make life at camp safer and more welcoming. Here are four lighting types every camper should own.

	WHAT THEY ARE	WHY THEY'RE AWESOME
STRING LIGHTS	Bulbs spaced evenly apart on a wire, like lights on a string. There's a great new crop of solar-powered string lights perfect for camping.	Frame tent doors with string lights for a cozy entrance and to light your front porch.
CAMP LANTERNS	Classic lights that illuminate in 360 degrees.	Hang them above work spaces such as a camp kitchen.
TASK LIGHTS	Directional lights that you can point in a specific direction.	A lifesaver for changing tires by the road or lighting up a campsite while you pitch the tent.
TENT LIGHTS	Lightweight soft beams that will hang from a tent's gear loft or roof.	Helpful for getting dressed and playing board games without a clunky headlamp.

067 FIND THE PERFECT HEADLAMP

Headlamps keep your hands free for all the important stuff—pounding in tent stakes, flipping pancakes, looking for your toothbrush, and reading bedtime stories to tuckered-out toddlers. There are tons of choices, from simple to super high-tech, and from cheap models that might not make it through the weekend to sturdy lights you can count on year after year. Here's what to look for.

ON/OFF SWITCHES Try before you buy. If you plan on using while wearing gloves, make sure you can manipulate the switch with sheathed digits. Some headlamps have a lock-out setting to prevent the light from being accidentally switched on, which is nice.

MODE CYCLING Most headlamps feature a single switch that turns the lamp on and off and cycles through the various high and low beam modes, colors, and possibly even signal flash settings. Some are straightforward, while others feel a bit clunky. Again, try them out.

TILT If a headlamp doesn't allow the unit to be tilted up and down, skip it.

COLORED LIGHTS Many models sport colored bulbs in addition to the standard white bulb. They can come in handy. Red lights not only save night vision, but help prevent you from keeping a tent mate awake while you read.

STRAPS High-quality headlamps should come with quick-release tensioning buckles that make it easy to adjust the length of the strap. You might be surprised at how often you adjust the headlamp so it will fit over ball caps, beanies, and heavy hats. For most applications, the single strap suffices. The over-the-head strap addition helps carry the load of headlamps with heavy battery packs, and keeps the light from bouncing up and down if you're running.

BATTERIES The increase in headlamp technology and choices has also brought about a corresponding complexity of battery choices. In general, go for a light that runs on AA or AAA batteries, or can be fired up with a USB connection. If you need extra batteries, the more common types are far more available in rural areas.

068 FALL BACK IN LOVE WITH AN ICON

Give credit to a part-time traveling salesman named William Coffin Coleman for lighting up untold numbers of campsites. He founded the Coleman Lamp and Stove Company in 1913, and a year later introduced the world to what he called "The Sunshine of the Night"–his single-mantle lantern fired by a pressurized canister of petroleum naphtha. The two-mantle lantern hit the market in 1927. The company has since sold more than 50 million lanterns. Propane canisters have largely replaced the old fuel tanks of white gas, but there's still nothing quite like the warm, homey glow of a Coleman lantern.

069 CHOOSE THE RIGHT KNIFE

No other piece of camping gear is called upon to perform as many tasks, in as many ways, under as many conditions, as a knife. It can spread peanut butter and fell a small tree. Cut a tent stake or a slice of summer sausage. Help start a fire or remove a splinter. And in a survival situation, a good knife can save a life. Here's a glossary of terms to help you choose the perfect blade for your style of camping.

A BELT KNIFE Also called a "sheath knife," this is simply a knife that is stored in a sheath and carried on a belt.

B EVERYDAY CARRY Highly functional knives that are designed to be clipped to a pocket or belt. Most EDC knives are folding models made with strong locks to keep the knife open during cutting tasks. Thanks to their ease of carry, EDC knives make great camping knives.

C SKINNING KNIFE Designed with plenty of "belly," which refers to the long, upswept cutting edge. They're perfect for hunters who skin game, but are also a good camping choice. The belly makes them great slicers and general task blades.

D BUSHCRAFT KNIFE Very strong, simple, fixed-blade design made for survival and general camp chores. A full tang and exposed handle tip allow a bushcraft knife to be batoned through wood. A short blade with a Scandinavian grind allows it to perform fine carving work as well as tough cutting chores.

E FILLET KNIFE With a sharp point to pierce tough fish skin and a long, slender blade, a fillet knife will flex around fish bones and remove every smidgen of meat. In shorter lengths they're great for general camp cooking chores. Toss an inexpensive one into your camp kitchen or toolbox.

F TRAPPER KNIFE This common pocketknife sports a pair of blades of equal length—a clip-point blade and a spey blade. Popularized by trappers around the turn of the 20th century, it's still very useful.

G BIRD-AND-TROUT KNIFE A smaller knife made with a slim profile and a sharp point. The slightly flexible blade is great for detailed camp cooking work. It's perfect for cutting up fish and meats.

H TACTICAL KNIFE A catch-all phrase for any knife—folder or fixed-blade—with military, rescue, or self-defense features. Most tactical knives have thick blades and non-glare finishes on the steel, and are built super tough. Tanto blades are common on tactical knives. They're fine for camp chores, but aren't great slicers.

070 PACK ONE KNIFE TO RULE THEM ALL

While it's become a darling of the hipster scene in recent years, there's perhaps no more versatile camping knife than the Opinel. This 125-year-old French knife is inexpensive and sharp, with an ingenious little safety ring that locks the open blade in place. It's a great slicer, rope cutter, mustard spreader, and campfire whittling blade.

Designed in 1890 by Joseph Opinel, the son of a sickle maker in Savoie, France, the knife gave rise to a dynasty that is still managed by the ancestors of its founder. The classic is the Opinel No. 8. It comes in both stainless steel and classic carbon steel, which requires a bit more TLC but takes on a gorgeous patina that deepens with use.

071 SHARPEN A KNIFE WITH A WHETSTONE

There's no mystery to sharpening a knife to a hair-shaving edge, but there is mastery. This time-honored and proven method is the best way to get started. And possibly the best way, period.

STEP 1 Place a two-sided (coarse and fine) whetstone on a wet paper towel on a countertop or table with the coarse side facing up. The paper towel will keep the stone from sliding. Place the heel of the blade on the whetstone and establish the proper edge angle. Most outdoor knives are sharpened between 15 and 20 degrees. Place the fingers of your free hand in the middle of the flat of the blade. You'll use these fingers to apply pressure to the blade and help maintain the sharpening angle.

STEP 2 While maintaining a constant angle, push the blade into the stone, drawing it across from heel to tip, using as much length of the stone as possible. Apply enough pressure until the flesh under your fingernails begins to turn white. Perform 10 to 15 strokes, depending on the condition of the edge.

STEP 3 Run your thumb perpendicular to the blade edge to feel for the burr–a small fold of metal on the opposite side of the edge you are grinding. When you have a consistent burr from heel to tip, flip the knife over and repeat steps 1 and 2 on the other side with the same number of strokes.

STEP 4 Repeat this entire process with the fine side of the stone. Use a decreasing number of strokes until you are passing the blade of the knife a single time across the stone with only the weight of the blade providing pressure.

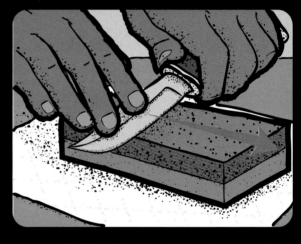

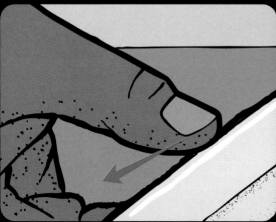

072 FIND THE RIGHT ANGLE

When it comes to sharpening a knife, it takes years of experience to be able to eyeball the correct blade angle on a whetstone. Until you get there, here are two ways to dial in the just-right angle degree.

THE INEXPENSIVE WAY This is as foolproof as it gets. Buy a set of inexpensive angle wedges. To use them, choose the correct wedge for the angle desired, place it on the side of the stone, place the blade on the wedge to establish the angle, and sharpen.

THE FREE WAY Fold the top right corner of a piece of paper so that it meets the left edge. You've now created a 45-degree angle. Fold the creased edge to the left edge once more, as if you're making the wing on a paper airplane. That's a 22.5-degree angle, which is very close to the 20 degrees at which many working knives are sharpened. Fine-tune the fold so the angle is just a bit more acute, and you'll have a paper guide to check your angle during sharpening.

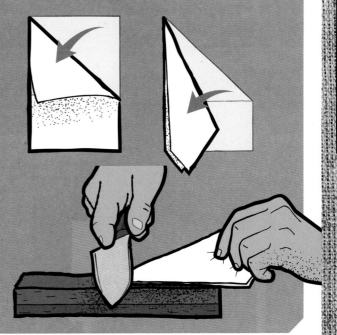

073 DIAL IN WITH A MECHANICAL SHARPENER

For those not comfortable hand-sharpening a knife on a whetstone, there are tons of commercially available sharpening tools that take the guesswork out of the process. While honing a knife on a stone has its advantages, you can definitely get a wicked edge using other methods.

SHARPENING RODS Ceramic rods and rods covered with diamond grit are used to put a fine edge on a knife. These slightly abrasive tools are handy for touching up an edge during use.

GUIDED SHARPENING DEVICES These ingenious sharpening systems hold abrasive materials in the proper position, removing the guesswork from calculating edge angles.

POWERED SHARPENING DEVICES Plug-and-play sharpeners involve powered belts and sharpening guides, enabling users to switch between grits for fine-tuning metal removal. They also typically include various angle guides for sharpening scissors, working edges, culinary knives, and axes and hatchets.

074 SHARPEN A SERRATED KNIFE

Serrations work like tiny saw teeth, and they're great for cutting through tough, fibrous materials such as rope. They can be a pain to sharpen, however, and honing serrations incorrectly will just wear them down to useless nubs. Here's the drill.

STEP 1 Use a progressively tapered diamond hone made specifically for sharpening serrated blades. Sharpen one tooth at a time by placing the hone on the beveled edge of the serration. Match the honing angle with the bevel of the serration and align the hone with the tooth so it is perpendicular to the deep gully of the serration.

STEP 2 Start with the serration nearest to the knife handle and push the hone down until the entire width of the serration is nearly filled with the hone. Rotate the hone slightly and repeat until you can feel a fine burr on the flat back side of the blade. Work your way down the blade, sharpening each serration.

STEP 3 When all serrations are sharpened, turn the knife over and grind off the burr with a ceramic rod or fine sharpening steel.

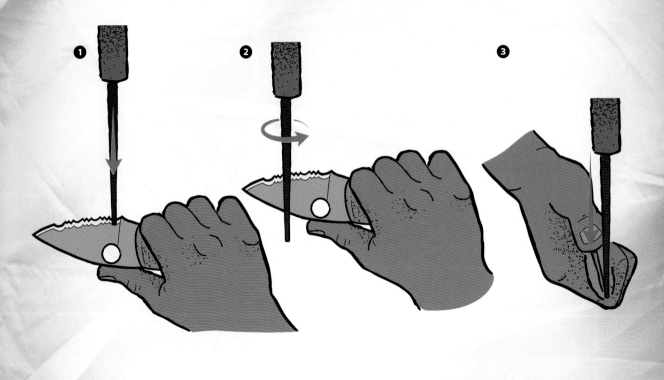

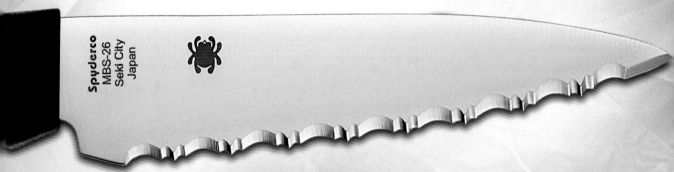

075 KNOW YOUR BINOS

A small pair of quality binoculars is a definite hit in camp and on the trail. You'll be able to see the antlers on moose across the river and identify birds above your tent. But having binoculars handy also helps in checking out stars and planets, and even butterflies and wildflowers.

Choosing the perfect binoculars involves a calculus of compromise. You might give up a bit of light transmission to gain portability, or pay more for expensive lens coatings that deliver purer color. These factors–plus price, of course–all weigh in on what makes a great pair of binoculars the best pair for you.

MAGNIFICATION For most general users, 7X or 8X is plenty. If you want to identify soaring raptors or distant features, 10X models will cut the distance. But they're not suitable for children and others who might have difficulty holding them steady.

EYE RELIEF This is the distance required between the glass and your eye for you to see what you're looking at. If you wear glasses, look for models advertised with long eye relief; 14mm is considered a minimum.

HINGE DESIGN An open bridge can reduce weight and allow for more gripping options. A single-hinge adds ruggedness.

CLOSE FOCUS If you're just as enamored with swallow-tailed butterflies as swallows, choose binoculars with a close-focusing function.

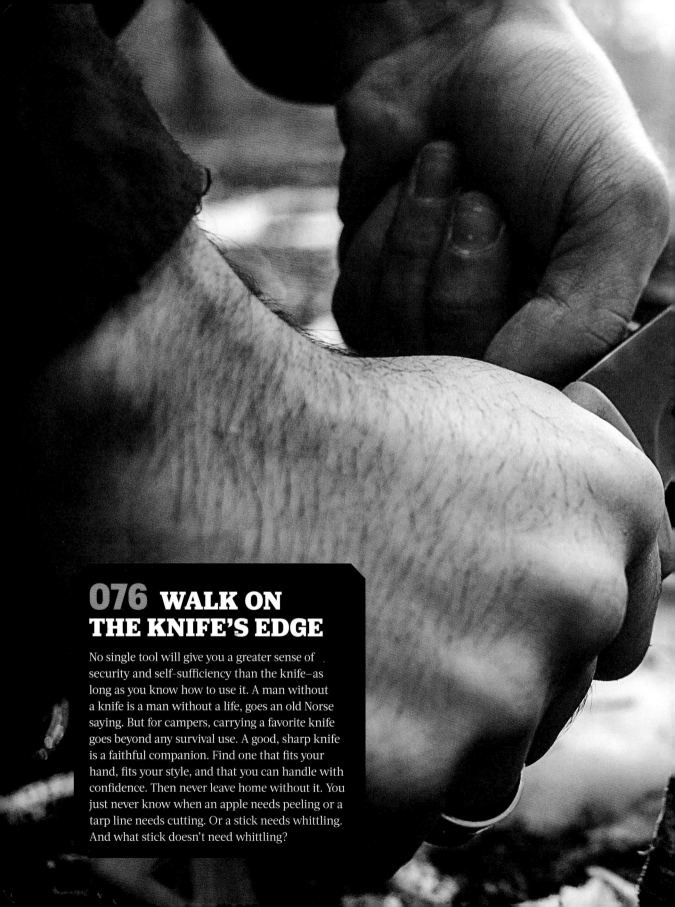

076 WALK ON THE KNIFE'S EDGE

No single tool will give you a greater sense of
security and self-sufficiency than the knife–as
long as you know how to use it. A man without
a knife is a man without a life, goes an old Norse
saying. But for campers, carrying a favorite knife
goes beyond any survival use. A good, sharp knife
is a faithful companion. Find one that fits your
hand, fits your style, and that you can handle with
confidence. Then never leave home without it. You
just never know when an apple needs peeling or a
tarp line needs cutting. Or a stick needs whittling.
And what stick doesn't need whittling?

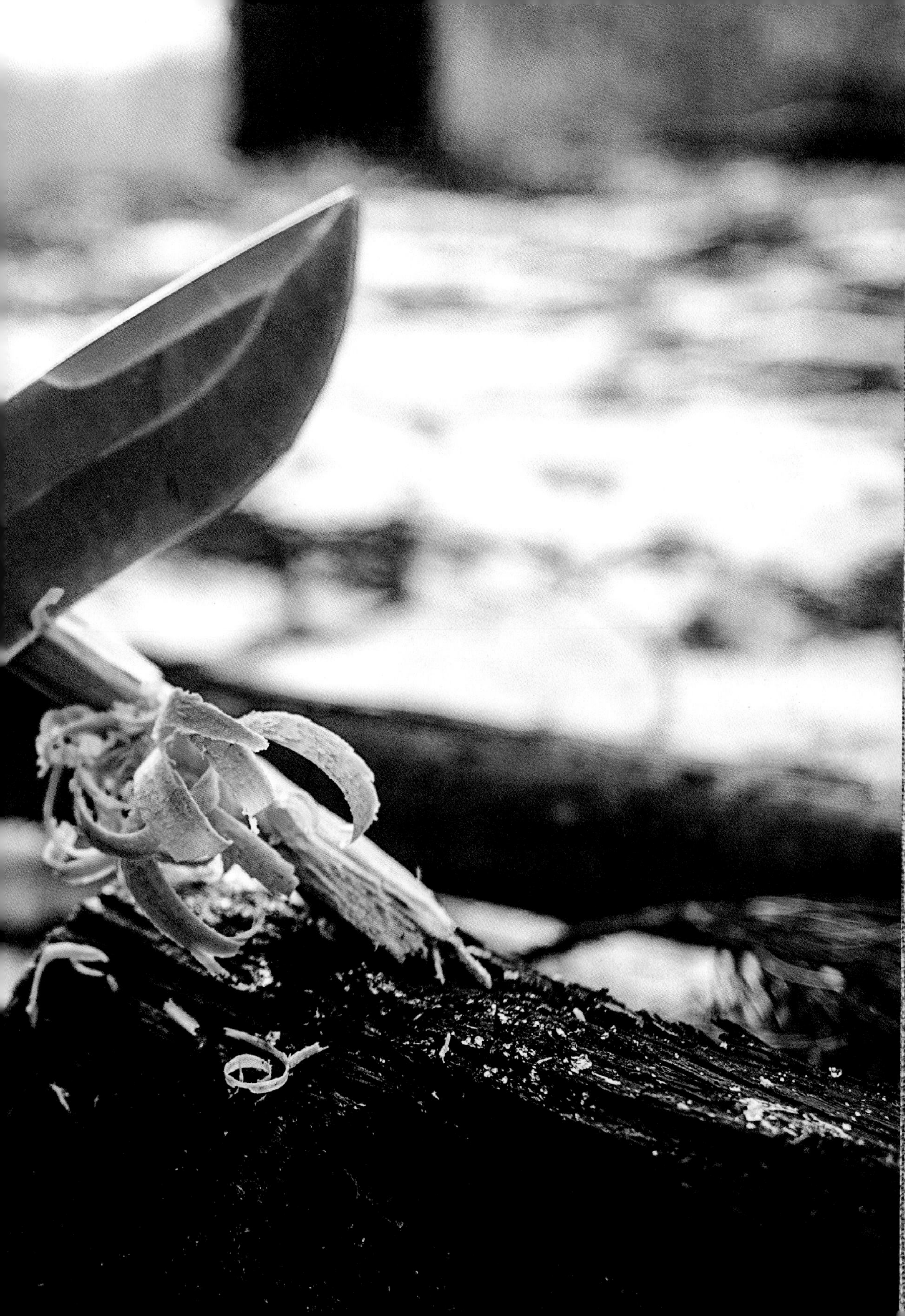

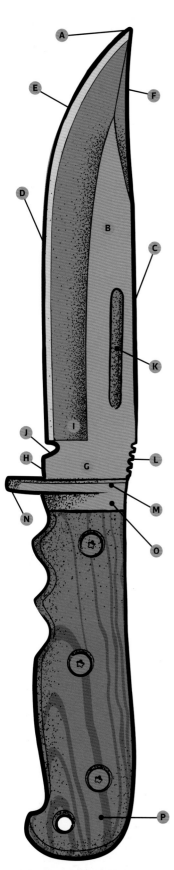

077 ANATOMY OF A FIXED-BLADE KNIFE

The sleek lines of a fixed-blade knife speak to the essence of outdoors competence. Fixed-blade knives consist of a blade, a handle, and a tang, which is the extension of the blade that carries into the handle. They are easy to clean and quick to deploy, with no moving parts to break or become gunked up. A strong fixed-blade knife can be batoned (struck on the spine) through wood. It can be twisted and torqued. Its strength comes from its seeming simplicity—although a cheaply made fixed-blade is no bargain at all. No fixed-blade knife is built with all the elements listed here, and many of them are found on folding knives, too. How designers choose among such a broad menu of options is what makes knives so endlessly fascinating.

A POINT Also called the tip. The sharper the point, the better a knife's piercing ability—though at the expense of tip strength.

B CHEEK The side of the blade, also called the face.

C SPINE The unsharpened back of the blade.

D EDGE The sharpened cutting surface.

E BELLY The curved section of the edge. A knife with lots of belly is useful for long, sweeping cuts like those used for skinning animals.

F SWEDGE A ground edge on the spine near the tip. A sharpened swedge increases piercing ability. Most are unsharpened and purely decorative.

G HEEL A general term for the section of the blade where it meets the handle or guard.

H RICASSO The short, unsharpened part of the blade between the edge bevel and the handle or guard. The ricasso allows for sharpening of the full blade without risk of marring the handle.

I PLUNGE LINE Where the cheek's grind meets the edge bevel.

J CHOIL An unsharpened, scalloped indent where the blade meets the handle. A large choil can be handy as a finger grip. Smaller choils serve as a stop for sharpening devices to protect the guard or handle.

K FULLER Often called a blood groove, this channel runs parallel to the spine. The fuller functions like an I-beam, reducing weight and adding strength.

L JIMPING Ground notches in the blade spine, and sometimes the handle, that provide traction for the user's finger.

M GUARD Designed to keep the hand from slipping onto the blade. Guards range in size, though many modern designs lack them.

N QUILLON An elongated point on the guard that provides added protection. Fighting and tactical knives often have double quillons, one on each side of the blade.

O BOLSTER A thick metal shoulder at the front of the handle, or separate pieces that sandwich the tang. Bolsters can be either separate pieces of metal or part of the blade and tang.

P POMMEL Also called the butt, this is the end of the handle. A stout pommel can be used to pound stakes.

078 ANATOMY OF A FOLDING KNIFE

In a folding knife, the blade swings around a pivot at one end of the handle. When open, it is locked into position. When closed, it is nestled inside the handle scales for safe carry in a pocket or pouch. From there, folding knife design varies widely. Much of a folder's design is centered on its greatest inherent weakness–the reliability of the lockup when open. Other aspects include speed of opening, beautiful handles, and sleek interior parts.

Manual folders that require the user to open the blade are still the most common type. Assisted-opening folders, in which spring mechanisms complete the opening process once the blade is partially opened, have joined the scene in recent years. Automatic folders–in which a spring mechanism exerts opening pressure on the blade with the mere press of a button–are growing in popularity as more states loosen knife restrictions.

The advent of the pocket clip ushered in a new way of thinking about carrying knives, complete with its own acronym: EDC, for "everyday carry." EDC knives are highly functional models designed to be clipped to a pocket or belt.

Fixed-blade and folding knives share plenty of common ground, but in many respects they're different species entirely. Here's the engineering behind the flick.

A **THUMB STUD** A metal stud or opening near the knife's pivot. By pressing or hooking a thumb onto the stud or opening, the blade can be swiveled open with one hand. Thumb studs are typically found on both sides of the blade to allow for ambidextrous opening.

B **PIVOT** The joint around which the blade swings. On some knives, the pivot can be manipulated to adjust the tension of the action.

C **LANYARD HOLE** Allows for the attachment of paracord or other cordage.

D **FLIPPER** A triggerlike protrusion on the blade that allows the knife to be flipped open with a finger. Not found on all knives.

E **OPEN FRAME** An open-frame folder has no backspacer. It can be cleaned easily, but the blade edge is exposed to loose change, keys, and other hard objects in a pocket.

F **STANDOFF** A metal pillar that provides the proper interior spacing for operation of the knife.

G **LINER** Thin plates, typically of steel or titanium, on the interior face of the handle slabs. The liners reinforce the handle; on liner-lock designs they serve as the locking mechanism.

H **POCKET CLIP** A metal clip that enables the user to clip the knife to a pocket for comfortable carry and quick deployment.

I **BACKSPACER** A strip of metal or tough synthetic material, such as G10, that spans the interior of the two sides of the knife handle. Metal backspacers are sometimes intricately filed.

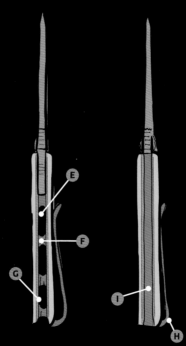
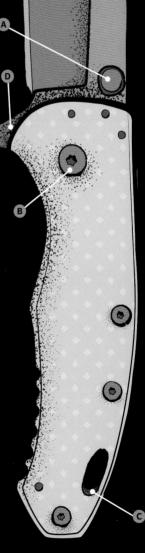

079 GET THE POINT

The shape of a blade determines how well that blade will perform specific tasks. It's a world of tradeoffs: Piercing ability, tip strength, slicing efficiency, and how much abuse a blade can take are all factors in deciding which knife blade profile is best for the task at hand. There's far more than looks involved when it comes to the shape of things that cut.

PROFILE	CHARACTERISTICS	BEST FOR	PROS	CONS
Ⓐ STRAIGHT BACK	A straight spine with an upward curving edge that rises to the spine to form a semi-sharp point.	Bushcrafting; kitchen tasks; learning sharpening techniques.	Very strong; easily batoned through wood; easy to apply force to spine with fingers or palm.	Not ideal for piercing tasks; not enough belly for skinning.
Ⓑ DROP POINT	A favorite of hunters, the drop point features a slight downward curve to the spine to form a lowered, or "dropped," point.	Field dressing and skinning; everyday carry (EDC).	Strong point retains a bit of belly for skinning; best for gutting animals, as the point angles away from organs.	With a tip less sharp than those of other profiles, it's not a great piercing blade.
Ⓒ TRAILING POINT	This blade's spine curves upward, and a trailing point provides a long, curved edge for slicing.	Skinning and caping animals; filleting fish.	Very sharp point; lots of belly; design gives lightweight knives additional length to the cutting edge.	Weak point; difficult to get in and out of a sheath.
Ⓓ CLIP POINT	The classic Bowie knife profile. A straight spine drops in a slight angle or concave curve to meet the tip, as if the spine were clipped off.	Skinning and caping animals; filleting fish.	Very controllable sharp point; decent belly; excels at piercing.	If the clip begins too far from the tip, the point of the blade can be weak.

Ⓐ   Ⓑ   Ⓒ   Ⓓ   Ⓔ   Ⓕ

PROFILE	CHARACTERISTICS	BEST FOR	PROS	CONS
E SPEAR POINT	A symmetrical profile with a spine that forms the centerline of the blade. Can be sharpened on one or both sides.	Piercing and thrusting; throwing knives.	Very sharp tip; can have a double cutting surface.	Not useful for non-fighting tasks.
F SPEY POINT	A defined, sudden downward curve to the spine that meets a curving, upswept edge. Commonly found on trapper-style pocketknives.	Traditionally used for castrating farm animals.	Easily sharpened; safe to use when a sharp point isn't needed.	That lack of a sharp point limits piercing ability; often a short blade.
G LEAF	This hybrid between a drop point and a spear point features a less aggressive downward slope to the spine with a more acute point.	Fine cutting that requires a sharp point; EDC; self-defense.	Easy to carry, as most leaf point blades are short.	Thin point can be weaker than that of other grinds.
H SHEEPSFOOT	A straight spine curves downward to meet a completely straight edge, with no sharp piercing tip.	Rescue work; use on inflatable boats; trimming hooves of small livestock.	Blunt tip can be very thick and strong; very controllable edge; easy to sharpen.	With no sharp tip, not useful for piercing tasks.
I WHARNCLIFFE	Similar to a sheepsfoot, with a downward curve or angle to the spine that starts closer to the handle of the knife.	Rescue work; self-defense; utility tasks.	Sharp piercing tip; strong, robust blade often built with thick blade stock.	No belly for skinning tasks.
J HAWKBILL	Shaped like a claw or talon—or a hawk's bill—the hawkbill profile has a sharply concave spine and cutting edge that meet at a downward point.	Utility work, such as cutting carpet and linoleum; self-defense.	Cutting webbing, heavy cordage and lines; sharp, inwardly curved tip is great for making long cuts.	No piercing ability; little utility for hunting and fishing.
K TANTO	Thick, with a straight edge that takes a sudden upward, uncurved angle near the blade tip to meet the spine at a straight or slightly convex angle.	Self-defense; EDC; general utility tasks.	Extremely strong and sharp tip; robust blade.	Tricky to sharpen; no belly for skinning.

At the turn of the 19th century, more than 200 different ax-head patterns were being manufactured in America. The choices are more limited today, but being able to swing an ax and deftly work a hatchet remain core skills for campers. Depending on your camping style you may not need both an ax and a hatchet. But you'll definitely need at least one. Or two. Or more. Here's what you need to know to match the edged tool to the woodsy job.

BIT BY BIT The bit, or cutting edge, profile is critical. A thin cutting profile works well when limbing felled trees or cutting branches into campfire wood. A more wedge-shaped profile excels in splitting log rounds.

CONSIDER THE CURVE A pronounced curve in the bit lessens bit-to-wood contact, allowing for deeper cuts. A flat bit cuts more evenly, but not as deeply.

GET A GRIP Proponents of curved handles consider them more efficient and easier on the hands. Straight-handle fans point out the strength inherent in wood grain running the length of the handle. Both camps claim greater accuracy. The best choice is the one that feels best in your hands.

SINGLE OR DOUBLE? A double-bit ax can serve double duty. One blade is sharpened to a narrow felling edge for taking down trees. The other is ground to a blunter edge for working through knots and cutting trees on the ground. A single-bit ax or hatchet has its own advantages. The poll can be hardened for hammering, but even an unhardened poll can be pounded with a wood baton to boost the cutting power of hatchet-sized bits.

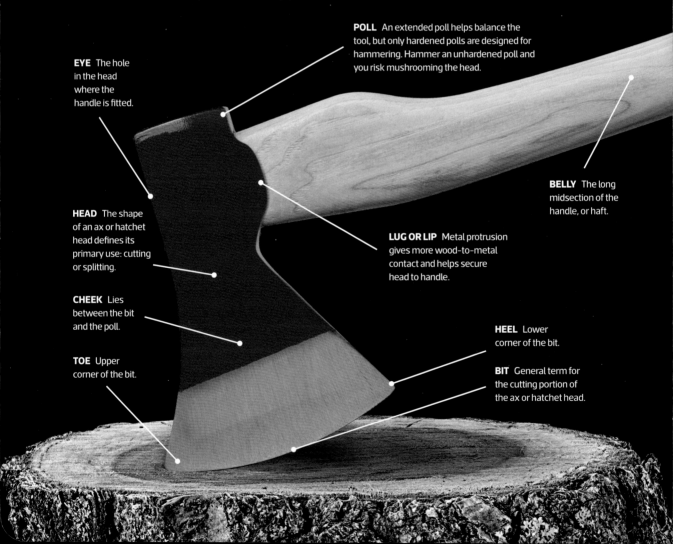

POLL An extended poll helps balance the tool, but only hardened polls are designed for hammering. Hammer an unhardened poll and you risk mushrooming the head.

EYE The hole in the head where the handle is fitted.

BELLY The long midsection of the handle, or haft.

HEAD The shape of an ax or hatchet head defines its primary use: cutting or splitting.

LUG OR LIP Metal protrusion gives more wood-to-metal contact and helps secure head to handle.

CHEEK Lies between the bit and the poll.

HEEL Lower corner of the bit.

TOE Upper corner of the bit.

BIT General term for the cutting portion of the ax or hatchet head.

THROAT The
sweep of the handle
towards the grip.

HANDLE Also
called the "haft."

GRIP The part of the
handle where the
hand holds the tool.
Can be textured for a
better purchase.

KNOB OR SWELL
Prevents handle from
slipping in sweaty hands.

081 CHOOSE THE RIGHT HAFT FOR YOU

Straight or curved? Ax handles come in a wide variety
of shapes, from ruler-straight hafts to various S-curves
and sweeping bends. The shape of a handle affects the
physics of the swing, and while the best choice is a
matter of experience and opinion, there are guidelines
to steer your decision.

Pioneering American woodsmen favored a straight
ax handle. Double-bit axes require a straight handle
so both edges can be used effectively.

Curved handles change the angle of your wrist
and forearm in relation to the handle and the head.
Many people prefer curved handles for their ease of
gripping. But too much curve in a handle, especially at
the bottom, can increase the chances of pivoting your
wrist on the swing, which decreases both the force
and accuracy of the strike. On many curved handles,
a swollen knob at the end, called the "fawn's foot,"
provides additional purchase.

With so many ax-head options to choose from, and so many various campsite tasks to handle, you might not want just one ax or hatchet in camp, but many. Try this list of suggestions to handle all of your chopping, cutting, and splitting needs.

AMERICAN FELLING AX

The classic American ax design, the felling ax evolved into dozens of regional variations such as the Dayton and Jersey axes. The thin, sharp bits excel at tasks that require cross-grain cutting,

HUDSON BAY AX

With a smaller handle and head, the Hudson Bay design was favored by fur traders traveling long distances by canoe. Hefty enough to work through medium-size logs, its relatively light weight makes it a good camping choice if you need an ax.

CAMPING HATCHET

With a handle around 18 inches (45 cm) long, a hatchet is designed to be used with one hand. It's the perfect camping tool for splitting kindling, chopping up branches, and pounding tent stakes.

SPLITTING AX OR HATCHET

One of the best camping tools around. The wedge-shaped head splits wood apart along the grain, and when you're splitting log rounds like those commonly purchased for camping, this hatchet is a miracle.

083 SHARPEN YOUR KNIFE WITH A COFFEE CUP

You might not have a sharpening stone handy, but a ceramic coffee mug will work in a pinch. They're common at country diners, and you should keep one in your camp kitchen kit. Turn it upside down, and you should see a raised rim with a dull finish. When ceramic mugs are glazed in a kiln, they rest on that rim, leaving an unglazed surface. That raw, unfinished ceramic is similar to what is used in a ceramic sharpening rod. Turn the mug upside down and place it on a non-slippery surface. Lay the knife blade on the rim at a 20-degree angle and stroke the edge into the ceramic with medium pressure. Count 10 strokes, then repeat on the other side.

084 SHARPEN AN AX OR HATCHET

Before you begin, place the head of the tool in a vise, with the head in a horizontal position. No vice? Use a stout C-clamp to clamp it to the edge of a workbench with the edge just hanging over the table. Pull on work gloves to protect your hands from the wicked edge these steps will produce.

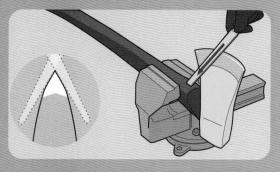

RESTORE THE PROFILE Using a flat, single-cut mill bastard file, establish a 15-degree sharpening angle and file away nicks, gouges, and turned edges.

SHARPEN Hold the file at 20 to 25 degrees, and use long downward strokes across the edge. Flip the ax over and repeat on the other side.

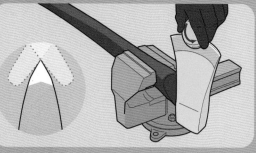

HONE Use a medium-sized whetstone with both a coarse and fine side. Starting with the coarse side, oil the stone, hold the ax head in one hand, and hone with small, circular motions all along the cutting edge. Repeat with the other side. Switch to the whetstone's fine side, and repeat the process.

085 DON'T FORGET A SAW

It's amazing how quickly a good saw can chew through tough wood. They're great for turning long branches into firewood-sized chunks, and excel at clearing roads and trails. These three saws cover a range of camp duties.

PRUNING SAW Short saws of about 8 inches (20cm) when closed can still work like a beast. Look for a saw made with heavy-gauge steel about .050 inches (.13 cm) thick, which will resist bending when working through dense wood. A slight curve in the blade will help start the cut and keep the blade in place when you're bearing down. A pruning saw is perfect to stow in a pack.

FOLDING SAW Many camp saws are designed with a blade that can be loosened and folded into the handle for easy storage and carry. They often fold into a single, straight piece, so they're easily lashed to or tucked into packs for longer trail trips.

BOW SAW Named for the bent handle, a bow saw is typically made of a metal frame and a stout, crosscutting blade. It's not the most compact saw, but it will chew through branches and logs up to about 6 inches in diameter. Great for car camping.

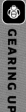

086 UP YOUR NET WORTH

Small nets and seines made for nature observation are great to have on a camping trip. Just remember to collect gently, and release whatever you catch quickly after taking a look.

AERIAL ANTICS A butterfly net can help ignite a child's love of nature. Or at least give them something to do while you make a camp dinner! Look for a lightweight net with a telescoping handle for easy transport and storage.

STREAM SCOOPER An aquatic sampling net is built with a stout D-shaped net frame with a "net saver" guard that reinforces the front of the net. You can use it to carefully scoop up frogs, salamanders, crayfish, and other stream creatures for study.

WINDOW IN THE WATER Pack a 3-foot (90 cm) length of window screening for a DIY creek seine. Have someone in the creek a few feet upstream turn over rocks and kick their feet around while you hold the screen vertically in the creek flow below. You can catch lots of bottom-dwelling insects for a quick nature lesson.

087 TIE THE KNOT WITH PARACORD

Don't leave home without at least 50 feet (15 m) of parachute cord, a.k.a. paracord. Originally used as suspension lines in military parachutes, it's now the four-wheel-drive of ropes and cords. It has as many uses as duct tape, from lashing broken tent poles to hanging food bags away from bears to serving as a camp clothes line. It was even used in outer space to repair the Hubble Space Telescope. But beware: There are tons of fake paracords on the market. The real stuff should be marked as "Type III 550." Comprising seven twisted strands wrapped in a braided outer sheath, it has a breaking strength of 550 pounds.

088 MAKE A MINI ROLL OF DUCT TAPE

Duct tape is famous as a jack-of-all-trades, but the rolls are bulky and heavy, and hikers and backpackers don't need to carry all that weight. Wrapping a water bottle or trekking pole with duct tape has been a favorite trick for stashing it in a convenient spot. Here are three other ways to make sure you're never in the woods without the sticky stuff.

WRAP A PENCIL Break off a pencil stub a bit longer than the width of duct tape, and wrap it with tape. Now you'll have both duct tape and a survival pencil, which you can use to write a note or shave into fire starter. You can also saw a 2-inch-long (5 cm) piece of plastic coat hanger and wrap it with tape.

UNLOCK POTENTIAL Stack two plastic hotel room key cards (one isn't quite long enough) and wrap duct tape around them, leave about a half-inch of one of the cards exposed. Then, drill a 1/4-inch (6-mm) hole in one corner. Now you can clip it to a pack or piece of webbing with a carabiner.

MAKE A KEY FOB You'll never be without duct tape if you carry it on your key chain. Break off a pencil about 2 inches (5 cm) long. Lay a paper clip along the pencil so one end extends beyond the top. Wrap duct tape around the pencil and attach the paper clip loop to a keychain.

089 GO BEYOND DUCT TAPE

Check out these three other sticky strips to have and to hold.

GORILLA TAPE It's duct tape 2.0, with a double-thick adhesive layer that even grips surfaces such as rusty metal, masonry, and lightly furrowed tree bark. The fabric itself is twice as thick as standard duct tape, with offset textile patterns that the manufacturer claims make it 145 percent stronger than original duct tape. Its only shortcoming: Gorilla Tape doesn't stretch.

TENACIOUS TAPE Made from tough nylon tent fabric, this strong repair tape closes up rips in tents, tarps, sleeping bags, packs, and down jackets. Designed for field use, it lasts practically forever, and ratty strips on a scarred-up coat are badges of honor. Unlike off-the-shelf duct tape, it leaves no sticky residue when removed. Available in a half-dozen colors, plus clear.

RESCUE TAPE This self-fusing silicone tape chemically bonds to itself, creating an air-tight, waterproof seal almost instantly. It's perfect for field fixes of leaky vehicle hoses. It stretches, so it's a go-to tape for field repairs and tool handle wraps.

090 PACK FOR CAMP COMFORT

Of course, you have to pack a tent and sleeping bag, cooking gear, and a flashlight, but beyond the basics are a few luxuries that will make camping life easier and far more comfortable.

SPREAD IT OUT You'll be glad to have a separate kitchen table. Camp stoves take up a lot of space, and it's a pain to both cook and serve on a picnic table. Collapsible kitchen tables stow easily and often come with handy carry handles. Buy one.

NOD OFF Forget all that business about filling a stuff sack with spare clothes to use as a pillow. Camping pillows come in various designs, from small versions that compress for packing to inflatable pillows that don't take up much space at all. Your neck will thank you.

TAKE A SEAT A great camp chair is almost a requirement, otherwise you'll be stuck sitting on a hard picnic bench or, even worse, a log. If you're car camping, spring for a collapsible camp chair with solid back support and arms. If size or weight are a concern, there are tons of lightweight chairs designed for backpackers and music festival fans.

KNOCK AROUND It's the simple things, and having an easy, slip-on pair of camp shoes by the sleeping bag will start your day off with a smile. Nobody wants to bend over and tie laces when they first crawl out of a bag. And it's a bonus to have a dedicated pair of slip-on shoes to wear around sooty campfires and muddy campsites. This is the time to rock Crocs with socks.

091 PERFORM THESE 3 IN-STORE TESTS

What can 5 minutes of poking, pulling, and burying yourself in a sleeping bag tell you about the gear you're about to buy? Plenty, if you take advantage of these in-store gear tests. Just ignore the stares of other shoppers, and think twice about buying from a store that won't let you put its products through these paces.

SLEEPING BAG Take off your shoes, spread the bag on a cot or the store floor, and climb in. Sit up in the bag and try to touch your toes. If it binds you, opt for a longer size. Next, lie back down. Zip the bag open and closed three times from the inside, and three times from the outside. If the zipper gets seriously stuck on the zipper tape or draft tube, keep looking.

BOOTS Shop in the late afternoon when your feet will have swollen up as much as they're going to over the course of a day. Be sure to wear the socks you prefer in the field. Put the candidate boots on and then lean forward slightly. Slide your index finger between your heel and the inside of the boot. There shouldn't be much more than a half-inch gap. Next, kick the wall. If your toes rub or bump the front of the boot, tie the laces a bit tighter and try again. Still bumping? Keep shopping.

FLASHLIGHT First, make sure you can manipulate all settings while wearing gloves. Headlamps, in particular, tend to have small switches. Next, tape a piece of unlined white paper to the wall of the store's changing room or bathroom, and turn off the light (if possible). Look for a bright central spot beam with enough spill–light around the edges–to illuminate the sides of a trail. Dark spots and circles show on the paper? Grab a different light.

092 LEARN THE TAO OF THE 5-GALLON BUCKET

Campers love new gear, and in our rush for the coolest, most cutting-edge gadgets out there we overlook some of the more common items–such as the lowly 5-gallon (19l) bucket. It may be the most useful piece of camping gear you never pack.

- Line it with a trash bag for the ultimate campsite trash can. Use two 5-gallon buckets, one inside the other, as a handy trash compactor.

- Slide a pool noodle over the rim and voila: A camp toilet.

- It's a great little stepladder.

- Shower tote–place your toiletries and towel inside for visits to the bath house.

- Add a clean bathroom plunger for a campsite clothes washing machine.

- Fill it with non-perishable food, and hang it in a tree to keep the mice out of your grub.

- And of course–turn it upside down and take a seat.

093 BRING BATTERIES BACK TO LIFE

When batteries give way in frigid conditions there are ways to pump them up with temporary new life. These techniques won't give you enough juice to battle your way to the next Call of Duty level, but you could get enough to lock down your location on a GPS or send a text.

BODY HEAT First, remove batteries from the device, when possible. Warm them next to your body. Armpits work well. Chest pockets do the trick, especially if you are moving and generating body heat. Overnight, toss batteries into the foot of a sleeping bag. They should be ready to fire up come dawn.

HAND WARMER If you have a granulated, air-activated handwarmer, place the handwarmer and batteries inside a closed pouch or a pocket. Better yet, duct-tape the handwarmer directly to the batteries.

SOLAR JUMP-START The principle behind a solar shower can revive dead batteries. Fill a zippered clear plastic bag with dark material–a black t-shirt, dark leaves, or a swath of black foam padding. Place the batteries on top of this dark material, close the bag, and place it in direct sunlight. The sun will heat the dark material, the resulting warm air will be trapped inside the bag, and the batteries should heat up sufficiently for a few seconds or minutes of emergency use.

094 TREAT WATER ANYWHERE

Getting away from it all sometimes entails getting away from a fresh source of water. Most public lands and private-ownership campgrounds will have a source of potable water, either from a bathhouse or a hand-operated pump. Elsewhere, you'll have to provide a means of filtering water for drinking and cooking. And even if you're off for a simple day hike, packing a small water filter will ensure that you'll stay hydrated and healthy on the trail.

There are lots of choices. One thing to note is the difference between water filters and water purifiers. They are not interchangeable terms. Water filters remove dangerous bacteria, protozoa, and nasty illness-causing cysts such as cryptosporidium and giardia. They also filter out sediment. Water purifiers kill all those nasties, as well, but also kill viruses. For most use in North America, a water filter is sufficient. For global travelers in places where human waste treatment is an issue, adding virus protection is a wise choice.

A STRAW FILTER With a small filter fitted inside a tubular housing, a straw filter allows you to drink directly from the water source. Just place the straw end into a creek, pool, or pot of water, and suck the water through the filter.
THUMBS UP Very compact, inexpensive, and intuitive to use.
THUMBS DOWN You can't store the water, so straw filters are only useful at the source. And using one requires you to lie down to access the water, or else scoop it up with a container and sip from it.

B PUMP FILTER A classic approach for backpackers and day hikers. Most include a tube that draws dirty water into the filter and a tube that drains clean water out. In between is a filter operated by physically pumping a lever.
THUMBS UP Proven design, some models remove viruses and can suck water out of shallow puddles.
THUMBS DOWN A bit heavy, and pumping the filters can require significant hand and arm strength.

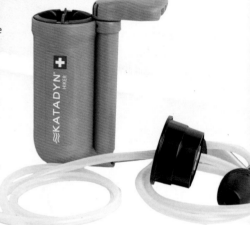

C GRAVITY-FED FILTER Let Mother Nature do the work: Fill a reservoir bag, hang it from a tree branch or post, and gravity draws the water down through the filter device and into a separate collection container.
THUMBS UP Hands-free once you set it up, great for larger groups.
THUMBS DOWN A little cumbersome to pack, more expensive than other types.

D UV PURIFIERS Utilizing UV light to kill bacteria, viruses, and dangerous cysts is quick and straightforward. You simply turn the penlight-shaped device on, and let it sit in a water bottle for 90 seconds or so.
THUMBS UP Very easy to use, portable, and lightweight.
THUMBS DOWN Requires batteries, won't purify large quantities of water, and does not filter sediments.

E **SQUEEZE FILTER** A receptacle bag holds the dirty water and is attached to a small filter. Squeezing the bag forces the water through the filter and out a small nozzle. You can either drink straight from the nozzle or output clean water to a container.

THUMBS UP Very light and easy to use, a great solution for one or two people, some models remove viruses.

THUMBS DOWN Slow and suitable for drinking water primarily.

F **BOTTLE FILTER** A handy unit integrated within a water bottle. You simply fill the bottle from a spring, creek, or other water source, and drink as usual.

THUMBS UP Lightweight, easy to use, very portable and perfect for day hikes and shorter outings when you know you'll be crossing creeks or staying near water.

THUMBS DOWN Limited volume and they can be slow. Best for one-person use.

095 BEHOLD THE ULTIMATE PACKING LIST

This checklist covers gear needed for two people for a weekend under the stars, with added ideas if you'll have the family in tow. Make a copy of this checklist and add to it as you gain more camping experience.

ESSENTIAL FURNISHINGS
- [ ] Tent, with stakes and footprint
- [ ] Sleeping bags
- [ ] Sleeping pads
- [ ] Camp pillows
- [ ] Tarp

PERSONAL GEAR
- [ ] First aid kit
- [ ] Water bottles
- [ ] Foam ear plugs
- [ ] Maps and compass
- [ ] Headlamps
- [ ] Spare batteries
- [ ] Knife
- [ ] Multi-tool
- [ ] Duct tape
- [ ] Paracord
- [ ] Zip ties
- [ ] SuperGlue
- [ ] Hatchet
- [ ] Folding saw
- [ ] 3 ways to start a fire—lighter, matches, spark tool
- [ ] Repair kit for sleeping pad, tent poles

FAMILY CAMPING ADD-ONS
- [ ] Books for reading in tent
- [ ] Small broom and dust pan
- [ ] Daypack
- [ ] Favorite stuffed animals

CAMPSITE COMFORT & FUN
- [ ] Indoor/outdoor carpet for doormat
- [ ] Lantern with fuel/ spare mantles/ batteries
- [ ] Camp chair
- [ ] Camp table
- [ ] Binoculars
- [ ] Field guides for birds and wildflowers
- [ ] Flying disc

FAMILY CAMPING ADD-ONS
- [ ] Board games and toys
- [ ] Clothesline and clips
- [ ] Screen house
- [ ] Camp shower
- [ ] Butterfly and stream net

CAMP KITCHEN
- [ ] 2- or 3-burner camp stove
- [ ] Pot set
- [ ] Collapsible frying pan
- [ ] Measuring/mixing cup
- [ ] Pot grabber
- [ ] Coffee pot or French press and mugs
- [ ] Medium chef knife
- [ ] Paring knife
- [ ] Mixing and serving spoons
- [ ] Spatula
- [ ] Metal tongs
- [ ] Stackable bowls, plates, and cups
- [ ] Forks, knives, and spoons
- [ ] Cups
- [ ] Biodegradable soap
- [ ] Quick-dry towels
- [ ] Pot scrubber
- [ ] Trash bags
- [ ] Charcoal chimney
- [ ] Bottle opener
- [ ] Corkscrew
- [ ] Spices, assorted
- [ ] Can opener
- [ ] Military can opener for backup
- [ ] Collapsible water container
- [ ] Aluminum foil
- [ ] Fire gloves
- [ ] Flexible cutting boards
- [ ] Thermacell with extra repellent pads and fuel
- [ ] Water filter
- [ ] Toilet paper
- [ ] Paper towels

FAMILY CAMPING ADD-ONS
- [ ] Tablecloth and clips
- [ ] Hammock
- [ ] Large fry pan
- [ ] No. 10 Dutch oven
- [ ] Dutch oven lid lifter
- [ ] Hand-powered blender

096 BRING ALL THE RIGHT STUFF

There's a simple way to make sure you pack all the right gear for any trip. Think through a typical day, starting with the crack of dawn, and work through each activity. You wake up, and what do you do? Drink coffee. (Coffee press, mug, stove.) Make a fire. (Lighter, firestarter, saw.) Eat breakfast. (Plates, knives, biodegradable dishwashing soap.) Imagine yourself throughout the day (toothbrush, shower shoes), and all the awesome fun you will have on hikes (trekking poles, binoculars, water filter, daypack) and relaxing at the campsite (camp chair, playing cards) with your dog (don't forget his food and treats). Come nightfall, you might turn in early (pillow, headlamp, book, earplugs) and you'll be glad you checked the weather (sleeping bag liner, sleeping hat). Taking an imaginary trip will help you remember some of those easy-to-forget items (oh no, you forgot the wine bottle opener!) that you'll have a hard time getting by without.

ESSENTIAL SKILLS

Find the Perfect Campsite
What to look for and what to avoid

Read Any Map

All Tied Up
Learn the only 6 knots you'll ever need

Bring Your Dog!
How to camp with a canine

Medical Kit
First-aid solutions for every camper

Survive Anything
Snake bites, lightning strikes, and how to stay found

097 CLAIM YOUR SPOT

In most campgrounds, there's a process for staking your claim to a campsite, and it's best to have a solid plan in place before you arrive. Unless you have a specific site reserved, you'll need to cruise the campground roads, choose your site, mark your territory with some piece of gear, then bolt back to the campground office to lock down your choice. At some campgrounds, camp hosts or officials are pretty chill about the process. Elsewhere, you'd better follow the reservation instructions to the letter, or you'll be booted to the back of the line.

MAP IT OUT Familiarize yourself with any online campground maps before you arrive, so you'll have a general sense of the layout and already know that Loop B runs by the creek, for example, while Loop G is too close to the highway. Print out a map to bring with you in case cell service at the campground isn't so hot.

TROLL THE WEB As with anything these days, there is no shortage of online reviews of specific campsites, and some even include photographs taken by recent campers. Sleuth out the ones that look promising and make notes on your printed map.

PLANT YOUR FLAG Once you choose an open site, you'll need to hold it by leaving behind a sleeping bag, cooler, or strong-willed child while you return to the office to fill out paperwork. Plan on what–or who–will be used as a marker so you're not unpacking half the car while the next group snags the campsite out from under you.

BRING CASH Many campgrounds, public ones in particular, only accept cash for payment of the nightly fee. Stock up on some folding money before heading out.

098 PUT UP AN A-FRAME TARP

If there's even the slightest chance of rain, string a tarp up as soon as you can. A tarp does more than provide a dry place for cooking and hanging out in a rainstorm (or give your family shade from a searing sun). It provides a visual anchor for the entire campsite, and turns a flat place in the woods into a homey outdoor living room. You can have a tarp up in two minutes if you have it pre-tied and follow this routine.

PREP BEFORE YOU GO Attach 15-foot (4.5-m) guylines at each corner of the tarp, as well as at the midpoints of the sides if there are grommets or loop tie-outs. In the tarp's stuff sack, stash at least 50-foot (15-m) of parachute cord for a ridgeline, another 10 sections of cord cut to 20-foot (6-m) lengths for extra guylines, and a dozen stakes.

DEPLOY IT IN THE FIELD If you're in a wooded area, use a trucker's hitch to tie the parachute cord ridgeline tautly to two trees. If there are no trees, you'll need a couple of tall poles and two helpers:

Each person holds a pole while you string the ridgeline between them, then stake out a pair of guylines to each pole to hold them in place. Once the ridgeline is up, drape one edge of the tarp over it and stake out the corner guylines or tie them to trees. Stretch the tarp out and repeat on the opposite edge. You can move the tarp along the ridgeline to change the shelter's apex if you want more or less tarp on either side. If needed, erect a center pole to peak the tarp so the rain runs off.

099 DRY BOOTS WITH A HOT ROCK

You almost made it across the creek–but now your feet are soaked, your boots are sloshing, and you're headed for misery. Here's how to dry your boots from the inside out.

STEP 1 Remove the insoles and set them aside. Pack boots with absorbent material: paper towels or newspaper if you have them, dry leaves and grasses if you don't. Remove the materials and repeat until you've gotten as much moisture out as possible.

STEP 2 Heat rocks in boiling water or near the fire, then carefully place in spare socks or a bandana. Test the stones for 10 seconds to make sure they don't scorch the material, then fill up the boot. Or pour boiling water into small water bottles and tuck them into the boots.

STEP 3 While your boots are cooking, work on the insoles. Press them between spare clothing, paper towels or dried grasses, and squeeze hard to express

water. Toss them in the bottom of your sleeping bag for the final overnight finish.

STEP 4 If you prop boots and insoles by the fire, go easy. Fire-baked leather will crack and synthetic material can melt. Insoles can harden in the heat without much of a visual warning. If you can't press your hand to the warmed boot and leave it there, move it back from the fire.

100 STAY WARM IN A SLEEPING BAG

There's nothing worse than waking up in the middle of the night with the shivers, so do what you can to make sure your sleeping system is toasty for the long haul. Here are six ways to sleep like a warm log all night long.

TURN ON THE "STOVE" Place a water bottle filled with hot water in the sleeping bag 30 minutes before you turn in.

FLEECE YOUR FEET Stash soft, dry clothing such as long underwear and a fleece vest in the sleeping bag's foot box. The garments will absorb foot moisture throughout the night and insulate your lower body. Bonus points: You'll have warm undies in the morning.

ESTABLISH GROUND CONTROL The cold ground can chill an air mattress, which, in turn, chills you. Add a layer of protection by covering your sleeping pad with a blanket before laying your sleeping bag down.

PULL ON A JACKET Zip up your winter coat and pull it over the end of the sleeping bag. Feet get cold first because they are a long way from your body's core.

BUNDLE UP Don't wait until you're shivering to pull on a layer of long underwear or dig your beanie out of the pack. Layer up before lights out.

GO POTTY Pee at the last possible moment. You'll stay warmer with an empty bladder, plus nothing brings on goose bumps like a midnight dash to the privy.

101 MAKE A NEST

The specific placement of the tent is critical to a good night's sleep. Before you pitch it, prep the ground where your sleeping bag will be.

STEP 1 Pace off the ground that will be under the tent and clear it of rocks and sticks.

STEP 2 Scrape leaves or loose soil into any divots and small holes under the tent space.

STEP 3 Dig or tamp down a slight depression in the ground—a couple inches is plenty—where your pelvis will be once you lay down. If you sleep on your back, this reduces painful pressure points on the small of your back. If you're a side-sleeper, your hip will nestle in the hole, keeping your spine aligned for a more restful snooze.

102 SLEEP UNDER THE STARS

When there's little chance of rain or mosquitoes, sleeping under the stars cowboy-style might change your camping approach. You'll watch tree limbs dance across the constellations and wake up to sunbeams on your face. You might be a bit unsettled at first, but it won't take long before you swear off tents forever. Here's how to snooze comfortably in the great wide open.

MAKE YOUR BED Sleeping sans a tent doesn't mean you drop and flop. First, spread out a space blanket or ground cloth, then center your sleeping pad and bag on top of it. The extra ground covering is nice if you need to stretch your arms outside of your bag, and it keeps ground moisture at bay.

WEAR A HAT Pull on a beanie to hold in some body heat, and dress warmly. Without the insulating and breeze-blunting properties of a tent, you'll need to prepare for a cooler night.

SET A NIGHTSTAND Place your boots near your head and drop a water bottle in one and a flashlight in the other. That way, you'll be able to find them quickly in the middle of the night.

103 IDENTIFY THE PERFECT CAMPSITE

The perfect campsite is as much about what it has as what it doesn't. It should have flat ground for the tents, decent access to water, and shelter from the winds. It should not have dangerous dead trees or blistering sun or an infestation of mosquitoes. And add bonus points if it has a view that makes you want to leap from the tent and high-five the rising sun. Here's what to look for when it's time to nest.

GO WITH THE FLOW Anticipate low spots, which will collect rainwater, and hills and ridges that could funnel water from a heavy storm under your tent. It's better to find another site than to dig unsightly trenches.

HAVE A POTTY PLAN If you're in a developed campground, consider your distance from the bathhouse. You want to be close enough to make an easy dash to the loo, but not so close that you're bothered by others tramping in and out all night long.

LOOK UP Study the overhead canopy for "widow-makers"–dead standing trees or large dead branches that could fall during the night and crush

or skewer a hapless camper. And avoid cliffs where loose rocks could tumble onto the tent.

HEAD UPHILL You'll want the flattest spot possible for the tent. Any incline and you'll roll off the sleeping pad into your tent mate or spend the night smashed into the wall of the tent. If you must pitch on a slight hill, have your head uphill.

TURN UP THE TEMP If you're cold-natured and grumpy on a chilly morning, camp higher rather than lower. Cooling air flows downhill during the night, and will make a valley campsite significantly colder at dawn.

FEEL THE WIND It's helpful to camp in the lee of a windbreak. That could be a stand of trees, a steep ridge, or a pile of boulders.

LET THERE BE LIGHT Think about where the sun will rise. If you don't want to be blasted at first light, pitch your tent in the shade. But it's a good idea to place the cooking and eating area in the sun for those early warming rays while you sip your coffee.

104 BOWLINE KNOT

Known as the "King of Knots," the bowline forms a single loop. It's very secure, won't jam no matter how hard you pull on it, and can be tied one-handed if you practice. It's the go-to knot for many rescue operators, but it has a million uses around camp even when there's no emergency at hand. Use it to hang a food bag, hoist loads, create a loop for carabiners, and tie guylines to tents and rainflies.

STEP 1 Remember the phrase: "The rabbit comes out of the hole, runs around the tree, and goes back in the hole." Make an overhand loop in your rope (the rabbit hole) and pull the working end (the rabbit) through the loop from the underside.

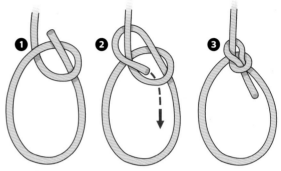

STEP 2 Circle that working end behind the rope above the loop (the tree) and then back through it.

STEP 3 Pull tight.

105 BUTTERFLY LOOP

This super easy knot creates a loop anywhere along the length of a rope or cord, and it's as easy to untie as it is to tie. Use it to create a handy gear-hanging line with multiple loops.

STEP 1 Hang a rope from your hand and wrap it twice to form three coils (a). Move the far right coil toward the left, over the middle coil (b). What was the right coil is now the center coil.

STEP 2 Move the new right coil to the left over the top of the other two coils (c).

STEP 3 Take the coil you just moved to the left and pass it back to the right, under the remaining coils, to form a loop (d).

STEP 4 Pinch this loop against your palm, using your thumb to hold it. Slide your hand to the right, pulling this loop (e). Tighten by pulling both ends of the rope (f).

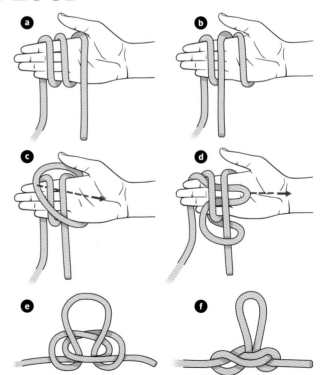

106 BONE UP ON THE DOG RULES

Why, of course! Everyone everywhere would love to hang out with your perfect dog. But that's not how the camping rules are written. There are lots of regulations regarding camping and your beloved canine–or cat, snake, or pet alpaca. And just because a place is "dog-friendly" doesn't mean it is "let-your-dog-off-the-leash-to-run-up-the-trail" friendly. Here's the general approach at most camping areas.

PRIVATE CAMPGROUNDS It's rare that a private, commercial campground will allow pets off a leash, but many put out the welcome mat with fenced dog runs and dedicated outdoor places for pets to relieve themselves.

NATIONAL PARKS Most national parks allow pets, and those that do typically have tight regulations. You'll likely have to keep your pooch on a leash at all times, including on trails and even in campgrounds. And in national park backcountry, you might not be able to bring them at all. Check with park authorities before you go.

NATIONAL FORESTS AND BLM LANDS These multiple-use lands are often the most pet-friendly. Leash laws might be in play inside designated campgrounds, but you may be able to let Rover roam off the leash while dispersed camping and in the backcountry. For the most part, though, keep your dog under your control, always clean up waste, and be ever aware that other hikers and campers may not be the dog fan that you are.

STATE PARKS AND FORESTS When it comes to pets, these lands can be as restrictive as national parks. Most welcome pets on a leash in campgrounds and on trails. But there can be exceptions, especially on public ocean, sound, and lake beaches. Know before you go.

107 DRILL WITH THREE TRAINING COMMANDS

You don't have to have the most finely trained hound in the world to enjoy camping with one. But you'll be doing your dog—and everyone else—a favor by having a solid grounding in these three commands.

THE RECALL COMMAND Whether it's "come" or "here," a recall command demands that your dog return to your side from wherever it's roamed. It's necessary to keep an off-leash dog from chasing animals or getting too far up the trail and bothering other hikers.

THE "LEAVE IT" COMMAND A stern command of "leave it" should be ingrained in any dog. "Leave it" means leave whatever you're messing with alone: Leave that half-rotten banana at the dumpster. Leave that fascinating pile of piquant poop. Put down that old animal bone. Drop whatever smelly, skanky, disgusting thing you've found and go about your business.

THE STAY COMMAND Every dog should have this one dialed in. It's as much about safety for your pooch as it is helpful for anyone traveling with a dog. "Stay" means "stay right here and don't move an inch." Every time.

108 DOUBLE UP ON DOGGIE ID

Nothing is worse than losing track of your trail pal, if only for a few minutes. Be prepared with these easy precautions.

CHECK THOSE TAGS Make sure ID tags are legible and solidly attached to the collar. Exploring the great outdoors is a great way to lose a poorly attached ID tag.

GO BEYOND THE ID TAG Microchip your pet. It's the best, cheapest investment for your peace of mind.

SHOW YOUR ID Make a laminated card with your pet's photo, identifying information, health history and concerns, and your contact information. Include microchip info if available. If your pet goes missing, you'll have a head start on identifying it to others in the area.

SMILE FOR THE CAMERA If you don't go the ID card route, at least take a good pic of your dog, showing any distinctive markings. Print out several copies so you'll have them ready if your bestie goes on a walkabout.

109 PRACTICE WITH YOUR POOCH

Before you head out to the wilds, have a trial run in your backyard and simulate a campground situation as much as possible. Keep the dog leashed, build a big fire, and have a friend or two over to hang out. You'll uncover any potential trouble spots. Some dogs love a campfire, for example, while others are anxious around a blaze. Create a short list of items you won't want to be without: a collar light, collapsible water bowl, doggie sleeping bag, and a doggie daypack if you think your pooch can handle it. And don't forget extra towels and waterless shampoo. They *will* romp through mud. They *will* roll in poop.

110 PREPARE FOR FIRST AID

Skunks, porcupines, exciting new smells, muck and mud, cactus, snakes—it's an exciting new world out there for the pooch. Be prepared with these items.

- First aid book for treating pets
- Contact information and directions to the nearest veterinarian or emergency pet clinic
- Booties for protecting injured paws or for thorny terrain
- Tweezers for tick removal
- Needle-nose pliers for pulling porcupine quills, cactus spines, and thorns

111 HELP A SKUNKED OR QUILLED POOCH

Camping dogs live the good life–until they stick their snouts where they don't belong. If your pooch has crossed paths with a skunk or porcupine, your camping trip is about to change dramatically. You might be able to deal with this in the field, but there's a good chance ol' Bowser will need a trip to the vet or spa. Here's the drill for each.

GET TO THE POINT According to veterinarians, a dog with a dozen or so quills stuck in the nose, chin, or lips is a DIY job. First, drape a towel over the dog's eyes to help it remain calm.

Next, grasp a quill firmly with pliers. Often the dog will instinctively back away at the first sensation of pain, and the quill will pop out. Repeat as necessary and spread the procedure out over an hour or two, if needed, to give the dog a break. Go for a walk, take a rest, and administer a dose of tasty treats in between sessions with the pliers.

If your pooch is pin-cushioned with more quills than you can handle, or if they are embedded in the mouth or tongue or near the eyes, you need to break camp and get to a vet. Trim the quills with sharp scissors to keep them from catching on brush or clothing, but leave enough of each exposed for the doctor to work with.

STOP THE FUNK If your pet gets sprayed by a skunk, you will quickly find out who your good friends are–and it's a safe bet you won't have many. Deskunkifying is a lonely task. If you're close to civilization, head for a pet store or outdoor sporting goods shop and hope they carry a commercial skunk soap. Otherwise, begin by bathing the dog with a solution of one quart (1 L) of hydrogen peroxide, 1/2 cup (120 mL) of baking soda, and 2 teaspoons (10 mL) of mild dishwashing liquid. Lather, rinse, and repeat. Again and again, most likely.

112 TAUT-LINE HITCH

This is a knot that will make you a hero when the winds blow and the rains come. It's the go-to knot to use on tent and tarp guylines because you can tighten or loosen the knot in a split-second to add or reduce tension on a rain fly or tarp. That keeps the cover fabric tight, which helps shed rain. Learn to tie it and you'll be able to adjust guylines in the dark, without a flashlight, just as the heavens open.

STEP 1 Pass the working end of the guyline around a stake, sapling, tree branch or other object. Make a half-hitch around the standing line, working towards the anchor.

STEP 2 Now make another half hitch, again working towards the anchor.

STEP 3 Finish with a last half hitch outside of these first two coils. Now the knot can be tightened

or loosened, and it will hold under a load. It's that easy. And that miraculous.

USE IT!
- Adjust a rainfly in a snap
- Tie a hammock to a tree
- Repair the Hubble Space Telescope (true story!)

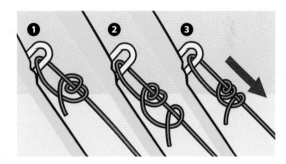

113 DOUBLE FISHERMAN'S KNOT

Despite its name, this knot has a thousand camping applications for all those times you have two ropes in hand and neither is quite long enough for the job. You can use it to fashion longer tent and tarp guylines, and it works great when combining lines of different diameters.

STEP 1 Lay the two ropes one atop the other, with tag ends in opposite directions.

STEP 2 Using one rope, tie a double overhand knot around the second rope (a, b).

STEP 3 Using the tag end of the second rope, tie a double overhand knot around the first rope (c, d). The tag ends should exit the knot on the opposite sides of the ropes (e). For example, the tag end of the top rope exits the knot below the bottom rope. Snug tightly.

USE IT!
- Join two ropes together when you don't have a long piece
- Make cool zipper pull loops out of any cord
- Make easily adjustable necklaces and bracelets

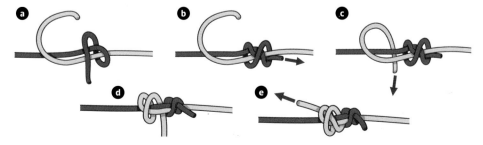

Leave behind nothing but . . . nothing. That's the philosophy behind LNT (Leave No Trace) camping. It's easy to pull this off, and actually fun to do all you can to camp like a ghost. Even at popular campsites it's just as easy to minimize your impact as it is to trash the woods. Here's how to vanish from the wilds, straight from the 7 Principles of Leave No Trace by the Center for Outdoor Ethics.

☑ PLAN AHEAD & PREPARE Think through your trip before you hit the road so you can plan on minimum impact.

- Cook on a stove instead of a fire.
- Plan one-pot meals when possible and minimize food waste.
- Remove foods from commercial packing at home and place in sealable bags.

☑ TRAVEL & CAMP ON DURABLE SURFACES You're not the only one living at your campsite. Minimize damage to vegetation and communities of organisms that can be trampled beyond recovery.

- Stay on trails. Do not shortcut!
- If in the backcountry with no trails, minimize travel on fragile terrain.
- If possible, camp on sites already highly impacted.
- Use an existing fire ring–do not make a new one.
- Camp a minimum of 70 adult steps from any water source.
- When breaking camp, naturalize the site. Cover scuffed areas with leaves and pine needles. Use a tree bough to rake flattened grasses.
- Vary your routes within the camping area to minimize the need to leave trails.

☑ DISPOSE OF WASTE PROPERLY From trash to poop, you need to have a plan to deal with your by-products–whether you like it or not.

- In most cases, burying human waste is acceptable. Check regulations; you may be in an area where pack-out systems are required.
- Poop in a cathole. Dig a small hole 6 to 8 inches (15 to 20 cm) deep and 4 to 6 inches (10 to 15 cm) in diameter. Do your business and tamp down the toilet paper with a stick. Fill the hole with the original dirt and disguise with natural materials.
- Pack it in, pack it out. No shortcuts. That means fruit peels, food waste, and every teeny piece of trash.
- Wash dishes with biodegradable soap a minimum of 70 adult steps from streams and lakes, and scatter the wastewater.

☑ LEAVE WHAT YOU FIND INTACT Leave no trace means leaving no evidence of your presence. It also means leaving stuff where you find it–including pretty rocks, shed antlers, and cool pieces of wood. When you remove natural objects, you steal the joy of discovery from the next person to come along.

- For the love of all things holy, do not carve your initials into anything.
- Do not dig trenches for tents or lash lean-tos or camp furniture.
- Do not drive nails or screws into trees.

☑ **MINIMIZE CAMPFIRE IMPACTS** Should you build a fire? This is a tough question. If you're in a developed campground with established fire rings, it's no problem as long as you collect firewood responsibly. If you're in pristine backcountry, probably not. Wherever you build a fire, minimize its impacts.

- Use an existing fire ring.
- Avoid scarring rock walls with black smudges that will last for years.
- Extinguish a fire completely. Use water, not dirt.
- Use a fire pan. Metal oil drain pans work great. Elevate it on rocks to prevent scorching the ground.
- Only collect wood that is "dead and down," meaning on the ground. Leave standing trees alone; they are home to many birds and insects.
- Burn all wood completely to a white ash. Soak with water and scatter away from camp.
- Camouflage new fire sites with natural materials.

☑ **RESPECT WILDLIFE** Remember, you're in their house. Do not disturb wildlife or plants for a better look at them.

- Do not feed animals. Ever. Anywhere.
- Keep your voice down at all times.
- Store food securely to avoid habituating animals to raid a camp.
- Avoid traveling at night when many animals are most active.

☑ **BE CONSIDERATE OF OTHER VISITORS** In other words: Be nice. We're all out there to get far from the madding crowd, so be on your best outdoors behavior.

- Consider tents and gear of neutral colors.
- Enjoy the music of the wind in the trees, moving water, and the calls of birds. Leave music devices at home or in the vehicle.
- Know the yield rules: Hikers headed downhill step aside to allow uphill foot travelers to pass. Hikers yield to equestrians, and bikers yield to both hikers and horse riders.

115 TRUCKER'S HITCH

Also called the waggoneer's or pulley hitch, this is a "tension hitch," great for cinching down a load and for maintaining or adjusting any kind of tight line. Use it for tying anything down to vehicle racks or when rigging guylines for a tent. Although this hitch lets you tighten down a load with cracking force, it's fast and easy to untie.

STEP 1 Twist a loop in the standing part of the rope, above the point of anchorage (for instance, the bar of a vehicle rack, a bumper, or a saddle ring).

STEP 2 Form a bight in the standing part of the rope below the loop, then pass the bight through the loop, pulling it tight to form a knotted loop in the standing line.

STEP 3 Now pass the working end of the line under the anchorage point, up through the loop, and back down. Pull down on the line to get the pulley effect, and cinch the load as forcibly as you like.

STEP 4 Lock the hitch in place with two or three half hitches to a solid point of anchorage.

USE IT!
· Tie a canoe to a vehicle rack
· Tighten up a tarp line
· Bundle firewood for easy carry

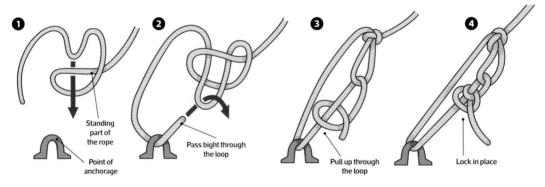

116 CLOVE HITCH

The clove hitch not only works as a quick way to tie a canoe, kayak, or boat to a piling or tree limb, but it's the foundation for many pole-lashing techniques. It's so easy to tie, you don't even need directions. Just follow this illustration.

USE IT!
· Start a cool lashing project
· Tie a boat to a log
· Leash a dog to a tree

117 DRESS FOR SUCCESS AGAINST BUGS

Mosquitoes and ticks don't play nice. Mosquitoes dive-bomb every square inch of bare skin. Ticks latch on to boot tops and pants bottoms and begin their insidious ascent into cracks and crevices of your nether regions that you don't even know you have. No wonder folks have devised a serious array of defensive measures for the biting and stinging hordes. To turn them back, start at the bottom.

BUG-REPELLANT CLOTHING Loomed of yarn treated with permethrin, anti-bug socks, underwear, and outerwear are the foundation for a full-body shield against the tiniest invaders. Most are good for 50 washings or more.

NET EFFECT Mosquito netting as clothing works pretty well, as long as the fabric isn't lying next to your skin. A better solution is clothing made with mosquito mesh affixed to an open weave of netting like a fish net. Mosquitoes can land on the mesh, but that second layer of netting prevents their proboscis from ever touching skin.

SOCK IT TO 'EM It's a classic technique: Pull your socks over your pants' cuffs for a decent barrier to bug entry. You can also duct tape your pants hems to your boots.

118 WAGE CHEMICAL WARFARE

Insect repellent sprays and lotions are the best line of defense against mosquitoes and ticks, and chemical technologies have improved dramatically. Choose one of these for a skin-level layer of protection.

THE OLD FAITHFUL Sprays and lotions with citronella and eucalyptus are meh. DEET is the big gun, developed for use by the U.S. Army after the hellish jungle warfare experiences of World War II. If using 100-percent DEET, know that it will melt plastic. Thankfully, products with 30 percent DEET work well. Go with a pump bottle to keep the stuff off your hands.

NEXT BEST THING For tender types who could never bring themselves to a dousing of DEET, Picaridin is a relatively new godsend. It's a synthetic repellent that won't irritate your skin or eyes, doesn't smell like a dead possum that's been stewed in turpentine, and won't melt your camera strap. Its EPA registration data suggest that a 20-percent concentration is effective against mosquitoes and ticks for 8 to 14 hours.

THE GAME CHANGER Few inventions have bettered the quality of camping life more than the Thermacell. The lightweight, portable apparatus creates an approximately 15-foot by 15-foot (4.5 x 4.5-m) zone of atomized insect repellant all around you. A small pan, fired by a compact fuel cartridge, heats a mat impregnated with allethrin, a synthetic form of a natural repellent found in chrysanthemum plants. The results are nearly miraculous.

119 FIX TORN MOSQUITO NETTING

Ripped mosquito netting invites a miserable night in the tent, not to mention a day full of itches and welts. Here's how to seal up a tear.

FIX IT QUICK For straight tears less than 2 inches (5 cm) long, thread a needle and stitch the rip closed. If you have extra netting in a repair kit, reinforce the tear with a netting patch cut a half-inch larger than the tear. In the field, any makeshift thread will work–dental floss, fishing line, or even plant fibers. You can always pretty it up with nylon sewing thread back home.

GET RIPPED For jagged, Frankenstein tears large enough for bats to fly through, heavier lifting is required. First, pull the edges of the tear together and tape with masking tape (duct tape is too sticky) (a). Next, tape a strip of paper over the tape to serve as extra backing (b). On the other side, brush on a layer of silicone-based repair adhesive (c). Give it two days to cure, then remove the paper backing. Dust the patch with body powder to knock back the stickiness and prevent it from picking up dirt or sticking to the rest of the tent (d).

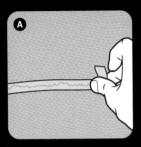
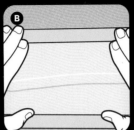

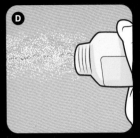

120 WIN THE CHIGGER WAR

Chiggers, AKA "red bugs," are actually the tiny larvae of harvest mites, and there are few things more horrifically itchy than a chigger bite. They find a place on your person where the skin is particularly thin. They insert tiny mouthparts, inject powerful digestive enzymes that dissolve your skin cells, then suck up the liquefied chigger spit and goo. Agony follows. Avoid such horrors by taking these four precautions.

TAKE A HOT SEAT Chiggers hate hot surfaces. When it's time to take a seat, look for a sunbaked rock.

SPRAY AWAY Standard mosquito repellants turn chiggers away.

So does powdered sulfur, called "flowers of sulfur," which is sold at most drugstores. Dust pant legs and waistbands, socks and shoes, and boots with it. It stinks, though, so try a half-and-half blend of sulfur and talcum powder.

STAY LOOSE Chiggers exhibit a behavior called "thigmotaxis," a liking for tight, cozy spaces. That's why wearing loose-fitting clothing can significantly reduce the number of places chiggers attach. If they can't find a place they like, they'll often just move off of you.

SCRUB NOW Get rid of chiggers quickly with a hot, soapy bath and

plenty of scrubbing as soon as you get out of the woods. In the field, rubbing exposed skin or suspected areas of infestation with a dry towel or cloth works wonders.

121 NIX THE ITCH

The noxious trinity of poison ivy, poison oak, and poison sumac have ruined many a camping trip. Each contains a chemical compound called urushiol, which causes mild to severe itching, scratching, and whining. The plants grow across North America, and are common in camping areas due to their love of open, shady forests. Here's how to stay the #@&(! away.

LEARN THIS RULE The best way to avoid a rash is to stay away from the plants. Poison ivy is the most common, and is easy to identify as it always sprouts clusters of three leaves. Poison oak can, as well, although it can also grow clusters with five or seven leaves. Just remember: Leaves of three, let it be! Poison sumac is less common. It grows in a cluster of 7 to 13 leaves, with one on the end by itself. Avoid such greenery like the itchy, pus-inducing plague it is. Note, too, that urushiol hangs on to dog's coats, clothes, shoes, and camping gear, so beware.

GET SOAPY If you come into contact, act fast to minimize the itchy outcome. There are great poison ivy–specific soaps available that break down and remove the oily urushiol. But a vigorous lathering of soap and water or rubbing alcohol is a huge help, as well.

SOOTH THE PAIN A poison ivy itch can be tamed with over-the-counter medicines. Calamine lotion works wonders, as does hydrocortisone cream. A compress with baking soda or oatmeal can also bring relief.

READ A TOPO MAP (EVEN THE DIGITAL KIND)

Thankfully, the digital age hasn't rendered USGS topographic maps obsolete. In fact, they're more prevalent than ever, as topo maps are now accessible by desktop, laptop, tablet, and smartphone. Here's how to read the lay of the land–literally.

LEARN THE BASICS Along the top and bottom of most maps are helpful blocks of information.

The map series relates to how much land area is covered by the map. The most detailed paper maps are 7.5-series maps, which cover 7.5 minutes of latitude and 7.5 minutes of longitude. Converted to miles, that covers a land area of about 9 by 16 miles (15 by 25 km). The 7.5 series was completed in 1992 and was recently replaced by the digital National Map.

Declination is the difference between true north and magnetic north, in degrees. The farther north your location, the greater the declination–and the greater the need to adjust when navigating by map and magnetic compass.

Scale is marked at the bottom of the map.

KNOW THE COLORS Background colors typically relate to vegetative cover.

Green: Woods, forests, and shrublands.

White: Open or semi-open lands, such as grasslands, agricultural lands, and deserts. Could include rock outcroppings.

Gray: On maps with large blocks of public lands such as national forests and national parks, gray will indicate private inholdings within public boundaries.

WATCH FOR WATER All water is marked in blue. Small streams are marked with a single blue line. Swamps and marsh are indicated by a blue pattern that looks like tiny cattails. Intermittent streams are marked with a blue line broken by three dots.

FOLLOW THE CONTOURS These are imaginary lines that trace elevation above sea level. Contour lines indicate changes in elevation; the closer the contours, the steeper the terrain. Cliffs can look like nearly solid blocks of merged contour lines. Contour lines that are farther apart indicate flatter lands.

There are three types of contour lines. Indexed contours will typically be marked with numerals that indicate elevation. Often, each fifth contour line is an indexed contour. Between the heavier indexed contour lines are lighter intermediate contours. These are not marked with elevation, but help express the general steepness of the terrain. In very flat areas, maps might be marked with supplementary contours, which appear as dashes. They indicate an elevation change of half of the total between the contour lines on either side.

Ridges will appear as a series of Us and Vs that point toward lower elevation.

The highest elevation contour on a ridge, hill, or mountain will be marked by an enclosed contour line. Sometimes the very peak will be marked with the elevation and an X.

A gap, pass, or saddle appears as an hourglass, where the contour lines from opposing ridges nearly touch.

NOTE ARTIFICIAL FEATURES Most human-made features are marked in black. Buildings and smaller structures are marked with squares of varying sizes.

READ ROADS AND TRAILS Large interstate and divided highways are marked in red. Other roads are marked in black. Secondary gravel and dirt roads are indicated with parallel lines. Broken parallel lines mark unimproved or 4WD roads. Foot and horse trails show as dotted lines.

LEGEND

- Woodland
- Shrubland
- Stream
- Intermittent Stream
- Swamp
- Building
- Large Road
- Road
- Dirt Road
- 4WD Road
- Horse / Foot Trail

123 ROCK THE RUTS

Don't let deep ruts turn you back. With a little bit of know-how and some teamwork with a partner, you can gingerly work your way through ruts so deep they would hide a cow.

LET IT OUT Let enough air out of the tires to decrease the pressure about 25 percent. That will help the tires deform around sharp rocks.

PICK A PARTNER Have a companion guide you through the ruts from outside the vehicle, bending low to make sure the undercarriage stays clear of rocks and roots.

RIDE THE RUTS (OR NOT) A rule of thumb is to drive in the ruts if it looks like there's enough ground clearance, and straddle them if not. If you're going uphill, try to straddle the ruts. And in wet conditions, it might be best to stay in the ruts so you don't slip into them and high-center the vehicle.

TAKE IT EASY In dry conditions, the turtle beats the hare. The slower you go, the more efficiently the vehicle can send power to the wheels with the most traction on the ground.

BUST FREE Dig shallow cuts at a 45-degree angle that lead out of the rut. Or pile rocks and branches in front of the tires to give the chassis more clearance, and rock the vehicle back and forth using forward and reverse gears.

124 SLOWLY DASH THROUGH THE SNOW

Unlike the surprise mud pit that appears out of nowhere, you know when you'll be traveling in the winter, so gear up. Swap out your street skids for all-terrain winter tires, and always carry tire chains and a shovel.

STAY STRAIGHT Scout a straight line through snow. You won't be able to change directions once you're into a pile of it. One of the best ways to bash through the white stuff is to lay down lines of packed snow that you can use to back out and then power forward with even greater momentum.

GO FULL MANUAL When you're plowing through heavy snow, turn off traction control settings, which prevent individual wheels from spinning faster than others–sometimes that's exactly what you need to punch through the Arctic. And keep an eye open for traction control indicator lights. Some

vehicles will automatically re-engage the setting if you change gears.

SLOW DOWN Unlike the bash-em-up approach that can work in mud, don't try to muscle your way through deep snow. Slow and steady–and back and forth–wins the race. And that's not true just for vehicle speed. Control your reaction time, as well. No wheel jerking or racing the engine. Once you lose traction, it's very difficult to retain.

DON'T STOP NOW ... As long as you're moving, stay on the gas. Spinning tires can still provide enough grip to get you through a snow drift.

... BUT DON'T DIG A HOLE Once you're no longer moving, don't continue to spin. All you'll do is dig yourself deeper into the snow hole. Instead, try rocking your baby back and forth, using forward and reverse gears.

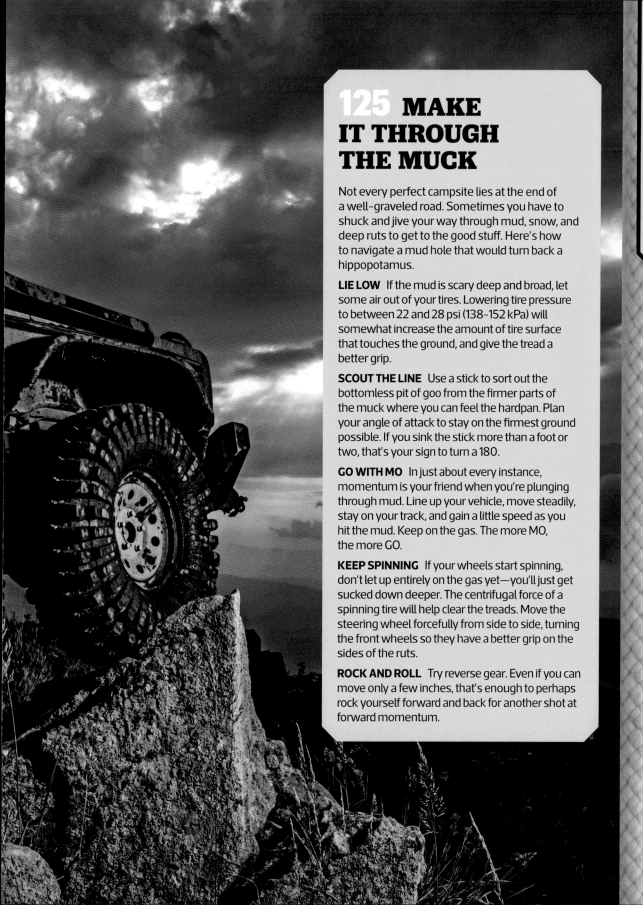

125 MAKE IT THROUGH THE MUCK

Not every perfect campsite lies at the end of a well-graveled road. Sometimes you have to shuck and jive your way through mud, snow, and deep ruts to get to the good stuff. Here's how to navigate a mud hole that would turn back a hippopotamus.

LIE LOW If the mud is scary deep and broad, let some air out of your tires. Lowering tire pressure to between 22 and 28 psi (138–152 kPa) will somewhat increase the amount of tire surface that touches the ground, and give the tread a better grip.

SCOUT THE LINE Use a stick to sort out the bottomless pit of goo from the firmer parts of the muck where you can feel the hardpan. Plan your angle of attack to stay on the firmest ground possible. If you sink the stick more than a foot or two, that's your sign to turn a 180.

GO WITH MO In just about every instance, momentum is your friend when you're plunging through mud. Line up your vehicle, move steadily, stay on your track, and gain a little speed as you hit the mud. Keep on the gas. The more MO, the more GO.

KEEP SPINNING If your wheels start spinning, don't let up entirely on the gas yet—you'll just get sucked down deeper. The centrifugal force of a spinning tire will help clear the treads. Move the steering wheel forcefully from side to side, turning the front wheels so they have a better grip on the sides of the ruts.

ROCK AND ROLL Try reverse gear. Even if you can move only a few inches, that's enough to perhaps rock yourself forward and back for another shot at forward momentum.

126 CHOOSE A DISPERSED CAMPSITE

No neighbors, no slamming car doors, no headlights in the middle of the night, no generators–there's no better way to experience the outdoors than setting up camp in a wild piece of the wide open. Many public lands allow dispersed camping outside of designated campgrounds, such as along forest access roads and in pullouts beside creeks and streams. A fire ring is the most obvious marker for a dispersed campsite. Otherwise, look for a place that hasn't been heavily used, but avoid making camp on ground that looks like it's never been touched. Pitch a tent, build a fire, exult in the solitude, and act like you own the place–which means treating it like home.

127 THE BACKCOUNTRY BEAST

Go off the grid, and things can get ugly pronto. You need a kit that's easy to carry and packed with everything you need to weather a three-day blow or a busted femur.

PACK IT IN The 6.10 Vertical Pouch from 5.11 Tactical is as straightforward as it is 1000-denier tough. Molded zipper pulls make for fast opening, and it's MOLLE-compatible—which makes it easy to connect the first-aid kit to the outside for quick access.

A Purifying water doesn't get any simpler than a LifeStraw: Insert into a cesspool. Drink. The filter removes waterborne viruses and protozoa including giardia and cryptosporidium.

B Pack a small glass signal mirror for maximum flash.

C Lash the Kinetic Two-Tine Gig Spear stainless steel spearhead to a shaft, and the wild is your grocery store.

D Leave a note with a Sharpie pen and the permanent ink won't run in the rain. While you're waiting for aid, use the pen to turn a sleeping pad or spare t-shirt into a checkers board. Stones and sticks stand in for the checkers. For good measure, wrap 10 feet (3 m) of duct tape around the marker.

E Have 30 feet (9 m) of parachute cord for the basics, and add 30 feet (9 m) of No. 36 tarred bank line for increased utility. The slightly tacky marine line holds knots more tightly than p-cord and won't absorb water.

F Supercharge the space blanket category with a SOL Survival Blanket. Pitch it like a tarp or wrap up burrito-style.

G The Bluetooth-enabled Kestrel Drop D3 environmental logger feeds temperature, humidity, altitude, and barometric pressure logs to your smartphone. Consider it an early bug-out warning system.

H Canned wild salmon or mackerel tastes good and is rich in protein and heathy fats—perfect survival grub.

I Bash, gouge, and dig with the Garberg's 3.2 mm-thick (0.12 inch) blade. The handle is nearly unbreakable, and the ground spine's angle shaves tinder like soap and showers sparks.

J Backcountry travelers need more than bandages. The small Hunter's Trauma Kit (1) includes a battlefield-tested SOF Tactical Tourniquet, a non-adherent petroleum gauze dressing and pressure bandage, antibacterial ointment, smaller bandages, and lip balm (2). It's a great foundation, but cover more catastrophes by adding a SAM splint (3), an antihistamine (4), and an epinephrine auto-injector (5) to your first-aid supplies.

K Goal Zero's Flip 20 recharger will rejuvenate most smartphones and USB-equipped headlamps at least twice.

L As a backup to your compass, bring a Garmin ForeTrex 401 wrist GPS to point your way home.

M Every situation seems a little less grim with a cup of decent java. Starbucks Via instant coffee packs are a backcountry godsend.

N The waterproof Black Diamond headlamp sports finger-tap beam adjustments and a light-up-the-night 200 lumens beam. A fail-safe lock feature prevents the battery from draining if you accidentally turn it on.

O Clif Bloks deliver an energy boost in gummy form.

P The Cammenga Destinate Tritium Protractor is the Humvee of compasses. Six Tritium microlights glow like kryptonite. There are four map scales, plus a map magnifying glass and waterproof and shockproof housing.

Q The Titan Stormproof Matches Kit contains wind- and waterproof matches that stay lit even after a dunking. Add a Pathfinder Glowing Survival Fire Steel as a 3,000-degree spark option; you can store tinder in the handle.

R The Gen3 stainless steel cup has folding handles and a perforated strainer lid; it serves as a pot you can set on a stove or hang over a fire thanks to pre-drilled bail holes.

S When it's bad enough to hail the choppers, the SPOT Gen3 is a lifeline to the satellites. There's one-button SOS to 9-1-1 responders, preprogrammed text messaging, and a tracking application that allows family to monitor your progress.

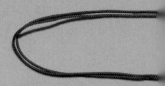

A

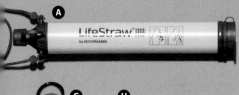

G · H

B

C

D

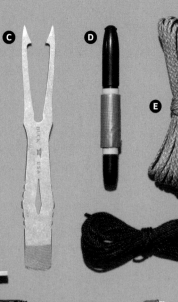
E

J3

J1

K

L

J2

J4 · J5

M

CLIF · O

Q

R

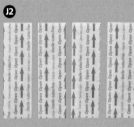

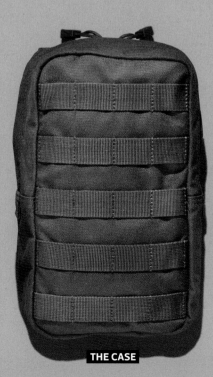

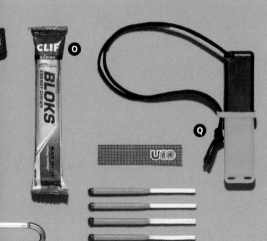

THE CASE

THE CASE

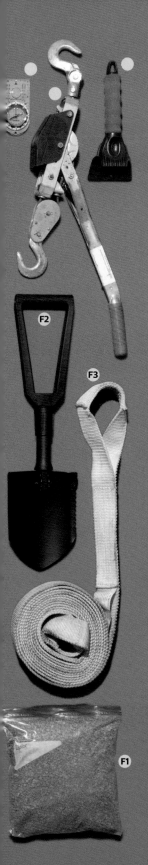

128 THE TRUCK CHEST

SURVIVAL KIT

A four-seasons truck survival kit should do it all: Help you shelter in place or pull off a rescue on your own, whether you bog down in a blizzard or burn up your transmission in a desert wilderness.

PACK IT IN Rubbermaid's 24-gallon (89-L) Action Packer is sturdy enough to stand on, with lockable latches and a nearly watertight lid.

A An on-the-fly truck repair kit should include replacement parts and enough stuff to MacGyver your way home. Hit the auto-parts store for JB Weld for fixing broken metal braces and patching an oil pan (1), two wire hangers and a tire reamer/plugger (2), duct tape (3), parachute cord (4), Fix-a-Flat (5), and jumper cables (6).

B Venison jerky and some freeze-dried meats can keep you nourished while you wait for the rescue crew.

C A gallon of drinking water to quench your thirst will make a major breakdown more bearable.

D A blue tarp will shed rain while you repair a punctured tire, provide shade in the desert, function as a makeshift sleeping bag, or catch rainwater for emergency drinking supplies. It's the duct tape of a truck kit.

E You'll need a fail-proof baseplate compass, with a lanyard, in case you have to hike out for help.

F Getting your ox out of the ditch is often job No. 1. Kitty litter (1) can provide just enough bite in moderate snow cover. Still spinning? Dig out with Gerber's E-Tool (2), a military-grade folding shovel with a

serrated blade and heavy-duty pick. A dedicated recovery strap (3) differs from a tow strap—it stretches to help snatch stuck vehicles, and there are no metal hooks that can be a serious injury hazard. A 2-ton cable puller (4) can be a last resort.

G Ever been caught without an ice scraper? Never again.

H The Savage Model 42 Takedown doubles firepower with a rimfire barrel over a .410 tube. Opt for the .22WMR for maximum small-game and rabid opossum firepower.

I Roadside flares not only alert other drivers to a broken-down vehicle but also serve as signaling devices and emergency fire starters.

J No sun? No batteries? No problem. Crank your way to communication with the Eton FRX5 hand-cranked and solar-powered AM-FM/NOAA weather radio with integrated smartphone charger.

K Include a few extra pairs of non-latex gloves with your first aid kit.

L It's a culinary multi-tool: Boil water in the Gen3 32-ounce (1-L) stainless-steel bottle, which nestles inside a bat-wing cup with a perforated lid for straining out coffee grounds and sassafras tea leaves.

M Stuck for the night? Bunk down in Klymit's KSB 20-degree synthetic sleeping

bag, which compresses down to bread-loaf size.

N Camp Chef's compact Stryker 100 is a rocket ship of a stove. With an integrated 1.3-liter pot, the package takes up little room but will boil a half-liter of water in two minutes.

O No one tool does it all, but Kershaw's Camp 12 Parang comes close. Need fire? Split kindling. Trail blocked? Chop it clear. The beefy, weighted blade is far more suitable for tough tasks than a vine-clearing machete.

P In addition to the first-aid basics, pack the small Hunter's Trauma Kit to help stop massive bleeding.

Q Sawyer's 2 Liter Water Filtration System filters more than a half-gallon (1.8 L) of water in one and a half minutes—leaving you more time to build a smoke generator for rescue.

R Double your fire-starting options with lighter and Titan Stormproof matches.

S Cram an old raincoat into the kit and you'll stay dry while wiring your tailpipe back to the frame with a coat hanger.

T Streamlight's Waypoint Rechargeable spotlight is a 1,000-lumen bright idea. An integrated kickstand turns it into a handy task light, and it's light and small enough to carry when you make a break for civilization.

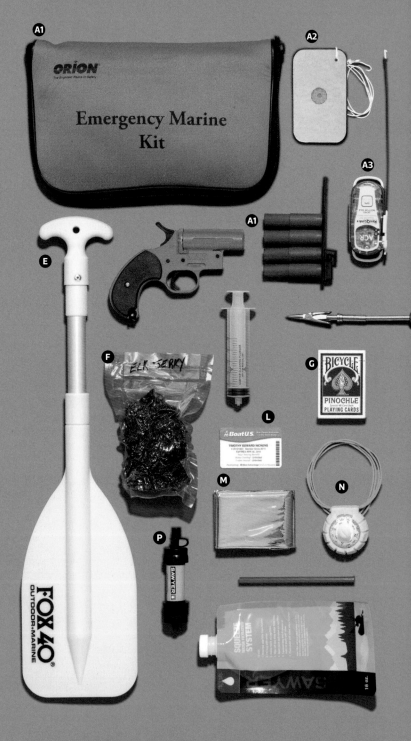

129

SURVIVAL KIT
THE WATER WORKS

When it's time to go, you may not have much time at all. The boat flips, and you grab the ditch bag. So, it better be packed with everything you need to survive.

PACK IT IN Watershed designed its Small Equipment Bag with input from the U.S. Coast Guard. It's completely waterproof, and has reflective tape, and includes a mouth valve so you can inflate it for emergency flotation.

A Stow multiple modes of putting out an SOS. Orion's Emergency Marine kit includes both hand-held and pistol-fired flares (1). A polished glass signal mirror (2) is good for 30-plus miles (48 kM). The floating ACR ResQLink+ (3) beams your precise location to the international Cospas-Sarsat search-and-rescue tracking system.

B Whether you need to cling to the hull or work on a stubborn outboard, a multitool and some basic supplies will boost your chances. Toss in a spare fuel bulb (1), fuel connectors, and hose clamps (2). Add duct tape (3) and p-cord (4). Round it out with the titanium-and-stainless-steel Leatherman Charge TTi with the Bit Kit add-on that includes slotted and Phillips screwdrivers plus Hex and Torx bits (5).

C The Spyderco AssistSALT's H1 steel won't corrode, and the heavily serrated blade will cut rope and webbing like butter. A survival whistle is built into the handle. Squeeze the knife while it's folded, and a hidden glass breaker emerges from the butt. 007 would approve.

D Cut the bottom out of a milk jug to form a cheap hand bailer.

E Shove a Fox 40 Telescopic Paddle under the handle in case the engine conks out.

F Pack some jerky—sealed in a waterproof bag—in case you get skunked while survival fishing.

G Break out a deck of cards for a game of Texas Hold 'Em or Solitaire. Just keep the emotions in check. You're all in this together.

H Kill some time—and dinner—with the Foldspear folding fishing spear and spear tip.

It breaks down to a tidy package and packs enough wallop to stab a meal.

I Stuff the shockproof, rain-proof Brunton Resynch 6000 into a ditch bag and forget about it until your smartphone goes dead. The integrated solar panels mean you're never out of juice.

J The waterproof 360-degree UST See-Me Light 1.0 runs for 44 consecutive hours.

K Packed with amino acids and sugars, a cold—or even lukewarm—round of hooch-free Jell-O shots will boost your get-up-and-get-home.

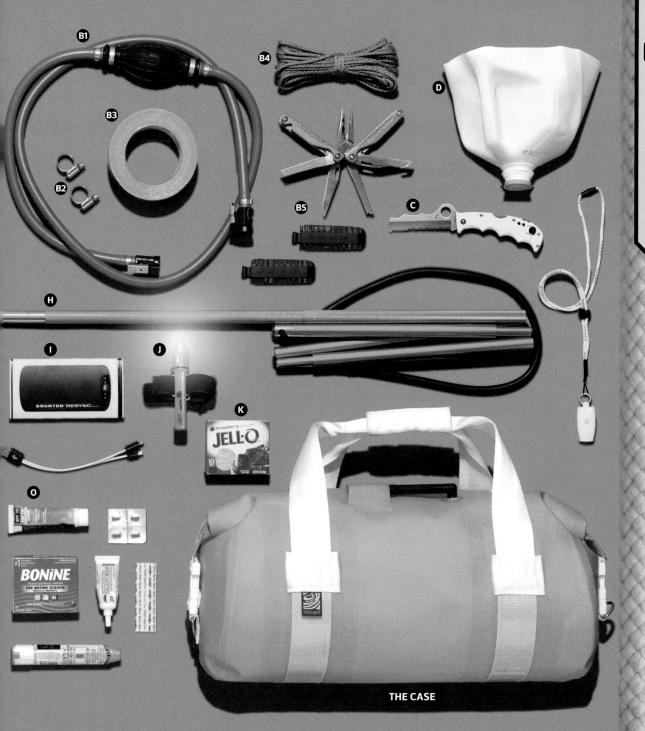

THE CASE

L A tow-service membership card is your secret weapon.

M Stay warm or rig a sunshade with the SOL Heavy Duty Emergency Blanket. The reflective material also serves as a daytime distress signal.

N The Ritchie SportAbout Hand Bearing Compass is a big, bright, waterproof direct-reading compass, so the bearing you read is the direction you face. That's just what you need while bobbing in the white-capped slop.

O Pack marine-worthy first-aid supplies. Sawyer Stay-Put sunscreen does what it

says, hour after hour. Add antibiotic ointment, bandages, antihistamine, an epinephrine auto injector, and Bonine, the best over-the-counter motion sickness remedy out there.

P If you're in a freshwater lake or river, the Sawyer Mini fixes that.

130 THE POCKET PROTECTOR

Here's the kit you grab every time you hike or camp. It's packed with the bare essentials, but they'll seem like luxuries when the only way out of a fix is to fix it yourself.

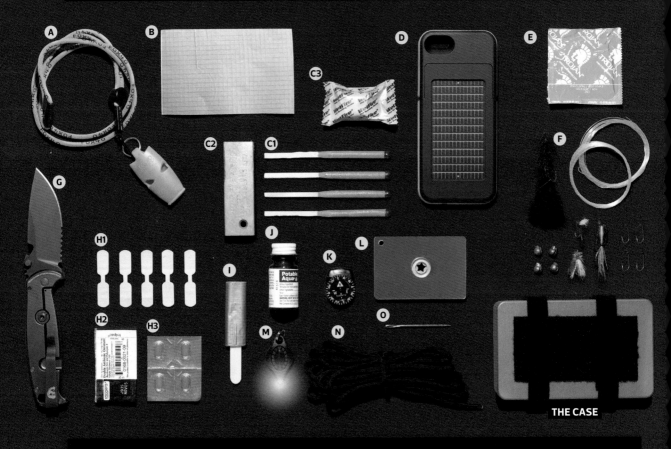

THE CASE

PACK IT IN Solkoa's SUMA Container is strong enough to double as a digging trowel, and you can boil water and fry grubs in it.

A Mountain lion got your tongue? Holler like hell with the pea-less Fox 40 Micro whistle.

B Tenacious Tape is strong enough to splint a broken fishing rod.

C You want two ways to turn on the heat: Titan Stormproof Matches (1) burn for 25 seconds and relight after a dunking. The SparkForce Fire Starter (2) is compact. Pair it with a WetFire tinder cube (3) for a 10-minute burn.

D Double the battery life of your iPhone with an EnerPlex SurfR solar battery pack.

E Pack a non-lubricated condom to carry water.

F Your emergency fishing kit should have: hooks, sinkers, wet and two dry flies, 50 feet (15 m) of mono and a 4X fly leader.

G A double-locking system turns the brawny DPx HEST/F nearly fixed-blade rigid.

H For first-aid supplies, bring butterfly bandages (1), antibiotic ointment (2), and an antihistamine (3).

I Wrap a few feet of duct tape around a tongue depressor, from which you can shave tinder.

J Potable Aqua tablets turn cruddy water safe.

K With a jewel bearing, rotating bezel, and luminescent markings, the Suunto Clipper stands apart from other button compasses.

L The StarFlash Floating Signal Mirror is easy to use and bright enough for overcast days.

M The Photon Freedom Micro flashlight is tough and bright.

N Ten feet (3 m) of 550 p-cord.

O A canvas needle's large eye and stout shaft can be paired with an inner strand of p-cord to stitch busted gear.

131 THE ULTIMATE SURVIVAL KNIFE

The ESEE-6 taps in at nearly 12 inches (30cm) long, with a fulll-tang 1095 tool-steel blade and micarta handles that could pound railroad spikes. Here are some uses for this bad boy blade.

BATON FIREWOOD Batoning is the act of using a short, heavy piece of wood to drive a knife blade by pounding on the spine. Center a small log with the middle of the knife blade, and baton down sharply.

BLAZE A TRAIL A big knife is a small axe: Mark your route Daniel Boone-style with easy-to-spot tree blazes.

SPLIT A PELVIS Expose the center line of a deer's pelvis, and pound the knife through the bone.

FLESH A HIDE A large knife can easily flesh a small hide. Just remember that you push the fat and flesh off the hide, so go easy on the pressure.

MINCE MEAT Use the knife as a makeshift meat cleaver to "grind" meat in the field.

CUT A SAPLING Surprisingly large saplings can be cut with a big knife. Bend the saplings over before cutting into the outside of the bend. Use multiple shallow cuts.

BREAK A CAR WINDOW The exposed tang in the butt can serve as a glass breaker. Side windows shatter more easily than windshields, which are made of a glass laminate that is difficult to break.

CARVE TINDER A sharpened top spine makes it easy to use the knife as a spoke shave for producing very fine tinder from a dry branch.

PLANE A BOW AND ARROW Use the knife blade as a field plane to shape bow limbs and arrows.

FELL A TREE Using a baton, girdle the tree with wedge shaped cuts.

FEND OFF A BEAR ATTACK If it comes down to this, make the most of the blade. Forget hacking and stabbing. Maximize the trauma by sticking the knife in and levering it back an forth.

After the fall down the ravine, the wrong turn on the trail, the icy plunge—could you make it through the night or next several days—and survive? Take this quiz and find out. Scoring high, of course, doesn't guarantee that you'll make it out. But scoring low means programming the remote is the riskiest thing you should do.

SCENARIOS

1 You are lost. It is very cold, with no snow on the ground. You somehow lost your fire-making tools. The sun will set in an hour. Which of the following is your best choice for shelter?

[A] A small cave with a protective overhang.

[B] A debris hut wedged between two fallen logs.

[C] A dense stand of conifers on a south-facing slope.

2 While prepping dinner, your knife slips and plunges into your thigh. Bright red blood spurts in frightful gushes. You're 2 miles (3.2km) from a road. You should:

[A] Apply a 3-inch-wide (7.5-cm) tourniquet between the cut and your groin. Bind the tourniquet very tightly for three minutes, then loosen for one minute. If blood flow resumes, retighten the tourniquet. After one hour, attempt the hike.

[B] Apply direct pressure to the wound with a clean cloth (if available), a dirty cloth (if that's all you have), or your hand. Wrap a dressing with some kind of bandage all the way around your leg. If more blood seeps through, put more dressings on top of

the old ones. When the bleeding stops, attempt to hike back to your vehicle.

3 After three days lost in snowy woods, your right foot exhibits the signs of serious frostbite— whitish skin that no longer has feeling. You should:

[A] Use your hands or someone else's body heat so slowly rewarm your foot.

[B] Act quickly: Soak the foot in the warmest water possible. Use urine if necessary.

[C] Do not attempt to rewarm your foot. Wrap it loosely in dry materials.

4 Your truck is out of gas. It is raining and cold. You have no matches, but these items are in the truck. Which is the quickest fire-starting option?

[A] Duct tape.

[B] Aluminum foil.

[C] High-carbon steel hatchet and a file.

5 You're soaked to the skin from a downpour and you're dressed in blue jeans, a sweatshirt, and a wetted-through lightweight shirt. It's almost freezing, you're shivering, daylight's fading, and car or camp is miles away. What's your plan?

[A] Keep moving. In these conditions, getting back to the truck is critical. You will be generating life-saving

heat (and possibly dry your clothes) while hiking. Take breaks, but begin moving again as soon as you start to shiver.

[B] Make camp now while you still have energy. Take off soaked cotton clothing and ring it out with all your strength. Put it back on, stuff dry vegetation inside, and replace the shell. Find a protected area away from the wind and tunnel into a debris hut.

[C] Recognize that you will become infamous for wearing all cotton in these conditions. Think up a new name for yourself in case you're still alive when searchers find you.

KNOWLEDGE

6 What does the phrase "deliberate offset" refer to?

[A] The practice of stacking kindling to the downwind side of a fire to compensate for a strong crosswind.

[B] The degree to which you purposefully veer off of a compass bearing.

[C] The tactic of setting a snare slightly off to the side of a small-game travel corridor.

7 Which of the following points towards the North Star?

[A] A line drawn between the two ends of a crescent moon and continuing to the horizon.

[B] The last two stars that form the outer edge of the Big Dipper's cup.

[C] The first two stars in the Big Dipper's handle.

8 H.E.L.P. stands for Heat Escape Lessening Posture. Which of the following is NOT a part of this lifesaving strategy to stay alive in cold water?

[A] Cross your arms and hold them firmly against your upper chest.

[B] Bring your knees close to your chest.

[C] Extend legs straight down to increase blood flow to lower extremities.

9 Which of the following describes the safest ice conditions?

[A] 6 inches (15 cm) of white opaque ice.

[B] 4 inches (10 cm) of clear or black ice.

[C] 5 inches (13 cm) of ice covered with 6 inches (15 cm) of snow.

FITNESS

10 Describe your current level of cardiovascular strength:

[A] I run for 20 minutes at least five times a week. (2 points)

[B] I get at least 30 minutes of cardio exercise three times a week. (1 point)

[C] I may not exercise, but I never forget my cholesterol meds. (0 points)

11 How many pushups can you do in 60 seconds?

[A] More than 40. (2 points)

[B] 25-40. (1 point)

[C] I technically can't do push-ups; my belly hits the floor before my elbows bend. (0 points)

READINESS

Score 1 point for each "yes" answer.

12 I can identify at least five wild edibles where I often camp and hike.

13 On every trip, at least one other person knows my location within half a mile (1 km).

14 I know how much declination to add or subtract from my compass bearings in the areas where I am traveling.

15 I have emergency water, fire-starting materials, and spare clothing in my vehicle right now.

16 When afield, I always carry a knife with a fixed or locking blade that is at least 3 inches (7.62 cm) long.

ANSWERS

Give yourself 1 point for each correct answer here:

1. [B] A debris hut built slightly larger than your body will hold heat better than a drafty cave or dense trees.

2. [B] Tourniquets should only be used after all other methods fail. They frequently result in the loss of a limb.

3. [C] Rewarming a frostbitten foot is extremely painful, and you'll lose your ability to walk.

4. [A] Simply unwrap the duct tape. Twist into a long match, and ignite with your truck's cigarette lighter.

5. [B] Burn up your reserves hiking and you'll be at an even greater risk for hypothermia. Answer C still applies, though.

6. [B] Say your vehicle is parked on a logging road that runs east-west. Instead of trying to walk a straight compass bearing to the vehicle, which is very difficult in irregular cover, travel several degrees to one side. Once you reach the logging road, you'll know whether to turn right or left.

7. [B] Follow a line from these two stars about five times the distance between them, and you'll find the North Star.

8. [C] Pull legs up to your torso to hold heat in the core areas of your trunk and groin.

9. [B] Here's why the others are dangerous: White opaque is logging weak, formed by wet snow freezing on ice. And a layer of snow can insulate ice and warm it.

RESULTS

10 OR LESS: Pathetic. Don't move an inch until you read the rest of this book.

11-12: Poor. You might survive a night outside...in someone's tool shed.

13-14: Fair. But work on your skills and knowledge before you hit the woods.

15-16: Good. You exhibit definite survivor-esque qualities.

17-18: Excellent. You are a 21st century Jim Bridger. (Subtract 5 points immediately if you don't know who he is.)

AROUND THE CAMPFIRE

Chop, Chop
Channel your inner lumberjack

Start a Fire with Your Food

Wood Work
Find fuel anywhere

Get it Going
Supercharge your flames

Build These 10 Awesome Fires

133 GATHER A FIRE'S BUILDING BLOCKS

The easiest way to get a fire going is to first gather up its three building blocks: tinder, kindling, and fuel. They work like a pyramid: You light the tinder to produce tall, hot flames that ignite the kindling, which in turn lights the fuel. If a fire fails, it's probably because the builder ran out of tinder and kindling, not the larger pieces of wood.

TINDER Dry, fine, easily shredded materials will catch a spark or a match's meager flame and burn quickly, with tall flames to light the larger kindling. Look for items about the diameter of a pencil's lead. For natural tinder, gather dry grass, pine needles, resinous pitch, cedar and birch bark, and milkweed fluff. At home, collect clothes dryer lint–a great, inexpensive option. Don't stop gathering tinder until you have two handsfuls.

KINDLING Sticks and split wood ranging from the size of a matchstick to finger-thick will catch the tinder's flame and kickstart the fire. Kindling needs to be very dry, so snap twigs and branches with your hands and discard any that bend–a sign of green wood. It's best to split wood so it has a rough surface for fire-catching ability. Conifers provide great kindling due to their high resin content. Don't stop gathering until you have a bundle the diameter of a basketball.

FUEL Larger pieces of wood provide the long, slow burn of a cooking fire and the tall flames of a warming fire. Wrist-sized fuel is best, because it has enough surface area to provide a long, coal-producing flame, but it's small enough that it won't smother the fire. Once you have a serious blaze, it's okay to feed it larger logs. Don't stop gathering fuel until you have twice as much as you think you'll need, especially if you're building a fire at night. Gathering wood after dark is dangerous.

134 SPARK

It is mesmerizing, this incandescent fusillade that leaps from your fingertips. But there is nothing mystical nor magical about a shower of sparks. Your task is pure physics: Aim at the delicate tinder. Shelter the smoking ember. Tease it to life with your very breath. A spark is a tiny, fleeting bit of fire, a few metal molecules that flare and die in less than an instant, and in that instant there is the possibility of heat and comfort, a warm meal, light for the path. But a spark is no promise. On the other side might lie darkness and cold and fear and death. A spark is an instant, and what happens in the instant after is up to you.

135 MAKE A SAFE PLACE FOR FIRE

The first step in building a fire is to create a safe space for your blaze where the flames and embers will be contained. In many campgrounds you'll find a designated site, with a metal or masonry fire ring and grate. In more dispersed camping areas, you might only find a circle of rocks. Elsewhere, it's your job to select a site that's away from anything flammable, and construct a fire bed and fire ring.

FIRE BED It's always best to build a fire on bare ground, so scrape away plants and grasses to form a circle approximately 2 feet (.5 m) in diameter larger than your intended fire. If you run into tree roots, move to another site. It's easy for roots to catch fire and carry a smoldering coal far underground. Also, avoid building fires under overhanging vegetation.

FIRE RING If rocks are available, circle the fire bed with them. This will help prevent sparks from igniting grasses and other dry ground cover. Avoid saturated river rocks, though, as they can explode when heated.

136 FIND WILD FIRE STARTERS

The first 10 seconds are the most critical when starting a fire, so make sure you have plenty of good, natural tinder on hand before you start. Here are two great fire starters, courtesy of Mother Nature, from each corner of North America.

NORTH

TINDER FUNGUS Look for bulbous blotches of blackish wood on live birch trees. The inside of the fungus is reddish-brown, and will easily catch a spark. Crumble it as a fire starter or use chunks to keep a coal alive.

BIRCH BARK The flammable oils in the papery bark of birches are a time-tested fire starter. Strip ribbons of bark from downed trees; it works just as well as bark from live ones.

SOUTH

LIGHTER WOOD The resinous stumps of southern pine trees last about forever. Knock off a few chunks of so-called "fatwood" and shave slivers for tinder. Carve feather sticks from it for kindling.

SPANISH MOSS Not a moist moss at all, but an epiphytic "air plant." Spanish moss is a great tinder, but don't carry it around—it's notorious for harboring chiggers.

EAST

CATTAIL FLUFF The cottony interior of a cattail spike can be fluffed into a spark-catching inferno. Have more tinder nearby, because this stuff burns up quickly.

CEDAR BARK Work over common cedar bark with a rock to smash the fibers. Pull the strands apart with your fingers and roll it back and forth between your hands to increase its spark-catching surface area.

WEST

SAGEBRUSH BARK Pound strips of bark with a rock, then shred them between your palms to fashion a tinder basket.

PUNK WOOD Rotten, dry wood will flame up with just a few sparks. Use a knife blade held at 90 degrees to file off punk dust that will ignite with a spark, and carve off pea-sized pieces you can then use to ignite the larger piece of wood.

137 START A FIRE FROM AISLE 3

Many common foods and other items from the grocery store will burn hot enough to draw out wet tinder or start a fire on their own. When Plans A, B, and C fail, break out the grub box and start a fire with your snacks.

SWEET HEAT Marshmallows will explode into flame, as any s'mores lover knows. That means they make awesome fire starters. The high sugar content ensures a steady burn slow enough to help catch a fire.

DIY FIRE LOG Soak paper towels in vegetable oil for a quick camp firestarter. They'll burn even longer if you stuff the oil-drenched towels into a cardboard tube.

DIP INTO CHIPS Many potato chips and other fried snacks burn like fury. The higher the oil content, the hotter the burn. Corn chips are a great fire starter, not only because of all the oil, but their thickness holds the flame longer. Puffed snacks such as onion-flavored Funyuns are another hit; the air pockets inside help fuel a strong flame.

138 TURN YOUR JUNK DRAWER INTO A BLAZE

Many common household items and medicine chest items can help start a fire whether you're in the backcountry or camping in the backyard. When you need a quick flame fix, rummage through your kitchen or work shop junk drawer for these flammable materials.

DUCT TAPE A fist-sized ball of loosely wadded duct tape is easy to light and will burn long enough to dry out tinder and kindling.

BICYCLE INNER TUBE Put a match to short strips or squares of a bicycle inner tube for a rank, smoky flame hot enough to dry small kindling. No bike? Try the rubber squares in a neoprene wader patch kit (don't forget the flammable patch glue) or a slice from a boot insole.

BEER CAN AND GAS Pouring gasoline on wet wood rarely results in more than a flare-up. Instead, cut the top off a soft drink or beer can, bury it so that the rim extends an inch above the ground, and fill it with gas. Stack a teepee of wet kindling over the can, and light the gas. If you can't cut the top off, fill the can halfway with gas and place it on its side so the opening is on top.

FIRST-AID BANDAGES Many bandages and blister pads will burn long enough to light stubborn wood.

LIP BALM The waxy content in most lip balms will catch a flame and burn. Smear lip balm on cardboard, paper grocery bags, or even sticks and twigs for an even longer flame.

HAND SANITIZER Most hand sanitizers burn like crazy. Look for those with high alcohol content for the hottest flames.

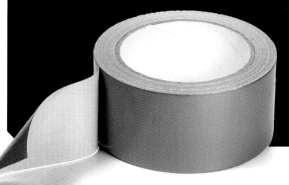

139 WHITTLE A FEATHER STICK

With a sharp knife you can turn a dry stick of wood into an excellent fire starter in no time at all. The thin, spark-catching curls of a feather stick will burn hot and tall, making it an easy, on-the-spot fire-starting solution. Here's how.

STEP 1 Cut a foot-long piece of soft wood such as pine, spruce, or aspen, and square up the stick with 4 flat sides, each measuring 1 to $1^1/_2$ inches (2.5-4 cm) wide. A knife with a flat grind is better for this task than a hollow-ground blade, but experiment to find a knife you can control with steady pressure.

STEP 2 Wedge the stick between your chest and a tree trunk, or hold it firmly against a chopping block at a 45-degree angle. Lock your wrist and use slow, steady pressure to push the knife edge down the corner to shave a thin, curly strip. This cut creates two more facets to work; bring the knife back up to the starting point, rotate the stick slightly, and begin another. Avoid sawing back and forth, but experiment with the orientation of the knife tip to create curls that trend towards one side or the other. Point the tip down and curls will come off to the right. Point the tip up and curls will shave off to the left.

STEP 3 Finish off with short, super-fine curls. Once you're done with one corner, rotate the stick and repeat on the remaining three.

140 STOCK UP ON FIRE AIDS

You can crumble fungus or shred cattails for fire-starting materials, but there are plenty of very good fire starters and fire accelerants available at camping and outdoor stores. Even if you want to start your fires the old-fashioned way, it's a smart idea to have a backup plan. A store-bought fire starter can be a literal lifesaver–and keep your family happy.

FIRE TABS There are tons of near-weightless commercial fire-starting devices, made from cotton, putty, and other materials impregnated with highly flammable ingredients. Many will burn whole, crumbled, smashed, stepped on or swimming in water. They'll ignite with a match or spark, burn with intense heat, and cool almost instantly when extinguished. Stash a few superlight fire-starting aids in your cook kit and survival kit.

FIRE PASTE It's a bit old-school, but it works. One advantage of this toothpaste tube full of fire is that you can spread it in long strips and smear it into cracks and crevices in the wood for better fire-starting.

WATER- AND WIND-PROOF MATCHES This is modern innovation at its finest: Matches that won't blow out in a hurricane, but burn for a solid 30 seconds and will relight after you plunge them underwater.

MAGNESIUM BLOCK A standard issue for military units. Shave flakes of magnesium into a tiny pile, ignite with a spark, and get to work with the resulting mini inferno.

FERRO RODS Ferrocerium is a mix of various metals that throws super-hot sparks. You can find ferro rods that come with small strikers, or just use the spine of your knife. Some are made with magnesium for even longer-lasting sparks.

TRIGGER-START PROPANE TORCH If you're going to cheat, cheat big. Those compact, lightweight workshop torches work wonders on a fire, and fit the same propane canisters that fuel many camp stoves.

WATER- AND WIND-PROOF MATCHES

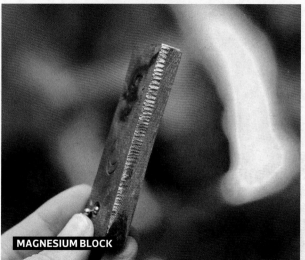

MAGNESIUM BLOCK

FERRO RODS

141 FLAME

This is the hunger. A small flame licks from the tinder. It needs fuel to grow. Feed it quickly. It eats chaos—the shredded and splintered, the broken and bent. The young fire is an ill-mannered beast, smacking its lips, cracking and popping and spitting in search of more. Let it gorge. There will be time to shape the flames and tame the blaze and make it what you want it to be. For now, give it what it needs, and take no chances that it might wither and flicker into smoke and smolder.

142 GATHER YOUR FIREWOOD

Many national and state parks and other camping areas ban the gathering of firewood, and a growing number of them prohibit travelers from bringing firewood in from other states or regions due to the danger of transferring non-native insects. So, be sure to check the regulations first. However, if gathering firewood is allowed where you camp, here's how to load up.

LEAVE NO TRACE The phrase to remember is "dead and down." In public campgrounds, don't saw anything off a tree. Look for wood that is dead and lying on the ground or caught in vegetation. Search for firewood out of sight of campsites and trails, especially downhill. The woods are less likely to be picked over there.

HIT THE HARD STUFF Hardwoods such as oak and hickory burn better, hotter, and longer than many softwoods such as pine and fir, so stock up on the denser woods. Coniferous trees do produce lots of flammable resin, so some pines in the mix are a good idea–they just won't burn down to hot coals.

FIND THE DRY Wood lying on the ground will soak up moisture. Look for the drier stuff leaning against trees and shrubs.

GO SNAG-FREE Dead standing trees are called "snags," and they provide critical habitat for many animal and bird species. Don't break off dead branches from standing trees unless you're in a survival situation.

143 SPLIT LOGS SMARTLY

Splitting firewood doesn't require the strength of an ogre. But cut without a plan, and you will generate more body heat than campfire BTUs.

CHOOSE THE TOOL A hatchet is not the best choice for splitting wood. Use an ax or 6- to 8-pound (2.7-3.6-kg) maul. The wedge shape will force wood fibers apart quickly. Err on the light side–velocity matters more than mass. Dulling the edge slightly prevents it from sticking in the wood. Set up a chopping block to provide a hard surface under the log, otherwise the ground will absorb the blow.

THINK BEFORE YOU STRIKE Look for splits in the log that extend from the center outward, or other cracks in the end grain, and exploit these weaknesses first. Otherwise, aim your first blows toward the barked edge of the round. It's easier to extract the blade with a rocking motion if it's on the edge. Use your next blows to walk the split across the round.

AIM LOW Strike as if the first 3 or 4 inches of wood don't exist. Visualize the ax or maul moving all the way through the wood. Make every swing count.

144 CHOP WOOD WITHOUT AN AX

In areas where it's permissible to gather your own firewood, a lot of the good stuff around most camping areas has been picked over, and the stuff left to burn is typically larger pieces that require working over with a saw or ax. Fortunately, there's an easy, safe way to turn a 15-foot-long (4.5-m) branch into campfire-ready smaller pieces, plus the kids can even pitch in. Let's call it the "break-and-bake" trick.

STEP 1 Find a sturdy, Y-shaped tree crotch about as high as your waist.

STEP 2 Insert a dead branch into the crotch so that a couple of feet stick out the back side. Now push or pull to one side until the wood breaks. You'll be amazed at how quickly you can stack up a pile of campfire wood that would make a lumberjack proud.

145 SPLIT WOOD WITH A KNIFE

A large sheath knife works better than a hatchet for splitting small sticks. The technique is called "batoning," and it's a swell way to get at the dry stuff inside wet firewood or crank out splints that you can whittle into tent stakes, survival traps, and thin shavings for starting fires. Compared to a hatchet, batoning with a knife doesn't take near as much room, and you don't need a chopping block. Batoning will turn a dry, seasoned piece of kindling into flame-catching chunks with just a few hard knocks.

GET A GRIP Have a campmate hold a wrist-thick stick of dense hardwood about 18 inches (.5 m) long. This is the baton.

POUND GAME The person holding the knife places it atop the end of the medium-size piece of fuel or kindling so that a few inches of the blade extend past the end of the round. The other person then taps the spine with the baton to set the knife steadily into the wood, then pounds harder to drive the knife all the way in. Next, whack the exposed knife spine sticking out of the log to drive the blade through the wood.

146 MAKE FIRE FROM FATWOOD

Commercially available pine fatwood is a great fire-building aid, but it can take an all-out flame to get it burning. You can easily process a couple of sticks of fatwood to create spark-catching fatwood dust, shavings, and kindling, and cut your fire-building time significantly. The best knife to use is a bushcraft or survival knife with a 90-degree ground spine that will file dust from the edge of a fatwood stick, but any knife will work. Start with a piece of fatwood 8 to 12 inches (20 to 30 cm) long, with squared corners.

MAKE SOME DUST Hold the fatwood against a firm surface. Place the knife's spine or edge along a corner of the stick and use a rasping motion to grind off flammable resin dust.

CUT THE SHAVINGS Use the knife's blade to shave thin slivers of fatwood from the remaining corners.

SPLIT FOR KINDLING Split the fatwood lengthwise into two pieces, then break each piece in half to create four pieces of fatwood kindling about 5 inches (13 cm) by half an inch (1.5 cm).

147 PULL OFF A CLASSIC SNIPE HUNT

The old-fashioned snipe hunt is a harmless rite of passage that involves a group of in-the-know participants who lead an unwitting group–often younger, but not necessarily–into the dark woods to hunt the elusive, enigmatic "snipe." Of course, there are no such night-loving woods birds (the true snipe is a marsh bird). But to watch a group of kids buy into the ruse, and run pell-mell through the woods with pillowcases in hand, desperately trying to trap birds that their imaginations have rendered in full detail–well, it's just good, clean fun. And when it works, it is bust-your-gut hilarious.

STEP 1 The group that's in on the game sets the stage: Describe snipe as dove-sized birds that live in the woods but rarely fly, and come out on dark nights because lights scare them away. You and your conspirators place the "hunters" in a straight line in the woods. Each should have a pillowcase and a short stick to be used to guide the birds into the pillowcases.

STEP 2 The conspirators steal away 50 yards (50 m) or so and stay quiet for a few moments, building the drama.

STEP 3 Start the snipe hunt with conspirators whistling and making crazy bird sounds as they move towards the hunters. Shine lights all through the woods and occasionally call out "Snipe! Snipe!" as if the birds are flushing. Pour it on. The louder and more confusing, the more you'll convince the victims.

STEP 4 Have a couple of conspirators get to the hunters first. Cry out, "There he is! Do you see him?!" and "Watch out, right behind you! Get him!" Most folks will start chasing imaginary birds. These front-line conspirators can toss sticks into the woods to create the illusion of a running snipe, or even carry their own pillowcases and fake "catching" the birds before they escape out of the pillowcase. The point is to make it as real as possible–before bursting out in catcalls of laughter once the duped victims are in on the joke.

148 BURN A WET LOG

Wet wood is the worst–unless you know how to carve a log into dry, fire-feeding tinder, kindling and fuel.

STEP 1 Find a solid log no more than 10 inches (25 cm) in diameter. A coniferous wood like pine or cedar works best due to its flammable resin. Cut a 12-inch (30-cm) section from the log.

STEP 2 Split the log into quarters. Lay one quarter on the ground, bark side down. Score the edge with two 1-inch-deep (2.5-cm) cuts, four inches (10 cm) apart. Shave off thin, 4-inch-long (10 cm) dry wood curls and splinters. Pound these curls with the back of the hatchet to break up the wood fibers, then rub some of these between your palms to separate the fibers further. This is your tinder; you'll need two handfuls.

STEP 3 Split pencil-size pieces from the wedge corners of a remaining quarter. Break these into 6-inch (15-cm) pieces for kindling.

STEP 4 Continue to split the quarters, utilizing the innermost and driest pieces. Use these as small and large pieces of fuel.

149 MAKE WIND YOUR FRIEND

Too much wind makes it tough to light a fire, but just enough of a breeze will turn a coal into a blaze. For starters, build the fire so the prevailing breeze isn't blocked with large logs. That will make it easier for the breeze to blow your flames into the fuel. Then, use these three tips to turn a fickle flame into a bonfire.

FAN THE FLAMES Use a pot lid or paper plate to gently fan air into a stubborn fire. A low, steady supply of fresh oxygen works better than an off-and-on puff. Make sure to get on ground level so the breeze doesn't create a mushroom cloud of ash, and keep it up at medium speed.

PUMP IT UP You won't believe this trick until you see it. Air blown from a battery-powered pump like those used to inflate air mattresses can supercharge a fire. Just go easy, because you can overdo it with too much of a breeze.

TUBE TOOL Attach 3 feet (1 m) of surgical tubing to a 5-inch (13-cm) length of copper tubing pipe for a precision instrument that can turn a puff into a fire blast. Place the copper tube near the embers and blow gently for as long as you can. Just be careful not to inhale through the tube.

150 WRITE YOUR WAY TO A BLAZE

Pencil shavings make great tinder. Toss a small, metal-bladed pencil sharpener and a good ol' No. 2 in your pack and you'll never be without a handy source for fire-building. Or, simply shave thin curls with a knife. You can also use the pencil sharpener to shave a twig into great fire-starting tinder.

151 TEASE UP A FLAME IN TOUGH CONDITIONS

The best time to build a fire is when it hasn't rained for days, the sun is shining, and there's plenty of dry wood all around. But all of that hardly ever comes together, so be ready to reach into a bag of fire tricks to get a blaze going under less than ideal conditions.

GET UP The soil in established fire rings is often sodden just below the surface. Start your fire on a small platform of dry sticks to keep humid air from being sucked into the blaze.

GET STICKY Use a small square of duct tape—sticky side up—as a base for tinder. The adhesive holds wispy magnesium flakes and fine grasses in place, and serves as a fire accelerant.

GET SPLIT Split wood will light more quickly, so use a knife to split twigs and branches lengthwise. That will expose the drier inner wood and present a rougher texture for greater flammability. And while you're at it, peel off the bark from woods other than birch and conifers. After all, most bark is there to protect the tree from fire, so it could hamper your initial blaze.

152 MAKE WATERPROOF MATCHES

These easy-to-make fire starters provide an all-in-one solution to starting a blaze: ignition, accelerant, and fuel in a single, handy, cheap package. To use, scrape the wax off the tip and strike against a rock. Each match will burn for five minutes or better.

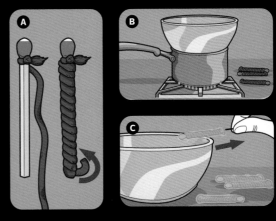

YOU'LL NEED

- Strike-anywhere matches
- Paraffin wax
- Cotton yarn or wicking
- Straight pins
- Aluminum foil

STEP 1 Tie an overhand knot in the yarn at the base of the match head and wrap the match shaft. Tuck the tag end of the yarn under the last wrap and pull snug. Cut excess yarn.

STEP 2 Melt paraffin wax in a DIY double boiler. Select an old pot that will nest in a larger pot. (A clean coffee can works in a pinch.) Fill the larger pot about half full with water and place on medium heat on the stove. Set the wax in the smaller pot and place it in the larger pot. Pay close attention. Paraffin wax has a low flash point and can burst into flame when overheated. When fully melted, move the setup off the heat.

STEP 3 Insert a straight pin into the non-striking end of a match and dip the entire match in the wax for a few seconds. Set on the foil to harden. Dip every match several times to build up a waterproof coating that also serves as fuel. After the last dip, remove the pin and tamp down the moist wax to seal the pinhole.

153 LET YOUR KIDS PLAY WITH FIRE

Kids are mesmerized by a campfire, and it's hard to keep them from playing around with smoking sticks and glowing embers. But there's a fun, safe way to let the kids play with fire: Toss a few common household items into the blaze to create flashes and colors and dancing sparks. You'll want to wait until after you've finished cooking on the fire to try this, but once the marshmallows have all been roasted, here are a few safe, easy-to-find items for a little campfire magic.

SWEET TOOTH Sprinkle sugar into the blaze to create tiny white sparks.

BAKING POWER Flour tossed into the fire will combust into a flashy burst. You don't need a lot; just a half-handful at a time.

JAVA JOLT Powdered coffee creamer will ignite into a shower of sparkly flashes.

SPICE IT UP Cast a small handful of ground cinnamon into the flames for bright amber sparks.

HEAVY SEASONING Sprinkle table salt into the blaze to create intense yellow flames.

CLEAN GREEN A smattering of common borax detergent turns on a bright green flame.

154 SPIN A ROUND ROBIN YARN

Everyone loves a good campfire story, especially kids. But it's often tough to get started. Do you tell a well-worn tale? A ghost story from out of a book? One great way to get the storytelling started is to tell a round-robin yarn. One person picks something that actually happened during the day—perhaps you spotted a fox running across a meadow, or you found a log that had been turned over by an animal rooting for grubs. That person sets up the story with a few simple sentences and then the next person picks up the tale, adding a few sentences more.

"That fox was running across the meadow because he was chased out of his den by his mother. All his brothers and sisters had left the den to find families of their own, but that little fox wasn't ready to strike out in the world. Until he had to. He saw that meadow and thought: Somewhere on the other side is where my life adventure will begin."

No one knows where the story is going, but everyone must listen closely because soon it will be their turn to keep the story alive.

155 WHEN YOU NEED AN ALL-NIGHT BURN: BUILD A LONG-LOG FIRE

Sure, you can craft a log-cabin blaze and feed the fire all night long, but there is a better–and much bigger–way. The Finnish *rakovalkea* fire is from a Scandinavian long-log fire tradition, and its slow-burning blaze produces a low wall of flaming warmth. Think of it as Mother Nature's version of a person-sized quartz heater. And this fire is as much fun to build as it is to burn. Setup requires some prep work with an ax, a couple of large logs, and a passel of good friends. So sharpen your ax, get swinging, then make like Logi–the Norse god of fire.

YOU'LL NEED

2 dry logs, 6 to 7 feet (1.8-2.1 m) long and about 8 to 10 (20-25 cm) inches in diameter, shorn of bark and branches

2 platform logs, 2 feet (30 cm) long

2 green branches, 2 feet (30 cm) long, about wrist-thick

Lots of tinder, such as birchbark and fatwood, and kindling

4 green stakes, 4 feet (1.2 m) long and sharpened on one end

2 green branches, 6 feet (1.8 m) long, about wrist-thick

2 nails

1 "threshold log," 6 to 7 feet (1.8-2.1 m) long and about 10 inches (25 cm) in diameter (not shown)

STEP 1 Chop out a flat surface along the entire length of both of the long logs (A). This isn't finish carpentry; the rougher the surface, the better the fire will be.

STEP 2 Notch the center of each platform log (B), and spread them out on the ground almost the length of the long logs. Place one long log into the notches of these platform logs with the flat surface

of the long log facing up. Position the long log parallel to the wind.

STEP 3 Lay the two shorter green branches across the first log about 5 feet (1.5 m) apart (C). Cover the flat surface with a thick layer of tinder and kindling. Place the second large log atop this layer, flat side down, like a giant hoagie bun.

STEP 4 Stabilize the fire by driving the 4 long, green stakes into place (D). For added security, anchor the free end into the ground and nail the other end of each 6-foot-long (1.8 m) branch to the top of the top log (E).

STEP 5 Lay down the threshold log a few feet in front of the fire as a backup in case one of the burning logs rolls off the fire.

STEP 6 Light the tinder and kindling along the entire length of the fire lay.

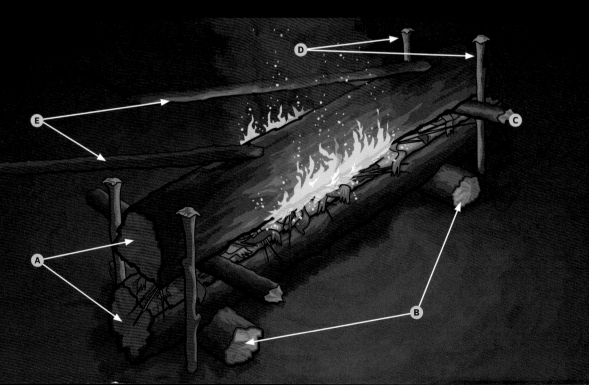

156 WHEN YOUR KIDS WANT TO HELP: CONSTRUCT A LEAN-TO FIRE

A lean-to fire appeals to kids because of its simplicity–there's no elaborate structure, and there's little hidden from view behind intricate layers of tinder and kindling. And with a lean-to fire lay, young pyros are less likely to burn themselves since they don't have to reach across flames and coals to add fuel. Lean-to fires do require a bit of maintenance, but that's another bonus from a kid's perspective: All that poking and messing and adding sticks to the fire actually helps.

STEP 1 Cut a support log 2 feet (30 cm) long. Lay it on the ground at a right angle to the wind. Have a second log similar in size to the support log ready to go. (Note: It's common practice to lay a lean-to fire so the large log acts as a windbreak, but that can starve the fuel of life-giving oxygen. Instead, lay the fire so the breeze runs straight at the support log.)

STEP 2 Pile tinder beside the midpoint of the support log, and lean thin planks of kindling against the log and directly above the tinder. Leave enough space between these sticks for air to circulate.

STEP 3 Light the tinder and feed the fire with progressively larger sticks of fuel. Once the kids have gotten bored with the fire, place the second log parallel to the first, and the lean-to fire is converted into a skillet-ready fire with the two larger logs serving as a cooking platform.

157 WHEN YOU NEED FIRE RIGHT NOW: BUILD A RIDGEPOLE-AND-RAFTER FIRE

This is an easy fire to love: Quick to light, fast-burning, pretty handy at shedding a light rain, and requiring just a few sticks and a small wad of dry tinder. You're not going to bake a potato or dry a drenched parka with a ridgepole fire, but this is a simple lay that makes a great base from which to build a larger blaze.

There are two approaches. The down-and-dirty is to simply shove a green stick into the ground at a 30-degree angle, and rafter finger-thick sticks across this ridgepole to form an A-frame over the tinder.

For a more substantial blaze, cantilever the ridgepole over the fire site. Cut a 3-foot (0.9-m) pole of green wood twice as thick as your thumb. Lay two heavy logs on the ground a couple feet apart. Anchor the pole by sticking one end under the first log and resting the stick on the second like a fulcrum. This stick should point into any wind or breeze. There's your ridgepole. Place tinder under this beam and rafter it with kindling. It's ready to light. The beauty of this design is that a backlog is already in place, making it easy to convert a quick-burning ridgepole fire into a more substantial lean-to.

158 WHEN IT'S HOWLING: BUILD A TRENCH FIRE

Wind blows. It blows out your match; it blows away a campfire's heat; it fans flames so they consume wood like crazy; it blows embers and ash into the surrounding woods. There's one solution to all of this: Start digging. In dry conditions this trench fire puts most of the coals safely below ground level, and since you're basically burning wood in a hole in the ground, fuel burns efficiently. That means less work–once you're finished with the trenching tool.

SITE WORK Avoid areas upwind of highly flammable trees such as pines and firs, and move to another site if you run into roots while digging the trench. Roots can smolder for a long time and eventually ignite a ground fire. Use topography to help tame high winds; look for low spots such as creek banks and gullies.

BE THE BACKHOE Dig a sloping trench approximately 4 feet (1.2 m) long and 1 foot (0.3 m) wide, with the shallow end facing the wind. The deep end should be about a foot (0.3 m) or so deep–the larger the fire you

need, the deeper the hole should be. Line the bottom of the fire hole with dry rocks (wet rocks can explode or shatter) or green logs (A). If possible, stand a large, flat rock on end at the deep end of the trench (B). This will reflect heat and help create a chimney effect to draw air up through the fire.

SIDE BUSINESS One major advantage to a trench fire is that it serves really well as a cooking fire. Use green sticks to create a grate over the coals or extend the deep end of the trench at a 90-degree angle, digging it a few inches narrower than your cooking pot.

DIRT DUTY Boost the fire's safety factor by mounding up the excavated soil in a C-shaped firebreak (C) around the deep edge of the trench. This will help prevent sparks from blowing outside the fire and keep the dirt handy for when it's time to extinguish the fire and fill in the trench. Take special care to put out a trench fire completely before using the excavated soil to fill in the hole.

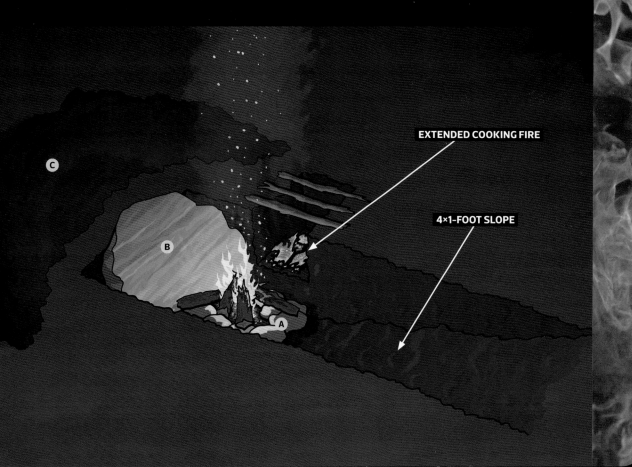

EXTENDED COOKING FIRE

4×1-FOOT SLOPE

159 WHEN YOU WANT TO COOK: BUILD A KEYHOLE FIRE

Flames licking a black pot, the smell of wood smoke and a simmering stew, with a table for two set under the stars–cooking in the wilds creates memories you can literally taste.

STEP 1 Create a keyhole-shaped fire ring: Build a 3-foot (0.9 m) diameter fire ring, and extend the two "rails" of the keyhole to 3 or 4 feet (0.9 or 1.2 m) long.

STEP 2 Build a hot fire in the round ring. As it burns down to coals, scrape the hot coals into the space between the rails, which serve as pot and grill holders. You can even lay skewers directly across the coals using the rock rails. Moderate heat and cook rate by adding coals or raising the skewers with additional rocks.

STEP 3 Keep the fire burning in the round ring. You can use its coals to stoke the heat under the pans and grills, and it will provide the perfect blaze for a sweet-tooth finish.

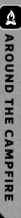

160 COAL

Sooner or later, the fire burns down to this. A constant, persistent glow. The roaring blaze is the adolescent fire, tempestuous and needy. This is the steady burn—older, wiser, something you can rely on. Coals will sear a steak and brown bread, and after the day is done, even as they fade, the dying flicker of coals carry promise. Five thousand years ago, Otzi, the famed Iceman of the Alps, died in the snow. He carried a copper ax, a longbow of yew, and a small birch-bark ember pouch. Once it held a tiny coal, the last glowing bits of his very last fire, and the seed of a blaze he would never live to build.

161 WHEN IT'S POURING: BUILD A TARP FIRE

Maintaining a fire in a downpour is no easy feat, but that's when you want fire the most. Rigged poorly, a tarped fire will smoke campers like jerky or turn a campsite into a deadly inferno. But there are safe ways to shelter a blaze. I once weathered a days-long southern Appalachian soaking in classy style thanks to backcountry guide Burt Kornegay's mash-up of an old-school cooking fire protected by a tarp. One big advantage to this method is that you can set everything up except for the tarp, then add it to the mix when the rain starts. That's a good safety feature, as rain helps cool the tarp fabric. Just remember the mantra: Tarp high, fire small.

HIGH-WIRE ACT Run a taut ridgeline of parachute cord between two trees (A) as high as you can reach, leaving an 8-foot (2.4 m) tag end of p-cord from the knot around one tree. Drape the tarp over this ridgeline to form an A-shape (B), leaving about 7 feet (2.1 m) of bare ridgeline between the tarp and the tree with the long tag end. Tie off the corners of the tarp (C).

POLE POSITION Cut a 10-foot-long (3 m) "push-up pole" (D) at least as thick as your wrist. Using the long tag end of the p-cord, lash the top of the push-up pole to the ridgeline 5 feet from the tree (E). Tie the end of the remaining cord

to the middle grommet of the tarp over the ridgeline (F). Now stand the push-up pole vertically. This creates a raised peak in the tarp, which keeps chimney smoke away from campers.

COOKING UTENSIL You could stop right there and build a warming fire just under the apex of the tarp, but take 10 more minutes to build a cooking fire. A "dingle stick" is a simple crane device used to suspend cooking pots over the fire. Cut another 10-foot (3 m) pole and lash this dingle stick to the push-up pole so enough of the stick extends over the fire pit to hold a pot over the flames (G). Anchor the rear end with rocks or heavy logs.

162 WHEN YOU WANT A SUMMER FIRE: BUILD A LOG CABIN COUNCIL FIRE

Summertime and the living is, well, hot–which makes a roaring campfire a bit of a problem. But if you lay the right foundation, you can build a great summer blaze that puts out plenty of light with less heat, burns a long time, and uses smaller pieces of fuel, so you don't break a sweat hauling huge logs back to camp. The log-cabin council fire is a pyro mash-up of a slow-burning, green-wood, log-cabin build on the outside, and a tepee fire that throws out tall flames within.

STEP 1 FRAME THE WALLS Choose slow-burning whole green logs of white oak, ash, or birch to build the frame that will hold the tepee sticks upright. Lay four stories of two logs each, starting with pieces about 2 feet (30 cm) long and using smaller logs as you go up.

STEP 2 STOKE THE FURNACE Inside the log-cabin structure, lay your tinder bundle and build a tepee of dry sticks and branches. Some of these pieces should be long enough to emerge from the top of the cabin by about 6 inches (15 cm). When burning, they'll supply plenty of light.

STEP 3 TOP LOAD Light the tinder inside your tepee, and feed the fire from the top as needed to customize the blaze–like a mood-setting dimmer switch. If the cabin walls start to burn too quickly, douse with water to knock back the flames.

163 WHEN YOU NEED AN EASY STARTING FIRE: MAKE A DUCT-TAPE FIRE

Out of dried bird nests, tinder fungus, and cattail fluff? Join the club. But surely there's a roll of duct tape nearby, and where there is duct tape, there is life. While you can't build an all-night blaze with nothing more than the sticky stuff, you can get enough of a fire cranking to dry and burn even wet wood. Start stripping.

STEP 1 Make a tinder bundle by stripping a 10-inch (25 mm) length of duct tape into ¼-inch (6 mm) strips and wadding them very loosely into a softball-size nest. A hot spark-thrower will ignite this bundle, but don't fire it up yet.

STEP 2 Twist strips of duct tape into tinder sticks 6 to 8 inches long. The adhesive side catches fire more quickly, so be sure to have as much gummy surface exposed as possible. You can make tinder sticks as large as your tape supply will allow, but a better idea is to wrap a few real sticks with tape. Remember: sticky side out. Rough it all up with a knife to increase flammability.

STEP 3 Light the duct-tape tinder bundle and feed the unnatural flame. Is it cheating? Well, sure. But doesn't it feel great to be alive?

164 WHEN THERE'S SNOW: BUILD A PLATFORM FIRE

Break through a frozen pond and you'll need to un-shiver your timbers pronto, but fire and water don't mix even when the latter is in the fluffy, crystalline form of snow. Digging through the snow to bare ground is best, but if the snow is too deep, you'll need a few degrees of separation to keep a fire burning in deep powder. This platform fire does the job nicely, and with a bonus: Simply building it will warm your cockles.

LOOK OVERHEAD It's always best to build a fire away from overhanging branches, but if you have no choice, don't lay your blaze under snowy branches. Use a long stick to clear the snow burden off the foliage so it won't melt into your fire, causing the ghost of Jack London to snicker in derision.

HEAVY FOOTWORK Stomp down the snow in an area (A) large enough not only for the platform fire but for extra wood, cooking gear, and your freezing backside. Tamp the fire site as level as possible. Once the blaze is going, the entire fire lay will most likely settle a few inches into the snow; starting off level will help keep wood and coals from sliding into the powder an hour into the burn.

BUILD A RAFT To raise the blaze, create a platform of two layers of wrist-thick wood (B), the greener the better. Break the wood into 4-foot (1.2 m) lengths. Lay down one layer, then the top layer perpendicular to the first, placing the sticks as close together as possible.

FLAME ON Start with a simple tepee fire (C). It will catch quickly and throw out heat and light for the task at hand. Build a log-cabin fire (D) around the tepee, feeding dry sticks into the chimney formed by the cabin walls. This helps dry out larger pieces of wood and creates a draft of hot, rising air to keep the tall, warm flames licking.

PHASES OF FIRE No. 4

165 ASH

These are the remains–curling wisps of calcium carbonate, drifts of deconstructed salts, traces of iron and manganese and zinc. After the crackling, the light-leaping, the blush of heat and revelry and the long silent staring as the flames flicker and die, these downy pillows of gray near-nothingness are good for soap-making and fertilizer. They will clean a skillet in a pinch. But most of that is from another time. These days, ashes are good for little but remembering. Stir them with a stick in the cold of morning and watch them rise, little bits of swirling laughter and fellowship from the night before.

166 WHEN IT'S THE LAST NIGHT AT CAMP: BUILD A MAGNUM BONFIRE

A bonfire is not a campfire. If you can roast a wiener in the flames with anything shorter than an 18-foot-long telescoping tree pruner, it's no bonfire. The only utility of this fire is to sear the memory of an awesome week at camp into the brain of every person nearby.

STEP 1 Carefully consider the fire site. If you're thinking about 6-foot (1.8 m) logs and flaming spare couches, you might need 50 clear paces between the blaze and the first row of spectators. Dig a shallow pit a few inches deep and encircle it with rocks or mounded soil. This keeps the fire from spreading but also helps prevent burning logs from rolling into the crowd if the bonfire collapses in an unplanned way.

STEP 2 To build a fire that will grow from a single match to a towering inferno to a contained bed of glowing coals all on its own, start with a 4-foot-tall (1.2 m) tepee fire in the middle of the fire ring, maintaining a safe few feet between the fire and the ring. The outer logs on the tepee should be 5 inches (12.5 cm) thick. Then build a towering log-cabin fire structure around the tepee. Keep every layer as even as possible.

STEP 3 Everyone's watching, so don't screw it up. Soak a roll of toilet paper in kerosene and tuck it at the base of the tepee fire. You don't have to light it with a flaming arrow shot across the dark sky. But, then again, you could.

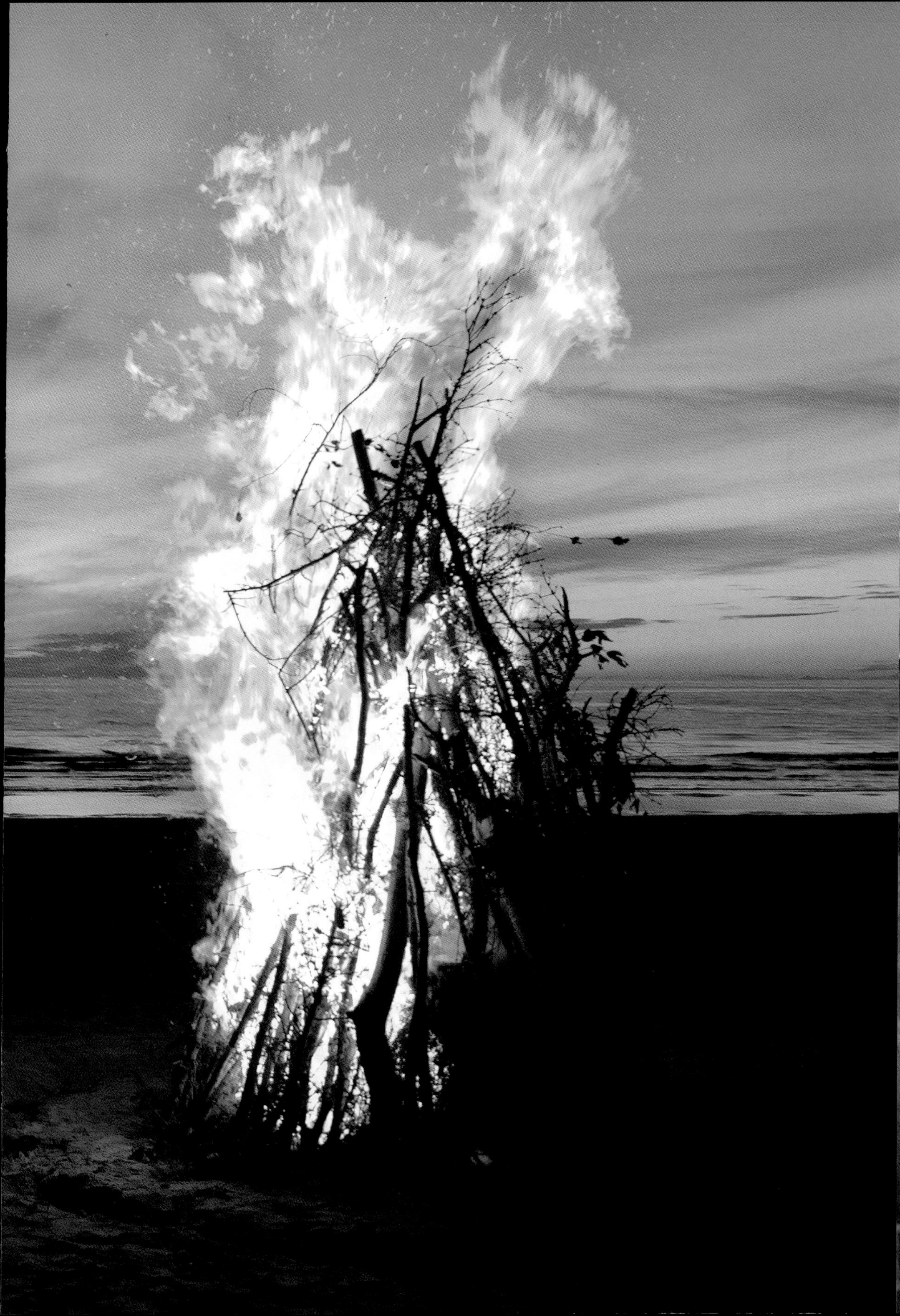

COOKING

Morning Joe
Brew perfect camp coffee

Grab a Handful
Trail snacks for every taste

Black Iron Magic
Do it all in a Dutch oven

Now Eat This!
Recipes for breakfast, lunch & dinner

Sweet Treat
Take s'mores to the next level

167 BE YOUR OWN BARISTA

Despite their hoity-toity reputation, there's probably no better way to make backcountry coffee than with a French press. There are some great camp models out there, so shop around. Some coffee presses are large enough to fuel an entire family, while others are sized for one person. Most are light, unbreakable and nearly fool-proof. Pour medium-ground coffee into the press, add hot water, wait three to four minutes, slowly press the plunger to the bottom of the mug, and jump-start the day. Always start with cold or cool water, never hot. And use good water. You can't dip a kettle into a muddy creek and blame the beans for the coffee's sludgy taste.

168 BUBBLE UP MORNING BREW

There are still plenty of folks for whom coffee isn't coffee unless it's made in a percolator. There's a down-side to such heritage, however: A percolator works because you boil the water, and boiling coffee releases tannins from the grounds, too much of which will give coffee a harsh, burned taste. To minimize the bite, watch the glass dome carefully and remove the percolator from the heat source as soon as the coffee's color is as dark as you want it.

169 MAKE JAVA IN A SNAP

Instant coffee has long suffered a terrible reputation as little more than black swill, but those days are over. Many newer brands work with small-batch coffee growers to ensure high-quality beans, and even partner with coffee roasters and freeze-drying facilities to customize taste. Brands such as Starbucks Via, Alpine Start, and Voila break the mold for instant coffees. They're a morning miracle for backpackers and even frontcountry campers who don't want to go to the trouble of brewing beans. And here's a pro trick: Use a dash of quality instant coffee to power up the feeble java you find in convenience stores and hotels while on the road.

170 CRAFT A CUP OF COWBOY COFFEE

Pecos Bill didn't fret about the extraction period of coffee solubles, but neither did he want his camp Joe sludgy enough to float a horseshoe. A perfect cup of cowboy coffee is hot enough to sear meat and strong enough to wake the dead, but that doesn't mean it has to be riddled with grounds and steeped with acid. Here's how to git 'er done on the trail with nothing more than water, beans, and fire. For the most impressive results, use a speckled enamel coffee pot—they're easy to find online—and Arbuckles' Ariosa Blend coffee, a cowboy favorite ever since it was developed in 1865.

STEP 1 Bring water to a rolling boil. Remove from heat and let it sit for 30 seconds. Spoon in 2 tablespoons = 24 g (15ml) of coffee ground the size of coarse salt for every 8 ounces (240 ml) of water. Stir the mix and let sit for 2 minutes.

STEP 2 Stir again, and give the grounds another 2 minutes to settle.

STEP 3 Use a spoon to sprinkle a bit of cold water on top, which will sink and help settle the rest of the grounds. Some folks insist on adding crushed eggshells to settle the grounds.

STEP 4 Pour slowly. It's best to brew just enough for a few cups, and start the process over if you want more java. Coffee that sits in the pot with coffee grounds will turn harsh and bitter. Like Pecos Bill after a Sante Fe Trail all-nighter.

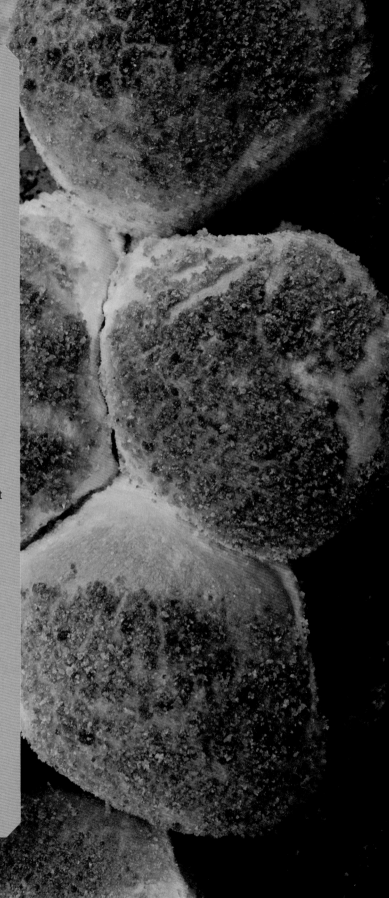

171 EXPLORE FLOUR POWER

Before the smartphone alarms go off; before the groans of middle-age men unfolding themselves from bunkbed mattresses; before all this I lay in my own deer camp bunk and listen to Tommy Krisulewicz in the kitchen.

Usually, by the time I'm awake, he's already sifted the flour: 4 cups (540 g), self-rising, hand-cranked through the sifter. He opens the freezer door. Tommy chills every tool he uses to make biscuits: sifter, pastry blender, butter knife, and cheese grater. He grates 2 sticks of butter into the flour, stirring the chunks with a butter knife to coat them well, then cuts the butter into the flour with the pastry blender. Thump-thump-thump.

The buttermilk, he says, is a feel thing. Maybe a cup or so to wet the mixture so he can form it into a ball. Out comes the rolling pin, and I can hear the old wood cylinder rattling in its spindle. He rolls the dough to a ¾-inch (2-cm) thickness, give or take, then folds it right to left and top to bottom. Rolls it out again and folds a second time: left to right, bottom to top. Rolls it out a final time, then cuts the round biscuit discs with the chilled cutter. Straight down and straight up, Tommy insists. Twist the cutter and the edges will harden.

He loads the cast iron skillet with biscuits touching "so they'll smoosh up together as they rise," he says. "Makes 'em rise taller. Trust me." And we all do.

The biscuits bake at 450°F (232°C) for 20 minutes, and by the time they come out of the oven, just about everyone is out of the beds, elbows on the tall counter, some ready to roll out in camo, others still in their underwear, all of us waiting on homemade, handmade Tommy K biscuits.

Pass me that jelly.

Where's that sausage?

A good day dawning. I can hear it.

172 COOK BISCUITS IN THE FIRE

There are lots of great ways to make a biscuit, and they can be as involved as building them from scratch, or as easy as busting open a can and daring your buddies to say a word. Here's the DIY route.

STEP 1 Mix 2 cups (270 g) flour, 3 teaspoons (15 g) baking powder, and 1 teaspoon salt (5 g).

STEP 2 Using a fork, cut ¼ cup (50 g) of vegetable shortening into the mix until it has a crumbly texture.

STEP 3 Add ¾ cup (180 ml) buttermilk and 3 tablespoons (45 ml) orange juice.

STEP 4 Fold the mixture over itself until it forms a dough.

STEP 5 Cut biscuits with a jelly jar.

STEP 6 Place biscuits in an aluminum foil tin, and cover with more foil. Cook in fire coals till golden brown.

173 COOK BISCUITS ON A STICK

Here's a super-easy campfire biscuit trick that kids love–and can pull off perfectly with very little instruction.

STEP 1 Cut one stick per person. It should be about 3 feet (90 cm) long to keep hands away from the fire, and ¾ inch to 1 inch (2-2.5 cm) in diameter. Shave off the bark 6 inches (15 cm) from one end.

STEP 2 Crack a tin of canned biscuits. Each person pats out a section of dough about 7 inches (17.5 cm) by 3 inches (7.5 cm). Cover the bark-free ends of the biscuit stick like a corn dog.

STEP 3 Bake over the fire till golden brown and cooked all the way through.

STEP 4 Remove the stick and fill with butter, maple syrup, brown sugar, and roasted nuts.

174 MAKE YOUR OWN TRAIL MIX

You could pay big bucks for pre-fab trail mix. Or you could keep some pocket change and make your own from a variety of pick-and-choose assortments:

THE BASICS Good Ol' Raisins and Peanuts (a.k.a. GORP), M&Ms, and granola.

THE TROPICAL Smoked almonds, butterscotch chips, dried banana chips, dried pineapple chunks, flaked coconut, dried papaya, and yogurt-dipped raisins.

THE HIPPIE SPECIAL Wheat germ, dark chocolate-covered coffee beans, macadamia nuts, chopped figs, salted sunflower seeds.

175 MAKE YOUR OWN JERKY

Jerky is an awesome camp food, because it's easy to make, easy to pack, great for snacking on the trail, and will hold up to being smashed in a pack or squished in a duffel bag. And it's a snap to make jerky at home.

STRIP BY STRIP For sliced jerky, use a sharp fillet knife to cut the meat across the grain, keeping the strips relatively uniform in size and thickness. Partly freezing the meat first helps with slicing. Using ground meat for jerky works well, too, though you'll need a jerky gun to squeeze out the strips.

SALT CURE Curing salt adds a measure of safety if you're not going to refrigerate the jerky, or if you plan to keep it for a long time. You can order the salt in bulk (it's easy to find online), but most jerky kits come with enough curing salt for 5 to 10 pounds (2.3-4.5kg) of raw meat. Mix both the salt and cure in a bit of cold water, and season the meat a few pounds at a time. Mix it well, then allow your meat to chill overnight.

FLAVOR BATH Marinate the jerky strips in your favorite flavoring agent for at least 12 hours. Try teriyaki sauce or a dry chili rub.

TURN ON THE HEAT Jerky can be dried in the oven on low heat with the door propped open. Use a 4-inch (10-cm) length of pencil and the grippy eraser end will keep the stub in place. A pellet smoker works well, too, as does a water smoker if you leave out the liquid pan. Dehydrators also make great jerky. Slow cook the meat until it's dry but you can still bend it without breaking. Store it in the refrigerator or freezer in zip-top or vacuum-sealed bags.

CAMP CHEF — TRICK No. 1

176 PERFECT THE DRUGSTORE WRAP

Cooking a fabulous mix of veggies and meat in a foil pouch is an honored tradition, but many a campfire meal has been ruined with a fire-blackened fail of this technique. Avoid the burn with the "drugstore wrap."

STEP 1 Tear off a piece of heavy-duty aluminum foil approximately three times the size of your pile of food. Place it shiny-side up on a flat surface. Put the food in the center of the foil.

STEP 2 Bring up two opposite sides to form a tent, and roll over tightly three times. Press tightly along the fold to seal the seam. Seal the other two ends with three tight folds.

STEP 3 Add a second layer of foil, with looser folds. This layer protects the inner layer from punctures and keeps it clean so you can use it as a plate once opened.

177 TOAST THE PERFECT S'MORES

STEP 1 Center a 2-inch (5-cm) square of a chocolate candy bar on half a graham cracker, and place this on a rock or grill grate near the fire. Set the other half of the graham cracker beside it. You'll want the chocolate to slightly melt, and the graham cracker to slightly toast, as you toast the marshmallow.

STEP 2 When toasting marshmallows, achieving the perfect balance of golden smokiness and creamy gooliciosity (that's a real word—you don't have to look it up) is no small feat. Start with a top-shelf brand such as Jet-Puffed or Campfire. Lesser brands burn way too quickly. Cut a plain, straight roasting stick approximately 30 (75cm) inches in length. Whittle to a point, and whittle or scrape off the bark on the pointy end.

STEP 3 Skewer the marshmallow onto the stick and hold it level over embers, not flames. It's fine to have flames off to one side, but they shouldn't be directly under your precious glob of sugary wonderfulness. Rotate the marshmallow slowly or a quarter turn at a time. Here's where the straightness of the stick comes into play: You don't have to move the marshmallow to a different place in the fire when you rotate it.

STEP 4 As the marshmallow turns a tawny golden color, it will sag on the roasting skewer. When a vertical slit appears where the stick and marshmallow meet, you know the insides are approaching that desired state of gooliciosity. It is time.

STEP 5 Pick up the piece of graham cracker with the chocolate. Lay the golden marshmallow on top, and make a sandwich with the other half of graham cracker. Press it all together slightly as you remove the stick.

STEP 6 Do not share. Nobody shares s'mores.

178 THINK OUTSIDE THE CHOCOLATE

While there's nothing wrong with a straight-up, traditional s'mores, getting a little crazy with the chocolate bar kicks this campfire treat to another level. Try Symphony bars for a bit of toffee crunch. Dark chocolate bars infused with orange are a big hit. A personal favorite is a dark chocolate candy bar filled with a bit of gooey cherry filling. Look around the grocery store and you should find plenty of gourmet chocolate bars to try.

179 SUPERCHARGE YOUR S'MORES

Achieving s'mores royalty status requires only a couple of easy-to-score extra ingredients.

First, whip up a batch of bourbon-glazed bacon. Line a baking sheet with parchment paper, spread out a dozen strips of bacon, brush with 2 tablespoons (30 mL) of bourbon, then drizzle with 2 tablespoons (25 g) of brown sugar. Bake at 350°F (175°C) about 25 minutes. Remove, cool, and hide the secret ingredient in a zippered plastic bag.

At camp, commence the age-old ritual, with golden marshmallows and chocolate bars melted gooey on a fire-ring rock. Now break out the bourbon-glazed bacon. A half-strip tucked between marshmallow and chocolate will leave your fellow campers stunned. But the show's not over.

Next up is a jar of caramel sauce for a second shot of sweet nirvana. The crowd roars. Your children fall prostate in worship. And if your campfire mates can handle a final enchancement, ditch the graham crackers for chewy oatmeal raisin cookies. Yes, you now rule the campfire cosmos.

My buddy Mike Shea breaks all the s'mores rules with his Nutella Peach S'mores–and I've never heard anyone complain. This approach requires a skillet to place over the fire, and it does omit the toasty marshmallow–though nobody says you can't double-deck this recipe with a perfectly golden puff of sugar. If you dare.

INGREDIENTS

Peaches	Butter
Sugar	Graham crackers
Cinnamon	Nutella

STEP 1 Cut each peach in half and remove the pit. Sprinkle with sugar and cinnamon.

STEP 2 Melt butter in the skillet and cook the peaches with the cut side down in the skillet until soft with a little crisp in the center.

STEP 3 Smear graham crackers with Nutella. When the peaches are cooked, make a

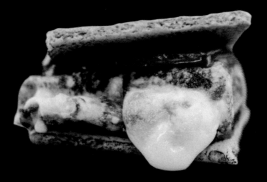

180 LOAD UP ON VACUUM BOTTLE VITTLES

Great vacuum bottles do more than keep water cold and cider hot–they'll hold serious loads of lunch grub for long day hikes far from your camping spot. And a hot trail meal is a welcome break from cold cuts and smashed sandwich bread. There's been a revolution in vacuum bottles over the last few years, with a welter of high-quality double-walled insulating containers hitting the market. Never mind that the technology has been around since about 1872, when Dr. James Dewar invented the double-walled glass flask.

DAWN PATROL PINTOS

For years my buddy and I ate beans for breakfast in a duck blind we called Pinto Point. To this day, I smell ham hocks whenever a flock of ringnecks whistles by. A vacuum bottle of beans makes a perfect, portable lunch or dinner side dish. Or a standalone, if unconventional, breakfast.

- 2   cans pinto beans
- ½   cup (120 mL) beer
- 1   small can diced tomato
- ¼   cup (13 g) chopped onion
- 1   teaspoon (5 g) lemon juice
- 1   teaspoon (5 g) chili powder
    Salt and pepper to taste

Mix all ingredients and simmer for a half-hour to reduce liquid. Pour into the bottle and you're good to go.

'MATER MIX

This vacuum bottle breakfast brew will warm you from the inside out, and makes a great side dish for a long day-hike lunch.

- 1   can tomato soup
- 1   can beef broth
- ½   garlic clove, minced (or powder to taste)
- 1½   teaspoons (7.5 g) oregano
- 1   teaspoon (5 g) basil
- ¼   cup (13 g) green pepper, finely minced

Black pepper to taste, then another shake or grind

Red pepper, ground or flakes, to taste

Tabasco sauce

Mix all ingredients and simmer for 15 minutes. Meanwhile, pour boiling water into your vacuum bottle and let stand for 5 minutes to preheat the bottle. Pour out the water and pour in the good stuff.

WASSAIL

In the 18th century, colonists in America would wander through apple orchards in winter, whacking the trees to drive evil spirits from the fruits. It was called "wassailing," and it led to a mighty fine spiced apple drink that has been the highlight of many a fine family camping trip. Or an adult camping trip, with the addition of whiskey or rum.

- 1   quart (1 l) apple cider
- 1   cup (240 mL) orange juice
- ¼   cup (50 g) sugar
- ½   teaspoon (2.5 g) whole allspice
- 1   12-inch cinnamon stick
- ¼   orange, cut into a wedge and studded with gloves

Heat all ingredients and steep for 20 minutes.

181 MAKE A GOOD REFLECTION

A reflector oven cooks by directing a campfire's heat down toward a cooking shelf that holds the food. You can buy a traditional reflector oven and use it time after time, or you can make your own from aluminum foil.

STEP 1 Cut two branched sticks about 20 inches (50cm) below the Y. Drive them into the ground at the edge of the fire ring, 18 inches (45cm) apart. Wrap a 22-inch (55-cm)-long stick with heavy-duty aluminum foil, place it in the forks of the Y-sticks, and unroll foil at a 45-degree angle away from the fire to the ground. Anchor the foil with another stick and unroll a shelf of foil towards the fire. Tear off the foil. Place four rocks on the bottom of the shelf. These will hold the baking rack or pan.

STEP 2 To create the oven sides, wrap one of the upright branched sticks with foil. Unroll the foil around the back of the oven. Tear off foil. Repeat on other side. Pinch the two pieces of foil together.

STEP 3 To bake fish, biscuits, and other foods, place them on the bottom of the reflector oven. Build a tall teepee fire, and keep feeding the blaze so flames reflect heat into the oven.

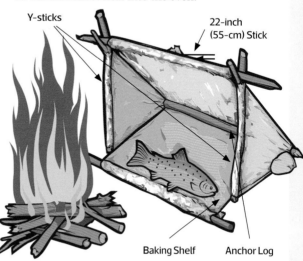

Y-sticks
22-inch (55-cm) Stick
Baking Shelf
Anchor Log

182 SOUS VIDE FOR EASY LIVING

Sous vide cooking is a game-changer for campers. You can cook steaks, chicken, pork chops, and other large cuts of meat at home, then pack them in the cooler. At camp, all you have to do is give them a quick sear on a grill or in a skillet, and a restaurant-quality main dish is ready. It's really that easy.

If you're not familiar with sous vide cooking, a quick primer: The machine is about as thick as your wrist and as long as a loaf of bread. You clip it to a tall pot of water, and the device heats the water to a preset temperature and circulates the water gently around the pot. You place a cut of meat inside a vacuum-sealed or zippered plastic baggie and drop it in. It will cook to the preset temperature in a few hours and never go past it. The slow cooking keeps tough meat parts from contracting under intense heat and mellows out

flavors. At camp, just pull the meat out of the cooler and let it come to an ambient temperature, then sear it for a crispy outside. Dinner is served!

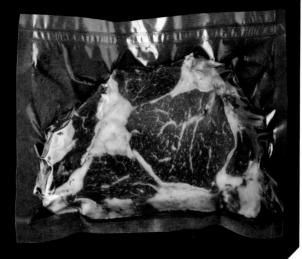

183 FORAGE FOR A FEAST

You don't have to have a PhD in botany to forage for amazingly tasty wild foods. Forests and fields are a pantry of possibilities, if you know how to grocery shop in the wilds.

MOREL MUSHROOMS Morel mushrooms emerge after the first few warm spring rains, just about the time oak leaves are sprouting.

Look for morels on sunny, well-drained hillsides, often near sycamore and poplar trees. Smaller black morels emerge first; larger yellow morels come on a week or two later. Cut them in half lengthwise and wash them thoroughly.

Sauté morels and serve alongside a good steak, or dip them in batter and deep-fry them. Big-city chefs pay a pretty penny for morel mushrooms, but if you know where to look, you can bring home buckets full for free.

RAMPS Ramps are a wild onion with a serious garlic punch. Legend holds that old Appalachian schools had separate classrooms for pungent ramp eaters in the spring.

Look near creeks in rich, moist hardwood soil. Use a trowel or hoe to get the bulbs out of the ground, but leave some to seed next year's crop. Wash off the dirt, peel off the outer thin skin, and cut off the end of the root.

Like onions, ramps can be grilled, roasted, sautéed, and eaten raw. For an Appalachian classic, stuff a fresh trout with ramps and butter, and pan sauté or cook in foil on a campfire.

BLACKBERRIES Blackberries begin to ripen in early summer, and there's good picking for a couple weeks after the first ones get sweet.

Leave the green and red berries alone for a few more days; focus on the darkest ones you can find, which are deliciously sweet. But watch out–the vines are covered in briars and, very often, ticks.

MOREL MUSHROOMS

RAMPS

BLACKBERRIES

Despite the seeds, blackberries are pretty good straight off the vine–but the Holy Grail of summer desserts is cobbler with a good scoop of whipped cream.

SASSAFRAS Sassafras makes a great tea and a pretty good licorice stick.

The small tree grows across much of temperate North America. It's easy to identify–few other plants have leaves on the same small tree with three different shapes: single, double, and triple lobes. Pull up knee- to waist-high saplings, and clean and skin the roots.

Chew on a skinned root for a licorice bite. Or fray a green twig for a DIY toothbrush. For sassafras tea, steep cleaned roots in water, strain, and sweeten.

SUMAC Smooth and staghorn sumac berries produce a tart drink, like Kool-Aid gone wild.

Look for ripe summer berry clusters in open sun, but pick before heavy rains dilute the potency.

After collecting, check for spiders, bugs, and other hitchhikers.

Place 6–8 clusters in a pitcher and add a half-gallon of cold water. Use your hands to rub off the red layer that has most of the flavoring. Steep for up to 2 hours; taste occasionally to monitor tartness. Strain through cheesecloth or a clean pillowcase. Add maple syrup, honey, or sugar to taste.

PERSIMMONS Persimmons are the largest native berry in the country, and trees are heavy with the fruits in the fall.

Pick a persimmon too early and the astringent fruit will pucker your mouth inside out. The fruits are ripe when you can shake them out of the tree.

Eat them raw, or skin and push them through a colander to pulp the flesh and make jelly, bread, pancakes, and syrup. Frozen pulp is a poor man's ice cream.

SASSAFRAS

SUMAC

PERSIMMONS

184 MAKE A 10-MINUTE BACKPACKER'S MEAL

When you've logged a bunch of miles—or wrangled the kids from sunrise to sunset—supper needs to be quick, hot, filling, and tasty enough to linger over. This quick one-pot wonder requires just a handful of ingredients and minimum cleanup. And it's easily customizable to your crew's taste—just swap out the smoked oysters for tinned chicken, salmon, or fresh veggies.

1	6-oz. (170 g) package of instant stuffing mix
3	tbsp. (45 mL) olive oil
12	sun-dried tomatoes
2	3.5-oz. (100 g) tins smoked oysters
1	8-oz. (210 g) can water chestnuts

STEP 1 To a 2-quart (2 l) pot, add the stuffing's required amount of water, plus 3 tablespoons (45 g).

STEP 2 Follow box directions for stuffing with these exceptions: (1) Replace butter with olive oil. (2) Toss in the sun-dried tomatoes and simmer for five minutes before adding stuffing mix. (3) After stuffing is ready, stir in oysters and water chestnuts. Mix thoroughly.

185 THROW A SOUTHERN BREAKFAST FEAST

Red-eye gravy is a Southern breakfast camp staple and turns ham drippings and coffee into an unforgettable breakfast meal.

- Slow-cook or 5-minute grits (never instant grits)
- 2 servings country ham
- ¼ to ½ cup (120–240 mL) strong coffee
- 1 teaspoon (5 mL) vegetable oil
- 7-Up

STEP 1 Prepare grits according to directions on the package.

STEP 2 Grease a cast iron or aluminum pan with vegetable oil and fry the ham for 2 to 3 minutes per side.

STEP 3 Add a few tablespoons of 7-Up and stir; the sugar in the soda will caramelize and help the ham stick to the pan. Scrape and stir the drippings in the bottom of the pan. Remove the ham from the pan.

STEP 4 Add the coffee to the drippings. Heat until just below boiling for 2 minutes, constantly stirring and scraping. Add the ham back to the skillet; stir to reheat thoroughly.

STEP 5 Plate the grits and ham and spoon red-eye gravy over it all.

186 MAKE A QUESADILLA PIE

Making a meal in a Dutch oven frees up the cook to sip whiskey and trade stories while pretending to be hard at work. This chicken quesadilla pie serves 10 to 12, and it's as easy as falling off the log you're sitting on while claiming to cook.

- 1 5 lb. (2.2 kg) chicken breasts, cut into stir fry-size chunks
- 2 medium sweet yellow onions, chopped
- 1 16-oz. (450 g) can corn kernels
- 2 green peppers, chopped
- 1 16-oz. (450 g) can black beans
- 1 large yellow squash, cubed
- 3 boxes cornbread mix
- 1 19-oz. (540 g) can enchilada sauce
- 3 eggs
- 25 small corn tortillas
- 1 cup (240 mL) milk
- 2 lb. (1 kg) shredded cheddar or jack cheese

STEP 1 Sauté chicken, onions, green peppers, and squash until chicken is nearly cooked through.

STEP 2 In a 14-inch (35 cm) Dutch oven, layer enchilada sauce, tortillas, cheese, canned ingredients, and cooked chicken-and-vegetables mixture.

STEP 3 Mix cornbread with eggs and milk according to box instructions and spread over the top.

STEP 4 Bake for 1 hour using 6 to 8 coals on the bottom and a tight ring of coals around the top.

187 COOK A CAMP CAJUN YAKAMEIN

Ramen noodles aren't just a dorm-room delicacy. A 25-cent brick of wheat flour, sodium and MSG has fueled many a long hike and backcountry camping trip, but there's an easier, healthier, and tastier way to put on a quick, hearty feed in the woods. Yakamein is a New Orleans mashup noodle soup staple devised by Chinese immigrants in the Big Easy. This version keeps the coonass seasoning and the street-food vibe but adds whatever meat you have on hand–steak, pork, and wild game work great–and a few easy-to-pack and easy-to-find ingredients.

AT HOME Pack a few green onions, a hard-boiled egg, one beef bouillon cube, and 6 ounces (170 g) of slow-cooked and shredded meat into a zip-top bag. Snag a couple packets each of ketchup, hot sauce, and soy sauce from a fast-food restaurant, and pack along your favorite shaker of Cajun spices.

IN THE FIELD Cook and drain spaghetti–about a golf-ball-sized handful for each person.

Bring 1 cup (240 mL) water to a boil. Add beef bouillon cube, meat, and a few hearty shakes of Cajun seasoning. Stir in one packet each of ketchup and soy sauce; save the other packets for additional seasoning if desired.

ON THE PLATE To serve, pour meat and broth mixture over spaghetti and top with a halved boiled egg and chopped green onion. Season with hot sauce.

188 DIG A BEAN HOLE

Digging a bean hole is a storied tradition in the North Woods, but there's no reason you can't do it anywhere. The wood smoke and molasses flavors in this dish can't be duplicated any other way.

- 10 cups (1.8 kg) dried Great Northern or yellow-eyed beans
- 1 lb. (.25 kg) salt pork, cut into 2-inch strips
- 4 tsp. (20 g) dry hot mustard
- 2 large onions, diced
- 2 tsp. (10 g) black pepper
- 2½ cups (600 mL) molasses
- ½ cup (110 g) butter

STEP 1 Dig a hole that's twice as deep and one foot in diameter larger than the Dutch oven you're planning to use. Next, toss a few rocks or a length of chain into the bottom of the hole. Fill the hole with hardwood, then burn the wood down until the hole is three-quarters full of hot coals.

STEP 2 Over your open fire (or on a camp stove), precook the beans by slow-boiling them for about 30 minutes. Drain and set aside.

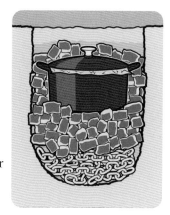

STEP 3 Place the salt pork in the Dutch oven, layer onions on top, and pour in the beans, molasses, mustard, and black pepper. Slice the butter and place on top. Add enough boiling water to cover the beans by ½ to 1 inch (12 mm to 2.5 cm). Cover the pot with aluminum foil and then the lid.

STEP 4 Shovel out about a third of the coals and put the bean pot in the hole. Replace the coals around the sides and on top of the oven. Fill the rest of the hole with dirt. Cooking time varies, but give it a good 8 hours.

189 COOK ON A ROCK

Before there were porcelain-coated grill grates, ceramic infrared bottom burners, and electronic ignition, there was a hot rock with a hunk of meat on it. Cooking thin medallions of meat and veggies on smoking-hot slabs of once-molten earth is still a great way to channel your inner Cro-Magnon.

STEP 1 Build a hot fire down to a good coal bed. While the wood is cooking, find a flat rock less than 2 inches (5 cm) thick. Avoid delicate shales and sandstones, and stay away from stream rocks; saturated rock can explode in a fire. Wash the rock surface and place it at the edge of the coals for 15 minutes to preheat. Move the rock to a shallow nest scooped into the coals.

STEP 2 When the rock is hot enough that a drop of water sizzles and vaporizes, brush on a film of flavored olive oil, such as chipotle, and plop on thin pieces of meat and onion slices about ¼ inch (6 mm) thick. Season with cracked black pepper. Cook the venison and onions for about 2-3 minutes. Using tongs, remove to a plate.

STEP 3 Turn the rock over and brush away the ashes. Drizzle with more olive oil. Place the medallions and onions on the fresh, hot surface, and top each medallion with an oil-packed sun-dried tomato. Cook another 2 minutes. Place a cooked onion slice atop each and serve.

190 TAKE A HOBO DINNER UP A NOTCH

A basic hobo dinner consists of hamburger, potatoes, onions, and carrots cooked in a foil pouch on the fire. But there's no reason to stick with the basics. What else to put in a foil pouch?

Whole boneless chicken breasts work great. Pork tenderloin and venison loin are stellar choices. Sausages and bratwurst are awesome. Steaks are a bit iffy, since they can overcook and get tough, but a thicker cut like a tender ribeye works.

For stepped-up vegetable options, add in pineapple chunks, sun-dried tomatoes, water chestnuts, and broccoli. And pump up the flavor with spices such as dried coriander, chipotle pepper, curry, and garam masala.

191 COOK A BROWNIE IN AN ORANGE

Move over, s'mores—here's some serious competition in the campfire sweet treats category. This citrus-flavored pastry meets all the requirements of the post-camp-dinner dessert: It's cooked on the campfire, you eat it with your fingers, there are no dishes to wash, and it requires just a few easy-to-find ingredients. It's not that a camper could ever tire of the venerable marshmallow-chocolate-graham concoction, but a campfire brownie cooked inside an orange? Sprinkle a few nuts on top, and it's practically a fruit salad. Here's how.

8   oranges
1   box of your favorite brownie mix, plus the ingredients required on the package
    Aluminum foil

STEP 1 Slice the top off an orange an inch or two from the top. Remove the orange flesh from both the cap and the rest of the orange, hollowing it out with a small knife or spoon. Repeat with the other oranges.

STEP 2 Prepare the brownie mix. Use a spoon to fill each orange with brownie mix about ⅔ full (it will expand while cooking).

Replace the orange caps. Wrap each brownie in two layers of heavy-duty foil. With the second layer, leave a short, twisted handle on top so you'll know which end is which, and to help lift the treats from the fire.

STEP 3 Cook in coals. Keep the twisted foil handle upright, and rotate the orange brownie bombs every 10 minutes for even cooking. Check one for doneness after 20 minutes.

STEP 4 Once cooked through, simply unwrap, discard the orange cap, and dig in. Plain ol' brownie mix works great, but uptown brownies such as turtle fudge or caramel are even better. If you're really feeling crazy, raid the camp kitchen for brownie toppings: M&Ms, GORP, even a few sprinkles of Frosted Flakes or a crumbled Pop-Tart.

192 OPEN A BEER WITH ANYTHING

Now this is an emergency: Miles from the kitchen and without a bottle opener. Don't despair. Get creative.

TRY BLADE WORK Hold the neck of the beer bottle tightly, with the top of your hand just under the bottom of the cap. Place the spine of a knife blade across the top of the third knuckle of your index finger, and wedge it under the edge of the cap. Then, pry the spine of the blade up carefully. Very carefully.

DRINK FOR A DOLLAR Fold a dollar bill in half lengthwise, crease the fold, and roll the bill up as tightly as you can, then fold the rolled bill in half. Crook your index finger and place the rolled bill on top, with the fold barely sticking over the edge of your finger. Hold it in place with your thumb. Hold the bottle tightly with your other hand. Place the fold of the bill under the cap and push upward with the bill.

UNLOCK YOUR BREW Hold the beer bottle tightly and place the tip of a key under one of the concave folds in the bottle cap. Pry the key to bend the fold outward, then bend out two or three neighboring folds. Insert the tip of the key under the worked edge of the cap, and pry it off.

193 CHANNEL YOUR INNER MOUNTAIN MAN

Grits and granola will do the trick for a day or two, but after a few mornings in the woods you may be ready for more. The venerable Mountain Man is a staple breakfast, and it is infinitely customizable to suit any family's tastes and quirks. The foundation of eggs, cheese, hash browns, and breakfast meat—bacon, ham, sausage, or some combination thereof—can be the final product or just a starting point. Add-ons can include sautéed onions and peppers, chopped fennel, garlic, and various cheeses. Our family favorite is roasted red peppers, coarsely chopped and sprinkled on top.

In a skillet, Mountain Man is more of a scramble. In a Dutch oven, it's a breakfast casserole. Either way, it will kick-start a day-long adventure, and it's so easy the kids can do the cooking while mom and dad sip coffee by the fire. Here's the drill.

1   pound (500 g) of bacon or sausage
1   26-ounce (730 g) package of freezer-case hash browns, or equivalent
1   dozen eggs
2   cups (225 g) shredded cheddar cheese
    Salt and pepper to taste

STEP 1 Brown the meat. Remove to separate platter and retain one-half of the cooking grease. Brown hash browns in remaining grease. While the hash browns are cooking, scramble eggs in a separate bowl.

STEP 2 When hash browns are cooked, dump in the cooked bacon or sausage, pour in the eggs, and mix. Season with salt and pepper. Cover and cook over medium heat, stirring occasionally.

STEP 3 When the eggs are nearly done, sprinkle cheese on top, cover, and continue cooking until cheese is melted.

194 GRILL FRENCH FRIES ON THE FIRE

Want fries with that? Always. And if you know how to cook French fries on an open fire, even the pickiest eaters will be happy with a smoky version.

STEP 1 Build a fire and burn it to coals. Scrape the coals to one side of the fire ring.

STEP 2 While the fire is burning down, slice potatoes into 1/2-inch (12-mm) French fry sticks. Rinse well and dry with a clean dish towel or paper towel.

STEP 3 Drizzle the potatoes with olive oil and season with salt, Cajun spices, or other favorites.

STEP 4 Place the potatoes on a grill grate and center it a few inches over the coals, balancing the grill with rocks. Cover with heavy-duty foil leaving the bottom of the grate exposed to the coals, and cook for 5 to 7 minutes. Flip the fries and give them another 5 to 7 minutes.

STEP 5 Wrap the potatoes in the foil, and place the package near the coals for another round of cooking. Test after 10 minutes to see if they're done.

195 LET THE KIDS COOK

Camping is the perfect time to let the kids get in on the kitchen fun. You can place a campstove on a picnic table or even the picnic table seat to lower the surface so it's far more kid-friendly, and it's no big deal when spaghetti sauce splatters the floor. It's only dirt!

MORNING MESSAGE Pancakes are super easy to cook, and even if your child burns one, you just toss it and go again. Get your young chef to experiment frying "monogram pancakes" by pouring the batter into the shapes of their initials. If you're really lucky, they'll try spelling out "I love you" one morning. Thankfully, there are no frying pans large enough for a golden-brown "when do I get my allowance" pancake.

COME AND GET IT For dinner, grilling shish kabobs over the fire ticks off all the how-to-make-a-kid-happy categories. They get to customize exactly what they want on their plate, and poke

around a campfire as their skewer of awesomeness sears to perfection. To pull it off, buy a set of long skewers with wooden handles to protect little hands from heat. Put together a smorgasbord of proteins and veggies, and add fun items such as pineapple chunks, shrimp, and slices of mango. Burn a fire down to a flameless bed of coals to minimize the burning effects of open flame, and use two larger pieces of firewood as skewer supports so they don't have to hold them.

196 COOK YOUR CATCH

A great fish dinner is one of the easiest meals to pull off while camping, and these methods make far less mess than any way you'd cook fish at home. Whether you catch your own or pick up fresh local fish from a market nearby, meals like these tie you directly to the natural world around you.

PAN FRY IT It's so easy it takes only six sentences to tell you how. Season the fillets liberally with Cajun spice and shake in a paper bag with fish breading mix. Pour enough peanut oil in a skillet to cover the fillets' sides but not spill over their tops. Heat the oil to almost smoking hot, and ease in a small piece of test fish to look for a rolling, sputtering boil around the edges. Gently add the other pieces. When the fish turns the color of caramel, generally about 2 to 5 minutes per side, turn carefully and only once. It's done when you can flake the fillet all the way through with a fork.

GRILL IT What a no-mess meal. Pack a small, foldable camp grill and sear your catch right over the coals.

FOIL IT Cooking fish in foil is a campfire staple, but think creatively about what you can stuff into the belly of the beast. Look for wild veggies such as ramps, mushrooms, and spring onions. Even wild fruits such as blackberry can lend great flavor to fish. Scrounge through the camp cooler: Bacon? Onions? Fry them up. Oranges? Apples? Cranberries and pecans from your trail mix bag? Heck, yeah! Drizzle with butter and spoon into the fish. Even leftover veggies like green beans, asparagus, and carrot strips will steam tender inside the fish, taking on the flavors of the wild.

197 SERVE UP FISH FRIED RICE

Fish fried rice is everything most other fish dishes aren't. It requires a single pan, one spoon, and zero cooking experience. Go low-tech with this recipe as is, or dress it up with slivered carrots, oyster mushrooms, or a tablespoon or two of Thai fish sauce. Mix the soy sauce, ginger, and spices in a small bottle at home, and complete in the field.

1½	lb. (0.68 k) fresh fish fillets, cut into bite-sized pieces
4	tbsp. (60 mL) soy sauce
¼	tsp. (1 g) dried ginger
½	tbsp. (2.5 g) Chinese five-spice powder
2	tbsp. (30 mL) peanut or sesame oil, divided
1	cup green peas
⅓	cup (17 g) sliced green onions
2	cups (500 g) rice, cooked and chilled
2	tablespoons (30 g) fresh parsley, chopped
3	eggs

Mix ginger and five-spice powder with soy sauce. Set aside. Heat 1 tablespoon of oil in a wok or large skillet, and stir-fry fish fillets 1 minute. Add peas and onions, stir-fry 2 minutes. Add soy sauce and spice mixture; stir well and remove from pan. Heat remaining tablespoon of oil and add rice and parsley. Stir-fry one minute. Scrape rice mixture to sides of skillet, leaving a doughnut-shaped hole in the middle. Add eggs, scramble, and cook for one minute. Add fish and vegetable mixture, mix thoroughly, and continue stir-frying until eggs are cooked, about 2–3 minutes.

198 GO BEYOND THE BURGER

Why stop your grilling with burgers, hot dogs, and corn on the cob? There are plenty of other tasty dishes you can fire up on the grate.

PEACHES Slice a peach in half, rub the cut surface with butter and place it on the grill. Count off 4 minutes then flip for another 4 minutes. The heat caramelizes the sugars in the fruit, boosting the sweetness with a kick of great char flavor. If you can resist the temptation to eat immediately, use these smoky grilled peaches in a cobbler.

POUND CAKE Grilling pound cake or angel's food cake is an awesome way to turn a cheap grocery store baked good into a dessert for the gods. Brush with melted butter and slap it on medium-low heat for a couple minutes on each side. Top it with fruit and whipped cream and call it a night.

PIZZA Forego the burgers for a slightly charred pizza crust. What a breeze: Brush olive oil on a pre-made pizza crust and lay it on the grill. Once it's slightly crispy and bears a few grill marks, remove the crust, load the grilled side with your toppings, and replace on the grill for another 3 minutes or until the cheese melts just the way you like it.

FRENCH TOAST Here's a great way to cook a fine breakfast and forget about cleaning dirty pans. Soak thick slices of crusty bread in a French toast batter of beaten eggs, cinnamon, and a touch of nutmeg. Fire up the grill, spray the grates with non-stick cooking spray, and grill the French toast about 2 minutes per side.

ASPARAGUS AND GREEN BEANS This will get the kids eating their veggies, and it's as simple as it gets. Drizzle the asparagus stalks or beans with olive oil and balsamic vinegar, and char on the grill. You can do this directly on the grate, although it's a bit easier with a perforated grill pan.

APPLES For a quick and (almost) healthy desert, cut apples in half and core them out. While you grill the apples, toss pecans on a sheet of foil and toast them on the grill. To prepare, drizzle maple syrup or honey into the scooped-out portion of the apple, fill with the toasted pecans, and feast.

AVOCADO It's not just for guacamole any more. Halve the fruit, remove the seed, brush with olive oil, and place it cut-side down for 5 minutes. Fill with salsa and start eating.

ROMAINE LETTUCE A grilled wedge salad is all the rage at fancy restaurants, but you can duplicate this divine side dish at camp. Simply slice a head of Romaine lettuce in half, drizzle with olive oil, and place on a hot grill until char marks appear. Top with bacon bits, chopped green onion, and julienne strips of sun-dried tomato. Dress with ranch dressing. Take a bow.

BANANA SPLIT If the kids have behaved all day, treat 'em right. Cut a ripe banana lengthwise, leaving the peel intact. Grill cut-side down for 2 to 3 minutes. Scoop off the grate with a spatula and place on a plate. Remove the hot peel with care, then load it up with whipped cream, chocolate sauce, and of course, a cherry on top.

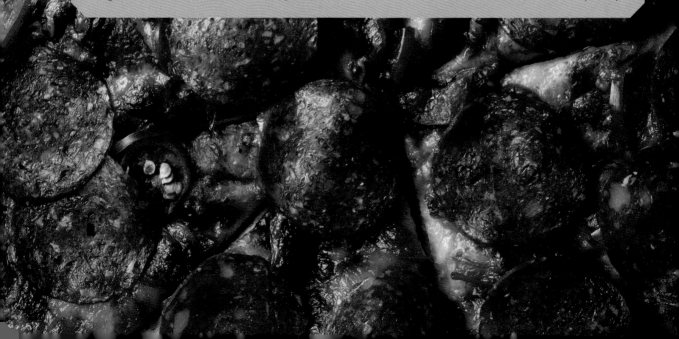

CAMP CHEF · TRICK No. 3

199 DIVVY UP K.P.

Doling out the kitchen patrol assignments is as much of a drag at the campsite as it is at home. Here are two ways to tamp down a revolt from your crew.

HAVE A LOTTERY Each night of the trip has a number, and whatever number you draw, you're responsible for that's evening meal, from preparation to clean-up. Have it catered, if you wish. Just don't ask for help.

USE THE BUDDY SYSTEM Assign 2-person teams for kitchen patrol: One to cook, one to clean. That way, no one misses out on the entire evening's festivities.

FIELD NOTES

200 MAKE A MOTH TRAP

For family campers, sunset is a mixed blessing. It's too early to hit the sack, but there's nothing to do after the first couple of s'mores are down the hatch. The answer: Rig up a light trap for night-flying moths. It's a great activity to start while you're cooking dinner.

Shine a light on a white sheet, and you'll be amazed at the gorgeous insects that will drop by for a visit. This is a perfect activity for young kids, since moths don't sting or bite. They'll stay fairly still while you watch them up close, and they'll fly away unharmed soon after you turn off the light and hit the sack.

GATHER THE GEAR You need a white bedsheet, some twine or cord, clothespins, and a good light source such as a strong camp lantern. You'll attract even more moths with a blacklight from a party shop.

SET IT UP Choose a site away from thick woods, such as a cleared field or meadow. String the cord between two trees at head height, drape the sheet over the span, and clothespin it in place. You'll want the sheet to drape along the ground for a couple of feet– some moth species prefer to land on horizontal surfaces. Weight the corners down to keep the sheet from flapping in the wind. Hang the light from an overhead branch so that it illuminates the upper third of the sheet.

WAIT AND WATCH Different moth species come out at different times in the evening, so it's fun to set up the light trap just as the sun sets one night, then an hour or so later the next.

FAMILY CAMPING

Moving Out
Pack up, pitch camp, and make yourself at home

Now What, Mom?
Awesome activities for every age group

Pitching In
How any kid can have fun with camp chores (Really)

Catch a Crayfish
And more fun nature activities for your family

Ultimate Backyard Campout

OL' TAJ

Julie had one requirement. If family camping was to be our family's "thing" we had to go big. She wanted a tent large enough for four inflatable camp mattresses, room for each of us to have our own duffel bag, a place for a Pack 'N Play, and a roof tall enough that she could change clothes while standing up. "Oh," she said. "And there's got to be room for a dog bed. Last time we camped, Biscuit pushed me off my sleeping pad. Put that on the list."

It was a tall order, but I found a tent beastly enough for the task: The Kelty Mantra 7, a 116-square-foot (11 sq m) nylon palace with a 6-foot (1.8-m) cathedral ceiling. Pitched on a state park tent pad, it flopped over all sides like a pancake too large for the plate. It looked like a lunar landing module. Actually, it looked like the garage a lunar landing module would fit inside.

But oh, the places we all went. Our tent, quickly dubbed by the kids as the "Taj MaTent," saw us through kids in diapers, kids in braces, and kids in high school. And three dogs. Over the years, we hauled Taj to the far corners of the country, and hosted unforgettable backyard campouts. Markie and Jack are grown and gone these days, but I keep the tent handy, where I can catch a glimpse of it in the basement now and then. Maybe we'll use it again. Maybe we won't. But ol' Taj shaped my family in ways that will never change. And all of them are good.

201 PACK YOUR CAR WITH A PLAN

Whether you're packing a van, sedan, SUV, or pickup, the basic rules of packing a camping rig apply. It takes some forethought, and requires some thinking, as you organize your gear in duffels and totes. But done this way, everything comes out of the vehicle in order of need, and the transition is a snap.

STEP 1 Whatever you need last, goes in first. That means stoves and cooking gear, camp chairs and furniture, toys and sporting equipment, and other odds and ends. Then layer in personal gear and clothing.

STEP 2 Whatever you need first, goes in last. That'll be the tent, sleeping bags and pads, and the tarp in case it's raining. If you're bringing in firewood, you might consider packing it last, if only because it will be easier to pull out of the vehicle.

STEP 3 Just before you close the trunk or hatch, stash a separate small duffel with raincoats, cold-weather jackets if necessary, and flashlights for everyone.

202 PACK FOR A FLIGHT

It took several trips to pin down the details, but my crew figured out the logistics of flying a family of four and all tent camping gear we'd need for a week. We made quite a scene at the airport: two adults, two kids, four carry-ons, and eight pieces of checked luggage, each of which weighed within a hair of the 50-pound (15-kg)-per-bag limit. But we pulled it off without any extra baggage fees over the typical allowances.

We had it down to a science. A 48-quart cooler was packed with stove, lantern, and cookware. Every man, woman, and child had his or her own duffel bag of clothing and personal stuff. A Canadian canoe-tripping barrel held anything breakable. And stuffed into a backpack was the Taj MaTent. Once on the ground, we rented a minivan, bought groceries, cheap camp chairs, and a square of indoor-outdoor carpet to serve as a front door mat, and we were off.

203 CUSTOMIZE A KID'S FIRST-AID KIT

Traveling with kids is always a roll of the dice. While camping, we've had to deal with strep throat, pink eye, a burst eardrum, and an ugly surfboard incident that required facial sutures. Think about your kid's needs–and injury proneness–and load up like a pediatric trauma specialist. I would pack two kinds of antibiotics, prescription eye drops for pink eye, EpiPens, butterfly sutures, anti-diarrhea pills, and those fabulous Vitamins A, I, N, and B–that's acetaminophen, ibuprofen, naproxen, and Benadryl.

204 CHOOSE FRIEND OR FAMILY ONLY?

I anguished over this. My sole purpose for putting a weeklong rafting camping trip together was to spend sustained one-on-one time with my 12-year-old daughter Markie, and allow for serendipitous,

meaningful moments of connection to happen of their own accord. I didn't want to be a chaperone to friends. I also was aware that the welcome mat between father and child might wear thin during a week of togetherness on a raft and in a tent.

In the end, Markie and I had a good chat about what this trip was all about–and we invited George and Katie, another father and daughter, to join us. I knew George would share my desire to center the trip on the bond between father and child, and their presence added immeasurably to our experience.

Markie had a blast with Katie, and we're glad we extended the invitation. But I also worked hard to maximize face-time with my daughter. We picked blackberries together and hunkered down in the tent to write in our journals. There were times when it was no easy feat to leave the grownups–with the grownup stories and grownup libations–to hang out with Markie one-on-one. But I'm glad I did. Being intentional with Markie led to moments of connection that we'll talk about for the rest of our lives.

205 GIVE THE KIDS A PLAY BREAK

When you first roll into the campground, it's always tempting to bail out of the family vehicle and jump right into the hard work of setting up a camp. But you'll be happier in the long run if you hold off on barking orders, and give the kids a 15-minute break to explore the nearby area. They've been cooped up during the drive, and stretching their legs will do their bodies good. More importantly, they'll show back up at the allotted time excited about the creek just down the hill or the cool patch of woods where they already found a turtle. And they'll be in a much better frame of mind when you tell them to grab one end of the heavy cooler.

206 LASH A TRIPOD

A great activity to keep the kids occupied while you detail the camp is to have them lash a tripod. It's easy and fun, and it has a ton of camp uses. It's great for hanging a pot over a fire or hanging a large garbage bag out of the way. Make it with stout branches and solid rope and you can even hang a swing in a tripod. Middle-school-aged kids should be able to pull this off easily with this illustration. Help them find three strong poles of equal lengths, and about 5 feet (1.5m) of parachute cord. Then they can take over. They won't even need a knife.

STEP 1 Lay the three poles beside each other. Tie a clove hitch around one of the outer poles, about 6 inches (15 cm) from the end.

STEP 2 Weave the cord in and out of the poles with racking turns, until you have at least 3 wraps around the poles.

STEP 3 In the two pole gaps, make two tight frapping turns so the cord travels up-and-down across the wraps, then finish with a clove hitch. To raise, simply spread the tripod legs apart.

207 GATHER FIREWOOD AS A FAMILY

After the tents are up and camp is snug, my family goes on a firewood-gathering assault. We've learned the dark, cold way that the answer to the question, "How much firewood do we need?" is nearly always, "More." Here's how to get the entire family in on the fun.

LITTLE HELPERS Younger kids can gather tinder, the fine, flammable materials that gets the fire going. Explain that you're looking for small, dry stuff that will burn super-easy and fast. Pine needles, strips of bark from standing dead trees, handfuls of brown grasses, and similarly sized items can work. Tell them to think like a bird building a nest–they shouldn't bring back anything a mama bird couldn't carry in her beak.

TWEENER TASKS Older kids are on the kindling team. Kindling can be sized from finger- to wrist-thick. The trick is that it has to be super dry.

No green, living wood. If they can break it by pulling it across a knee, that's a great size. And broken, split wood catches fire quicker and burns better than whole round sticks.

TEEN TROOPS Put older middle schoolers and high schoolers on fuel duty, gathering the large pieces of wood that will burn long and provide lots of coals. When scrounging for dead-and-down fuel, the best bets are often larger, longer dead limbs that have sheared off of hardwood trees. Tell your fuel squad to look for wood that's off the ground, as it will be drier and more rot-free. Branches that have fallen and are leaning against other trees are the easy find.

EVERYBODY DO YOUR SHARE

Camping is a lot of fun when it's not a lot of work. Cleaning up after mealtime can be a grind, and it's not fair to the parents to have to do it all. Here's a task-specific job plan for the dreaded Kitchen Patrol that makes it seem like less of a chore, because no one does it all and everyone gets a break.

YOUNG KIDS The picnic table and benches will be the KP workspace, so younger children can clear one half of the picnic table to be used for dish drying while the other is the designated washing station. Scrape plates into the garbage, and stack up pots and pans near the camp stove. That might be enough to ask of tykes, so cut them loose.

MIDDLE SCHOOLERS These kids can do the actual dish-washing work, so tell them they have a few minutes of free time while the rest of the family clears the dishes. Set up a wash basin or three along one edge of the picnic table.

OLDER TEENS Let them handle the hot stuff: Get a large pot of boiling water simmering on the stove for washing (let it cool a bit before using) and fill a smaller wash basin with warm water for rinsing. Call those preteens back to the picnic table to do the actual dishwashing work, or have your older kids do the scrubbing. But pull them off the sudsy jobsite before they get bored and put them on fire duty: They'll need to build up the blaze that's sputtered out during mealtime, so everyone can cozy up with a marshmallow roasting stick.

209 MAKE RAINY DAYS GAME DAYS

Sleeping pads make perfect game boards, and there's no better way to pass time during a downpour than with a rousing brain-smash of chess. Or a spirited tic-tac-toe challenge, if you'd rather.

PREP YOUR PAD You'll need to prep at home for this rainy-day fun. First, use a warm, wet rag to clean the pad of dirt, sweat, grime, and smashed-in candy bars. While the pad is drying, pull out your favorite board games, a ruler, and permanent markers.

DRAW YOUR GAME Sketching out a chess and checkers board is as easy as drawing squares and coloring between the lines. Backgammon is bit more complicated, but still doable. And there's always tic-tac-toe. If you have kids, a boiled-down board of Chutes and Ladders isn't that difficult to draw. You could even go hardcore and sketch out Monopoly if you like.

CHOOSE YOUR TOKENS For backgammon, rocks and pebbles will work just fine. Die-hard chess fans can snip out cardboard cutouts of pawns, queens, and other pieces, and store in a pack pocket for a rainy day. The most fun is checkers. Use yogurt raisins, M&Ms, or nuts. Each time you jump an opponent's piece, you get to eat their checker.

210 LEARN TO HAND-GRAB A CRAWDAD

If you ask yourself why in the world anyone would want to catch a crayfish, you might not have what it takes from the get-go. You can't be a scaredy cat. You can't flinch or hesitate–that's a good way to get pinched, and a decent-sized crayfish can draw blood. You don't have to catch them by hand, of course. It's possible to net crayfish or pin them down with a stick. You can catch a crawdad by scooping up a double handful of muck and silt with the crustacean all mixed in, and hurl the whole mess towards the creek bank. But those are the sissy ways. It's best to simply dial up your courage and go in for the quick snatch. There's something to be said for the direct approach.

Move gently upstream and gingerly turn over every rock larger than a softball. Lift the downstream end of the rock first, so the creek water swirls into the void and stirs up a plume of sediment that will hide you from your prey. As the water begins to clear, get your mind right for the grab–you have to grasp the crayfish in the sweet spot right behind the pincers. Too far back or too far forward, and a five-inch crawdad will light you up.

211 PULL OFF A CAMPING PRANK

Camp pranks are a harmless way of dialing up the fun, and kids can't get enough of them. Here are four safe pranks for any ages.

POOP DUDS Brag to your young campers that you've always been known for your ability to identify different kinds of animal poop. Plant chocolate-covered raisins along the trail, and taste-test a few in front of your horrified children.

KNOT A SNAKE Tie a half-dozen knots into a length of rope, and push the rope under a tent while it's unattended. Make sure it winds under the floor and under a sleeping pad or two. Then, once the campers are nodding off, slowly pull the rope under the tent. Snakes!

SCARY EYES Pack a few toilet paper tubes and glow sticks. At camp, cut angry eye shapes into the sides of the paper tubes. As someone tells a few ghosts stories, have another camper activate the glow sticks, place them inside the tubes, and hide the tubes near–or inside!–the tent.

BAGGING IT Toss pine cones in the bottom of a victim's sleeping bag. It's a tame way to give them a jolt as they settle in for sleep.

212 LEAVE A CAMPSITE SPOTLESS

The very last thing we do at camp before the ride home is set everyone loose for a "micro-trash" scavenger hunt. Micro-trash is all the itty-bitty stuff that gets left behind. Tiny pieces of aluminum foil and paper. Teeny snippets of rope and parachute cord. Orange peels and potato skins. Anything that's not natural. Tell your kids to stay away from broken glass, but offer them a dime for every piece of micro-trash they can find. They'll have a blast, and you'll leave behind a spick-and-span site for the next family.

213 TRACK A WILD ANIMAL

Studying animal tracks with a young camper is the ultimate game of "Where's Waldo?" When you find a track, start sleuthing.

WHO GOES THERE? Hoofed animals such as deer and elk are easy to identify with their heart-shaped tracks that show two distinct toes. But figuring out whether it's a buck or a doe is a challenge. Look for a few clues: A buck leaves a larger track, and the tips of its prints are a bit rounder. Also, a buck can have a wider chest and narrower hips than a doe, so their hind prints tend to be slightly inside the front prints.

Animals with paws can be trickier, but there's more to learn than the animal's identity. Study the crispness of the track's edges in the soil. Do the sidewalls seem crumbly? That can indicate an older track. Have tiny balls of mud that might have come off the side of the track adhered to the ground or are they still unattached? Moister soil at the surface could mean the animal is just around the corner.

STRIKE THE TRACK When you first cross a track, take a moment to look around and ask questions about the environment. Is the track following a creek? If so, the animal could be hunting for food. Do the tracks lead to thick woods and brambles? That could indicate an animal looking for a place to rest or sleep. Help young campers connect the animal with the natural environment.

BELLY DOWN Carefully lay down with the track in between you and your child, so your eyes are mere inches from the print. Get young minds thinking with creative questions. Is one hoof worn more than the other? Are there scrapes and smudges in the dirt that might indicate the critter was running? Learning to be an observant and creative thinker is more important than a precise identification of the track's maker.

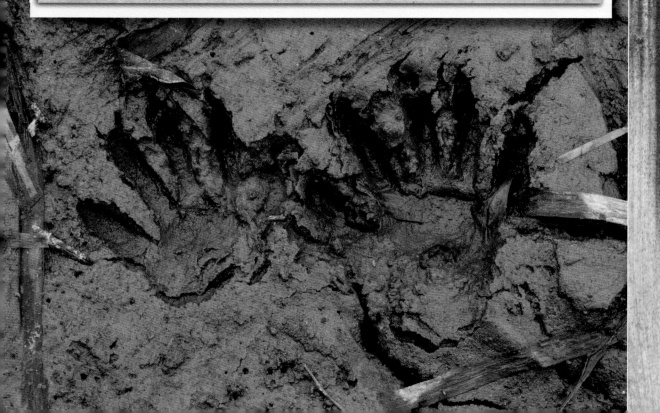

Pulling off a backyard dress rehearsal for a camping trip is a great way to ease young kids into the exhilarating, but potentially unsettling, aspects of sleeping outdoors. It's also a super way to tune up your skillset if you're a first-time camper, so you don't pitch the tent upside down or forget to bring a flashlight. For young, first-time campers, a backyard overnighter has one specific purpose: Do what it takes to keep the kids happy, all the way from sundown to sunrise. Here's your 10-part plan for success.

1 PACK LIKE YOU'RE GOING SOMEWHERE Part of the fun of camping, whether in the backcountry or the backyard, is making an event of it. Get your kids together to pack duffel bags of personal gear, clothing, and favorite toys. Head outdoors with tents and sleeping bags stashed in their stuff sacks, and pretend you're rolling up to a distant campsite.

2 MAKE IT PLUSH This is no time to scrimp on comfort. Double up on sleeping pads. Bring extra quilts and pillows. And, yes, there's room for the nearly life-sized stuffed unicorn. Whatever it takes to get to sunrise!

3 PLAY GAMES Adults can spend hours gazing into a campfire's flames and telling stories, but young kids can't. Have both an indoor and an outdoor plan: Cornhole and badminton before sundown. Story time and checkers played with M&Ms when you're ready to tuck in. Boredom is the enemy, especially when the television is only a few steps away.

4 COOK OUTSIDE There's a lot to manage when it comes to first-time campers, so it's OK to dial back the dinner menu. Hot dogs on sticks work just fine, and it's perfectly acceptable to order up a pizza delivery if you think cooking on a fire or grill might be too much trouble.

5 HAVE A SOUND PLAN Sleeping outside means you're surrounded by unusual noises. Owls hooting, local traffic, laughing and talking out on the street, the occasional raccoon fight down at the park–it can all cause young children some stress. Be prepared and talk through what your child might hear before you hit the sack.

6 SKIP THE GHOST STORIES As if you didn't already know this.

7 WATCH A MOVIE The point of a first-time backyard campout is to make it through the night, so don't sabotage your effort with an iron-clad "no electronics" rule. Set a limit and expectations, but it's better for the tyke to hunker down with a frozen princess on her tablet than bail to her bed. Better yet, string up a white bedsheet and project a favorite movie a bit before bedtime. If you're lucky, your campers will be sleepy-eyed and ready for the sack.

8 BAN THE BUGS Do everything you can to deal with biting insects. One way is to let the kids make "bug bombs." Work together to bundle together fresh sage, bee balm, lavender, and mint and stash the bundles in the campfire coals to smolder. It works pretty well, but the psychological benefit is the big win.

9 MAKE S'MORES ANYWHERE Many major municipal areas will allow a small backyard fire as long as it's being used for warmth or cooking. If you don't have space for that, no sweat: Toast s'mores in a terra-cotta planter. Fill the saucer with sand or soil and line the planter with aluminum foil. Arrange three layers of charcoal briquets, and fire it up. Every kid can have their own mini s'mores fire, which rachets up the fun.

10 SHUT THE ESCAPE HATCH This is tough love, beginner-camper style. If you live with a spouse or significant other, double up in the backyard so escaping inside with daddy isn't an option. Or have your significant other spend the night away, so it's the backyard or nuthin'. You don't want to terrorize your kid, but you might lose the game if you make it too easy to quit.

FIELD NOTES

215 BUY A TICKET TO A FIREFLY SHOW

North America is home to more than 135 species of fireflies, and lightning bugs are most common in areas with dark nights and lots of natural vegetation. That means campers often get a front-row seat to their spectacular nightly light show.

One of the most common species is *Photinus pyralis*, the males of which trace a yellow "J" against the sky every seven seconds. Females answer with their own burst of light, most commonly a single flash. The male descends, flashes once more, and proves anew that summer is for lovers.

Some firefly species love grasses and meadows, while others hang out in wooded edges. Wetlands can be great places to catch a lightning bug show. Here are three super camping spots known for stellar firefly displays.

TRY THE GREAT SMOKY MOUNTAINS The South's most spectacular light show is made by a species that lights synchronously, *Photinus carolinus*. In the Elmont region, thousands of bugs blink six quick-fire flashes in perfect unison. It doesn't last long–perhaps a couple of weeks in early June–but it's a mind-blowing sight.

SPRING FOR FLORIDA Many lightning bug species like to hang out near water, and the natural springs in many Florida parks are a huge draw. Check out Blue Spring State Park for a great show.

CLIMB THE ALLEGHENY MOUNTAINS Another hotspot for synchronous fireflies are the parks and forests of northwestern Pennsylvania. There's even a Pennsylvania Firefly Festival that celebrates the phenomenon.

216 TEACH A KID TO READ THE NIGHT SKY

You need a dark evening, a broad treeless view of the horizon, and no more than a half-hour to teach a child a handful of night signs that will serve her well for life. Grab pillows and sleeping pads, and reach for the stars.

TAKE A DIP First, find the Big Dipper. Help your child trace the Big Dipper to the outermost two stars of the cup, then follow those "pointer stars" five times the distance between them to a bright star called Polaris—the North Star. Explain that no matter the time of year, a line drawn straight from Polaris to the horizon points north. Now, with your little stargazer fixed on Polaris, show her how the North Star is also the first star in the handle of the Little Dipper. How cool is that?

QUEEN CONSTELLATION Continue the imaginary line from Polaris another distance equal to that between the Big Dipper and Polaris. Boom: You're in the middle of five stars that create a big, lazy "W" lying on its side. That's Cassiopeia, the once arrogant queen who now eternally hangs her head in shame.

STELLAR STEED Extend the imaginary line to a big square of four bright stars and say hello to the Great Square of Pegasus, which forms the torso of the famous flying horse. Your little girl is practically a Greek scholar by now!

TRUE NORTH, ER, SOUTH Can't remember which star is which? Pound two sticks in the ground a couple of feet apart. Have your kid crouch behind one stick and line up a star with the top of the two sticks as if she were sighting a rifle. Get comfortable and watch for 5 minutes. If the star shifts to the left, kiddo is looking north; to the right, she's facing south. If it rises, she's facing east; if it falls, west.

HORNS OF THE MOON On nights with a high crescent moon, point out that the tips of the moon look like a bull's horns. Now have your kid draw an imaginary line from tip to tip and on to the horizon. She'll be looking roughly south.

217 HAVE A CAMP SPA DAY

On week-long camping trips, we always plan a midweek half-day Camp Spa Treatment. By then, all those half-washed dishes from late-night dinners can use a scouring. The same for socks and underwear if you are in the backcountry and packed light. Not to mention your smoky, grimy hair and faces. Pack a solar shower for an almost-hot blast of clean–it's definitely worth the trouble. Boil water and give pots, pans, and dishes a disinfecting scrub with biodegradable soap and elbow grease. Tidy up tents and common areas. And fire up the washing machine. Nothing says "home sweet home" like socks and undies simmering on the stove.

218 FENG SHUI YOUR TENT

The Chinese philosophy of feng shui is to arrange living spaces so that they create a place of balance, peace, and serenity. That's a tall order inside a nylon hovel awash with dirty socks, candy bar wrappers, and wads of used bathroom tissue. Here are three cheap, easy ways to introduce some feng shui love to your mosh pit of a tent.

RESTORE ORDER Use a shoebox-size plastic tub or tote as a tent organizer. With the top on, it works as a perfectly-sized nightstand beside your sleeping bag, holding a reading lantern and your water bottle. You can also use it as a storage box for stuff that gets scattered all over the tent—headlamp, glasses, pocketknives, ear plugs, and all the junk that's accumulated in your pants pockets over the course of the day.

LET THERE BE LIGHT There are tons of easy-to-hang LED tent lights that will clip to or hang from the tent dome and illuminate every corner of your nylon mansion.

HOLD THIS Keep a small plastic bag of binder clips in various sizes. They're much easier to use than clumsy toggles and ties when you want to keep tent doors and mesh open so they don't dangle in your face. And they're handy for hanging wet socks and other light items to dry.

TAKE THE KIDS FISHING

No, it's not as simple as it sounds. Turning good intentions into a good morning on the water with a 7-year-old isn't the easiest thing to do on a Saturday. Here are a few ideas to make sure those first fishing trips lead to many more.

HUNT FOR LIVE BAIT Let your kids scrounge for worms, crickets, and grubs around the campsite. They'll need to be careful turning over logs and rocks–always use a stick in case there's a snake under there. But filling a tin can full of dirt and fish food is almost as much fun as the fishing itself. Plus, you will have already caught something without ever leaving the campsite: Bait.

DOUBLE UP ON RODS Take two rods. One is for your child. The other is for when your child birds-nests the reel beyond a quick field repair or drops the first one in the drink. The larger lesson is this: Don't try to fish yourself, at least not at first. Focus all your attention on the young angler. Explain the basics of baiting hooks, casting, and playing fish, then let them have at it. It's frustrating for a beginner to watch the old pro succeed effortlessly, so give the kid all your attention and all the water.

MAKE IT SAFE Avoid potential disaster by smashing down each and every barb on each and every hook. Each and every time.

FRY 'EM UP Plan on a fish fry. Most kids will love taking a few fish back to camp. They like to feel as if they're providing for the grownups for a change, and eating what they keep is a valuable lesson in the proper role of the ethical angler. But don't get hung up on size. I've fried up a world of 3-inch (7.5-cm) fish fingers, all to make a point. And a tasty one at that.

KNOW WHEN TO FOLD 'EM If you're not catching fish and your kid is getting antsy, by all means go chase bullfrogs or butterflies instead. Some kids embrace the challenge of close-mouthed fish by trying new strategies. But others will remember a long afternoon of an enthusiastic parent saying, "Five more minutes!" for the last hour-and-a-half. Don't be that way.

220 LEARN TO THROW A KNIFE

Throwing knives don't have sharp edges, so they're actually quite safe as long as basic measures are in place–mainly, that no one stands in front of the thrower. And kids love to throw things, so a quality set of throwing knives can keep them entertained around camp for hours. There's a lot of trial and error to getting the throw down pat. But that's part of the fun.

The first phase is to learn a single-turn throw, in which a knife, held by the handle, makes one full revolution in the air and hits the target point-first. Tack a playing card to a board or a standing dead tree and give it a hurl.

STEP 1 Stand about 10 feet (3 m) from the target. Grip the knife by the handle as you would a hammer, with your thumb along the top of the spine. Keep your eye on the bull's eye and throw the knife with an overhand motion, releasing the knife just as your arm becomes horizontal.

STEP 2 Watch the point of impact carefully and make adjustments. If the knife sticks with the handle pointed downward, you are too close to the target. Back up a half step and try again. If the knife sticks with the handle slanting up, you're too far back. Take half a step towards the target, and let fly. Keep practicing until the knife sticks close to horizontal.

STEP 3 Time to stretch it out. Step back 5 full paces from the target. Try again. Adjust your distance from the target as needed until the blade sticks.

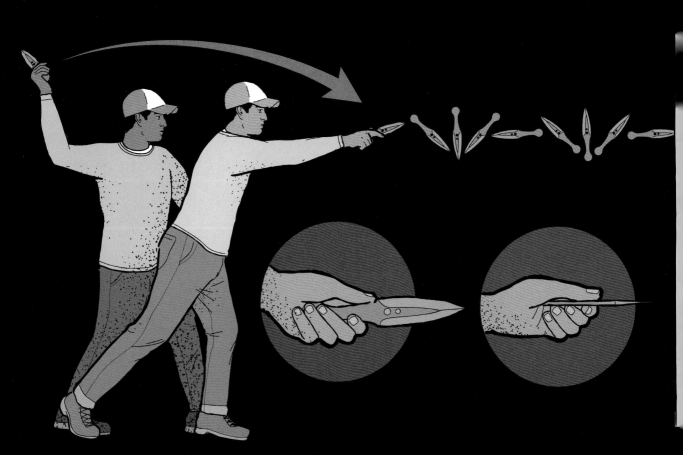

221 SCHOOL A KID ON KNIFE SAFETY

How old is old enough for a knife? That depends on the maturity level and physical dexterity of the child, but it's never too soon to talk about knife safety and demonstrate how to safely use a knife. Here's a step-by-step guide to bringing up a knife-savvy child, one ready for a lifetime of learning the knife skills that make life in the outdoors more fun.

START WITH WOOD Some knife companies sell wooden knives and knife kits. For kids too young to handle the real thing, they're a great way to introduce safety concepts.

DO A HACK JOB Use a rotary tool to grind down the blade on an inexpensive small knife such as a folding Swiss Army Knife. That will spark plenty of early conversations about knife safety and pay off later when they're ready for a real blade.

GET KITCHEN HELP Cooking with a child is a great way to introduce safe knife-handling skills. It's easy to provide close supervision, and there's plenty of knife work to be done in the kitchen, which keeps boredom at bay.

222 TEACH THE HAND-OFF

One of the first knife skills anyone should learn is how to pass a knife to another person. It's not the time for indecision or wishy-washiness–someone could end up bleeding. It's easy with a folding knife: Close it up and hand it over. But a fixed-blade knife is a bit trickier. Here are three ways to practice with younger kids.

PUT IT DOWN The safest way to pass a knife is to not pass the knife at all. Place it on a table or counter, and then let the other person pick it up.

USE A CRADLE HOLD Hold the knife by the handle, edge down (A). Next, pinch the bolster between your thumb and index finger and swing the blade forward (B) at a slight angle, away from your palm. The knife handle should end up canted toward the other person,

with the spine resting safely between the base of your thumb and forefinger (C). As the other person takes the knife from your hand, ask, "You got it?" When the reply is "yes," gently move your hand downward.

HAND IT OFF HANDLE-FIRST Hold the knife blade with the tip pointing toward you and the edge facing away from your palm between your thumb and fingers. As the recipient grasps the handle, ask, "You got it?" Upon confirmation, gently move your hand away from the knife.

223 BRING PRACTICALLY EVERYTHING

What does it take to pack up a family of four and camp at the beach for a week? For starters, a big truck.

For several years I hauled my bride and two teenaged kids 1,000 (1,600 km) miles to Florida's Bahia Honda State Park for 6 nights of Spring Break bliss. We camped on the Keys beach in a monstrous tent, cooked pancakes for breakfast, snorkeled and fished and swam and rode bikes and took long walks and marveled in the awesome tackiness of Key West. Needless to say, we took more than a couple of roller bags. Here's a fairly complete list of what we packed–not including clothing and personal gear. It all fit into the back of a Chevrolet Silverado extended cab pickup truck outfitted with a camper shell. You ain't doing this in a sedan.

BAHIA HONDA PACKING LIST

SHELTER
7-person tent
4 sleeping bags
5 air mattresses
   (includes one spare)
Tent broom
Sheets, towels,
   blankets & pillows
Large screen house
Large tarp
Medium tarp
Paracord, 300 feet
2 box fans
30-amp converter
Drop cord

KITCHEN
2-burner stove
Backpacking stove
3 pots, various sizes
Dutch oven
French press for coffee
Mugs for 4
2 frying pans, various sizes
Plastic dinnerware for 4
Plastic tableware for 4
2 cutting boards
2 camp knives
Various spatulas, spoons, etc.
2 camp tables
Picnic table cloths and clamps
2 portable sinks
5-gallon (118-L) water jug

MISCELLANEOUS CAMPING GEAR
4 headlamps
2 battery-powered lanterns
2 backpacking-
   style hammocks
4 camp chairs
125-quart (118-l) cooler
Clothespins
Sunscreen
Bug dope
Thermacells
Backpack for hauling a day's
   worth of gear to the beach
Daypack for shorter trips
Large square of indoor-outdoor
   carpet for tent door mat
First aid kit
5-gallon (19-l) bucket

FUN STUFF
1 3-person inflatable raft
2 1-person inflatable rafts
Canoe anchor and line
Rechargeable air pump
Foot pump
2 fly rods and reels
2 spinning rods and reels
Flies and spinning tackle
Baseball gloves and ball
Board games, playing cards
Snorkel gear for 4
Camera gear and tripod
2 bicycles

OUT THERE

Beyond the Picnic Table
Spread your wings in the backcountry

Pack that Boat
Bring it all in a canoe or kayak

Face Your Fears
The real truth about bears, snakes & more

A Field Guide to Clouds

Hunker Down!
The best camping game ever

224 JUST A LITTLE FARTHER

This is the temptation of wild places: Just a little farther—over the next mountain, around the next river bend, another half-hour down the trail—awaits even greater adventure. Whether you get there by canoe or kayak, hiking boots, horse, or raft, getting off the beaten path—and gravel road—pays dividends in empty valleys, empty skies, and empty waters. Empty, of course, except for the incredible wonder that fills every square inch.

There's a logical progression at work here. Get your feet wet camping at a state park and you might strike out for a national forest next. Learn to cook on a camp stove and you might soon be ready for the open fire. Before long, you'll be thinking about a canoe-camping trip or a horseback adventure.

And the backcountry doesn't have to be halfway off the charts to hold an allure. Somewhere just beyond the campground loop is a place where you can put your gear and skills and spirit to the test. Get out there.

225 PACK A CANOE OR KAYAK

Think of canoes and kayaks as giant, 16-foot-long duffel bags with few dividers, compartments, or pockets. Packing one for a camping trip can be a mess if you don't have a plan, and a poorly packed canoe or kayak can be an unwieldy, dangerous craft. The right approach takes into account heavy gear, light stuff, gear you won't need till darkness falls, and items you'll want close at hand, such as an emergency kit, map, compass, or bug dope. Whether you plan to paddle a canoe or a kayak, here's the 4-1-1.

HOME WORK Arrange your gear in three piles. One is for stuff you won't need until you're making camp—tent, sleeping pad and bag, cooking gear, water, and most food. Another is for gear you might need while paddling, such as a fleece jacket or binoculars. The third pile is for gear you'll want within easy reach: raincoat, sunscreen, camera, VHF radio, map, compass, safety gear, and light snacks. Pack gear in multiple dry bags so it will be easy to adjust, and keep the load centered side-to-side and low in the boat.

CANOE TO-DO LIST There are two schools of thought when it comes to loading a camping canoe:

Pack everything in multiple smaller bags to make it easy to trim the boat for efficient traveling, or load up larger waterproof packs to make gear-schlepping easy. Unless you're crossing big water and need maximum paddling efficiency, opt for the latter strategy.

Divvy up the gear by function: All the food and cooking tools go into one pack. Another holds all the shelter items: tent, tarp, sleeping pads and bags, and the like. Add a personal gear bag for each paddler, and that makes for a load that can be moved around to keep the boat trim. Pack easy-to-reach items in a small bag that you tuck under or behind the seat. You'll want those close at hand so you won't have to tear the boat up looking for your lip balm.

Small coolers are handy on a canoe-camping trip. They can serve extra duty as cutting boards and camp chairs. Just be careful to either tie them tightly to a thwart or wedge them snugly in place with other gear bags. A heavy cooler that shifts around in a canoe can make the boat dangerously tippy.

'YAK ATTACK Pack gear in waterproof dry bags and think small; any bag with a diameter greater than a dinner plate likely won't fit in kayak hatches. If you don't have dry bags, pack in heavy-duty contractor bags and seal with zip ties.

Light items such as sleeping pads and bags go into the stem of the bow and stern. Heavy items such as water, food, and liquid stove fuel ride in the bottom of the boat and centered side-to-side. Moderately heavy gear—tents, cookware and stoves, and clothing—can go on top of the heavy items. Keep tent poles separate, and stuff them low in the boat between other gear bags. Large soda bottles are great for extra water. You can shove them into nooks and crannies where other gear won't fit.

Space behind the seat is perfect for the small drybag of gear you'll need on the water, plus a bilge pump and a few spare water bottles. Keep the deck free of bulky items that will throw off the boat's balance or catch the wind. Stow a spare paddle and waterproof map case under the deck bungees, but that's it.

226 STAY TRIM IN THE BOAT

The boating term "trim" refers to how much of the boat is in contact with water and how evenly weighted are the bow and stern. When loading a canoe or kayak for a multi-day trip, keep the weight low and centered in the boat. Multiple small bags allow you to "trim" the boat so it's not too heavy at either end.

In a canoe, shift the gear until a double handful of water pools just behind the center thwart. You can mop it up with a sponge or rag, but this is a great way to test a canoe's trim. For a kayak, pack the boat so it sits at level trim, which means flat in the water with the bow and stern evenly weighted. A bow-heavy boat is sluggish and difficult to turn, while the bow of a stern-heavy kayak will catch the wind. If there's a little chop on the water, it's okay to be a little bit stern heavy. That will help the boat ride up and over small waves. With gear in multiple bags, it's easy to adjust weight to keep the load centered side-to-side and low in the boat.

227 TIE A CANOE TO YOUR RACKS

To correctly tie down a canoe to a vehicle, follow the rule of twos: two tie-downs across the boat, two bow anchors, and two stern anchors.

STEP 1 Place the boat on the canoe racks upside down and centered fore and aft. Tightly cinch the boat to the racks using one cam-buckle strap per rack or ⅜-inch (10mm) climbing rope finished off with a trucker's hitch. Do not crisscross these tie-downs. It's critical to snug the tie-down straps or ropes directly against the gunwales where the straps cross under the racks.

STEP 2 Run two independent bow anchors by tying two ropes to the bow, and the end of each rope to a bumper or bumper hook. Repeat for stern anchors. Do not use the same rope or strap to create one long V-shaped anchor. Otherwise, if one end comes loose, everything comes loose. Pad these lines wherever they run across the hood or a bumper edge.

STEP 3 Test the rig by grabbing the bow and shifting hard left, right, up, and down. Do the same for the stern. You should be able to rock the entire car or truck without shifting the canoe. After 10 minutes on the road, pull over, test the rig again, and tighten if needed.

228 PLAY HUNKER DOWN

Hunker Down is tug-of-war with a twist. Instead of pulling another person or team across a line, two people square off on wobbly stands, trying to pull each other off-balance with a rope stretched between them.

SET IT UP Place the two stands about 15 feet (5m) apart and stretch the rope between them with the middle of the rope at the midpoint between the two stands. Each Hunker Down warrior stands on a ammo can, bucket, or log round facing his or her opponent, holding the rope so it extends behind them.

GAME ON The crowd calls out: "One-two-three Hunker Down!" At the final countdown each player begins tugging and jerking on the rope, letting go when the opponent tugs in order to maintain balance on the tippy stands. You fake a pull, you let the rope slide through your fingers as your opponent is pulling, you give slack at just the right moment and jerk the rope at others. There's a bunch of teetering and tottering and smack talking a-plenty. And when one person takes the Hunker Down tumble, there will be no shortage of folks clamoring to be the next player up.

229 ANCHOR A TENT IN THE SAND

It can be a challenge to anchor a tent or tarp on a beach, river sandbar, gravel bars, and other soft places where standard tent stakes won't hold. Those tent sites are often open to high winds, but their views make them prime camping spots. Here's how to firmly stake your claim so your tent doesn't sail off without you.

BARE MINIMUM Fill garbage bags or empty stuff sacks with sand, tie a knot in the opening, then tie the tent's stake loops and rainfly guylines to the bags. A few bags of sand placed along the inside tent edge will help keep it anchored.

NEXT LEVEL Bury a sand-filled bag in a 10-inch (25-cm)-deep hole, and attach guyline to the bag. Repeat around the tent. If you don't have bags, rocks or dead-man stakes can be used. To make a dead-man stake, cut a stout branch 18 inches (45cm) long, wrap the guyline around it, and bury the dead-man at an angle perpendicular to the guyline.

A STORM'S A-COMING Picket stakes boost the holding power of tent stakes; use them on the guylines attached to the side of the tent that faces the wind.

Drive the primary stake at the desired location and attach the tent guyline to it. Create a picket line by tying an overhand loop in one end of a 16-inch (40-cm) length of guyline or paracord. Attach this to the first stake by looping the running end of the picket line through the loop and cinch it tight against the stake.

Next, drive a second stake–the picket stake–into the ground 8 to 12 inches (20-30cm) from the first stake so that it is in a straight line with the guyline. Wrap the running end of the picket line around or through the picket stake twice to create a round turn, then tie off with two half hitches.

230 MAKE LANDFALL AT THE PERFECT CAMPSITE

Nothing beats a sandbar or a sandy beach on a river bend. The upstream and downstream ends of islands can often hold perfect campsites, too. They offer flat spots for tents, superb views, and plenty of room to spread out. Sparse vegetation holds down biting insects, and you're just steps away from catching a fish dinner. In many states, all land below the normal high-water mark is public, so you won't have to have landowner permission in hand. You'll need to monitor river levels, though, and have a plan in mind if the water starts to rise.

FIELD NOTES

231 KNOW YOUR POOP

Well, not *yours*, necessarily. But identifying animal poop, known as "scat," is a great way to deepen your understanding of the natural world. And few things will make kids happier than a poop scavenger hunt. Here's how to get the drop on droppings.

WHO POOPED?	POOP CLUES	WHERE TO FIND IT
WILD TURKEY	Droppings from a gobbler are elongated and measure about two inches, with a J-hook or club-like bulb on one end. Hen dropping are often looped or spiral, and more globular, shaped like popcorn.	Easiest to find on bare ground, such as dusting areas, or in scratchings where turkeys have fed.
COYOTE	Tubular with tapered ends, often with twisted fur and hair or berries	Where it can be seen by other coyotes—trail crossings, in the middle of roads and paths, and along field edges.
RACCOON	Poop can be blackish or reddish or even gray, depending on diet. Looks like dog poop but smaller, with seeds, fish scales, or bits of crayfish shell.	Often piled up in raccoon "latrines" along logs or at the bases of trees.
DEER	Dark brown oval pellets in small, scattered piles. Can be lumped together depending on diet.	Deer poop on the go, so they can be anywhere.
BEAR	Tubular poops 5 to 12 inches long. Could contain berries and grasses.	Bear don't use scat as a marker, so their poops are widely scattered.
BOBCAT	Hard, segmented, and tubular, from 3 to 5 inches long. Look for bones and hair.	Cats mark their territory with scat, so look for it in and along trails and crossings.

WILD TURKEY   COYOTE   RACOON   DEER   BEAR   BOBCAT

Even if you're not in bear country, it's a good idea to hang your food bag. I've had my grub pilfered by raccoons, opossums, mice, coyotes, and even an armadillo. Here's an easy way to keep your food to yourself.

STEP 1 Tie one end of a 40-foot (12-m) length of paracord to the drawcord of a small stuff sack. Tie a loop in the other end of the cord and clip a small carabiner to it. Fill the sack with rocks and throw it over a branch that's at least 15 feet (5m) off the ground (A). Dump the rocks from the sack.

STEP 2 Clip the carabiner to your food storage bag, as shown (B). Grasp the paracord near the small stuff sack and run it through the carabiner. Pull on this end to raise the food bag against the branch.

STEP 3 Find a sturdy twig and, reaching as high as possible, tie the twig to the cord using a clove hitch (C). Stand on a rock or cooler for additional height if possible. Slowly release the cord. The food bag will drop down until the twig catches on the carabiner to keep the food bag hanging (D).

STEP 4 When you need to retrieve your food, pull the rope down, remove the twig, and lower the bag.

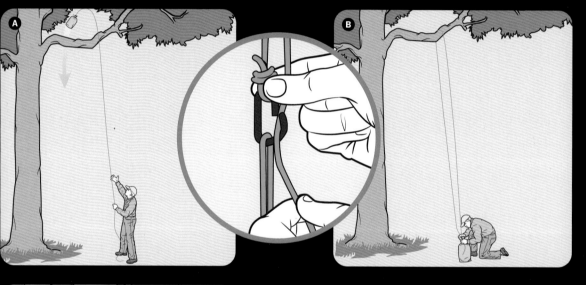

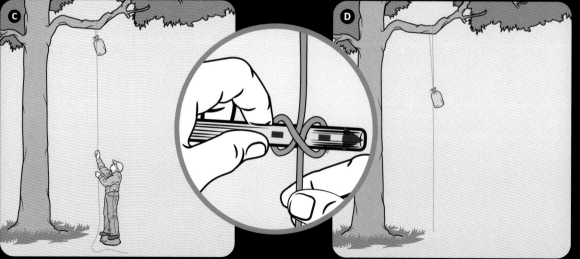

233 BE A CLOUDSPOTTER

You don't have to travel at all to check out some of the most incredible natural wonders–clouds. Cloudspotters are folks who love to learn about cloud formations, and knowing a few basic cloud types will not only enrich your time outdoors, but it might help keep your hair dry. Plus, it's a good activity for engaging the kids.

CLOUD TYPE	HOW TO ID	WHAT IT MEANS
CUMULUS	Big, puffy, cottony clouds with flat bases	Clear sailing—for now. When white cumulus clouds turn gray, grab your rain gear.
CIRRUS	Thin and wispy. Means "lock of hair" in Latin.	Cirrus clouds can't produce rain, so plan for a full day on the trail when you see them.
STRATUS	Looks like a thick blanket in the sky.	Rain or snow is coming. And it might stay awhile.
CIRRUS UNCINUS	Also called "mares' tails," these curly, hooked clouds are thin and high in the sky.	Often form when a warm front is coming. It will likely rain the next day.
CUMULONIMBUS	A cumulus cloud that grows higher and higher to crystallize into ice.	Can produce heavy rain, lighting, and hail. Get inside and tighten the tent guylines.

234 COOK WITH A FORKED STICK

Forked sticks were the original duct tape—they can be used to make snares, make repairs, and hold up a fishing pole. And they play a big role in one of the most useful of all backcountry skills: Getting a pot boiling.

TECHNIQUE A allows you to raise or lower the pot by adjusting the placement of the log.

TECHNIQUE B is used on ground that's too hard to drive in a stick.

TECHNIQUE C is for true gourmet chefs: Unhook the long stick from the short forked stick and you can easily swing the pot away from the fire.

Should you be careful and alert while in the back of beyond? Of course. Should you be frightened? Only if you believe in ghosts. Here's a short bestiary of the creatures, great and small, that cause campers the most concern—and why a little bit of common sense is the antidote to fear of the unknown.

	THREAT EVALUATION	STAY SAFE	TAKE ACTION
SPIDERS	Spiders kill about as many people in the U.S. every year as snakes. That's typically less than 10. But that might not make you feel better.	Turn boots upside down and knock them together. Zip up your tent. Avoid walking in tall grass. Wear gloves when gathering firewood.	Most bites, even from venomous spiders, aren't deadly. If you are sensitive to insect stings, however, prepare for possible anaphylaxis and get to medical help.
BEES, WASPS, AND HORNETS	Allergic reactions to these stinging hordes can be severe. About as many people die from bee, wasp, and hornet stings in the U.S. each year—the average is around 55—as are killed by lightning.	If you see just a single bee or wasp hovering over the ground, back up and circle around; it's likely you've encroached upon a ground nest of yellowjackets or hornets.	Start running with the first sting—it won't be the last. Slap at exposed skin but keep your hat on. If you are sensitive to insect stings, take an antihistamine and monitor symptoms. At the first itchy welt or swollen lip, head for the hospital.
SNAKES	Snake bites are uncommon, and thankfully, deaths are rare.	Don't blindly step over logs or climb where you can't see your hands. Avoid rockpiles and other sunny places in cool weather. And be super careful when gathering firewood.	Keep the victim calm. Keep the bite location lower than the heart, and get to a doctor. No cutting and sucking.
WOLVES	The number of wolves in North America is growing, but wolf attacks are extremely rare.	Keep dogs on a leash. When in wolf country, stay aware whenever you see a wolf or coyote. The very few instances of attacks often involve sick animals.	Don't run. Stand and defend yourself. If you're with a group and are under attack, stand together and approach the animals aggressively.
MOUNTAIN LION	Mountain lion encounters are becoming more common as more people venture into the backcountry.	Keep alert for tracks. Keep young children within sight at all times and close to you when in woods or brush.	Do not crouch or bend over. Try to make yourself appear as large as possible: Raise your pack over your head. Open your jacket wide. Start looking for a club or large rock.
BLACK BEAR	Black bears in popular camping areas can get habituated to people—and people food. Secure food and cooking gear to minimize problems.	Don't get between a bear and whatever it seems to be interested in—your cooler or food pack most likely. And sing out when traveling through dense brush.	Back away slowly and make lots of noise. If you're attacked, fight like crazy.
GRIZZLY BEAR	Grizzlies are magnificent totems of the wild, but you must prepare when camping in their habitat. Stay alert.	Make your presence known—often. Sing loudly on the trail. Study meadows carefully before crossing. Keep a clean campsite.	Hit the ground facedown with (hopefully) a pack protecting your torso. Lace fingers behind your neck and play dead for as long as you can.
CHUPACABRA	Fact: Every confirmed attack of a human by these blood-drinking, bear-like creatures with heavily spined necks has resulted in death.	Twist your garlic necklace counterclockwise three times. No garlic necklace? Uh-oh.	There is no hope.

236 SPRAY A BEAR INTO RETREAT

Bear spray stopped charging grizzlies in 92 percent of test studies and prevented injury 98 percent of the time. Those are pretty good odds, but you need to practice using bear spray before you need it. Buy two cans of inert bear spray—this stuff is harmless, and the bright colors help with learning how to aim—and spend 10 minutes working out the kinks. It's not difficult, but shaking knees and a pounding heart won't make it any easier. Here's the drill.

DRAW Practice readying the can: Slip off the safety strap, push the nozzle safety clip free, and grasp the can with two hands for accuracy. If pack straps hinder these movements, move the straps or tuck them away. Speed is of the essence. A charging bear can move at 44 feet (13.4m) per second.

AIM LOW Pace off 50 feet (50m) from a shrub, tree, or other inanimate object. Practice drawing the can and spraying a short, two-second burst, moving the can from side to side in a Z pattern. Aim slightly below the target. Bear spray will billow up from the ground into the bear's face. Aim too high and the bear could run under the spray.

STRIKE TWICE Practice discharging a second plume of spray to back up the first. Yell loudly while aiming.

GO ALL OUT Practice emptying the can to get a sense of the total load available. Most cans will spray for about nine seconds. In a true attack, your last step will be to empty the can in the bear's face.

QUICK DRAW Now repeat the drill with the second can, but imagine close-quarters combat: You're surprised by a bear so close there's no time to draw. Practice discharging the can from the hip or shoulder strap.

237 LEARN TO IDENTIFY FROST

Frosty the snowman. A frosty glass. Frost on the pumpkin. Frost is associated with happy times, but what is it, actually?

For one thing, it isn't frozen dew. Frost skips the middle step of the gas-liquid-solid cycle. Moisture in the air condenses directly from vapor to ice, and clings to surfaces that have cooled below the freezing point. There are lots of different kinds, some of which give you clues about the state of the atmosphere. Here's how to identify frost like you would animal prints.

RADIATION FROST On cold, clear nights when cooler air hovers near the ground, radiation frosts will sheathe grasses, branches, tents, picnic tables, and other objects that have cooled below the freezing point. These frosts might be a light covering of tiny ice crystals, or they could be hoarfrosts–dendritic stalks like the white beard of an old man.

WIND FROST Also called "advection frost," this forms when a cold, wet breeze blows over a cold object, such as leaf edges or tent poles. Tiny ice crystals grow like saw teeth into the oncoming wind.

FEATHER FROST OR FROST FLOWER Layered like phyllo dough, this frost looks like cotton candy, or can be shaped like a frozen, white feather. Look for it along trail edges in high mountains and on wet fallen logs where the ice is pushed out of pores in the wood.

RIME ICE Not a frost at all, rime forms when water droplets in fog freeze fast to whatever they can find, such as tree branches.

SUN CRYSTALS When a cold night follows a warm day and water evaporates from within the snowbank, sun crystals freeze on the surface. The snow will actually glisten and sparkle from a blanket of tiny crystal facets.

238 SURVIVE A CAPSIZE IN COLD WATER

Cold water kills weak swimmers, strong swimmers, the fit, and the slobs. And it kills quickly. An adult has only a 50-percent chance of surviving for 50 minutes in 50-degree (10°C) water. When you go overboard in frigid water, your first challenge is to simply survive long enough to have to worry about hypothermia. The first danger is "cold shock." Hit cold water quickly and your body involuntarily takes a few gasps of breath followed by up to three minutes of hyperventilation. You can literally drown while floating, before you even have the chance to freeze to death.

STEP 1 Keep your face out of the water. If you're on wind-blown water, turn away from the waves and spray. If you're not wearing a personal flotation device (PFD), float on your back until you catch your breath.

STEP 2 Don't panic. Cold shock passes after a minute or two. Only then can you think rationally about your next steps. Hypothermia can set in quickly, so once you have your wits, get to work.

STEP 3 The more of your body you get out of the water, the better. Crawl up on anything floating.

STEP 4 The more you flail around, the faster your body cools off. Unless you plan to swim to safety, stay still in the water.

STEP 5 Assume the H.E.L.P. (Heat Escape Lessening Posture) position. Hold your arms across your chest and firmly against your sides–basically, give yourself a bear hug–and pull your legs up toward your chest. This buffers the core areas of your chest, armpits, and groin, and will conserve as much body heat as possible.

239 PLAN YOUR NEXT TRIP NOW

The river ran 15 feet (5m) from the camp stove, and I shuttled back and forth from the water to the frying pan, swapping out a spatula for a flyrod. I could get a solid half-dozen casts in the water before I had to run back and flip the smallmouth bass fillets, sputtering in hot peanut oil. I didn't want to miss a moment of one of the best days of my outdoor life.

Before lunch we'd landed bruiser smallmouth up to four pounds (1.9kg), wading waist-deep in a back slough of the river. We ran whitewater rapids at midday, and wound up on this gravel bar, casting to rainbow trout within sight of the tent, with just an hour of daylight remaining.

Now, I sprinted from fish in the river to fish in the pan, gnawing every little piece of summer fun from what remained of the day. I wanted all the good stuff. I didn't want to leave a morsel of awesome behind.

It's been like this on nearly every camping trip I've ever taken, and my hope is that it will be like this on every camping trip to come.

Soak in every ray of light. Breathe in every whiff of pine and campfire. Milk every minute for all it's worth. And on the drive home, start planning for your next night under the stars.

ACKNOWLEDGMENTS

From the Author, T. Edward Nickens

The road between the initial phone call from Weldon Owen president Roger Shaw and this book in your hands was paved with joy and creative expression–but also significant weeping and gnashing of teeth. That's pretty typical for the process of making a book, but there's nothing typical about my relationship with Weldon Owen, the San Francisco-based publishing house. This is my sixth book published with Weldon Owen, and the second designed by the talented–and patient–crew at Waterbury Publications, and each one seems a wonder. I'm very fortunate to work with Mariah Bear and Ian Cannon as they herd words and images and ideas into the finished product. And I'm grateful for the *Field & Stream* crew, led by editor-in-chief Colin Kearns, for sending me on wild adventures. And thanks, also, to Backbone Media, Big Agnes, Camp Chef, and HEST/Greg Sweney for many of the stunning photographs in this book that capture the joy and wonder of sleeping on the ground. I'm headed back out there as soon as I finish typing this sentence.

T. EDWARD NICKENS

For more than three decades, T. Edward Nickens has reported on conservation, the outdoors, and sporting culture for the world's most respected publications. He is editor-at-large and columnist for *Field & Stream*, and a contributor to the brand's numerous media projects. He is also the author of *The Last Wild Road*, a collection of his best writing for *Field & Stream* across nearly two decades. He splits time between Raleigh and Morehead City with his wife, two dogs, a part-time cat, the occasional sightings of two grown children, 11 flyrods, 3 canoes, 2 powerboats, and an indeterminate number of tents and sleeping bags.

FIELD & STREAM

Since 1895, *Field & Stream* has brought its audience adventure stories, humor, commentary, reviews, and–above all else–outdoor skills. The tips that teach sportsmen and sportswomen how to land a big trout, the tactics that help you shoot the deer of your life, the lessons that show you how to survive a cold night outside–those are the stories that readers have come to expect from *Field & Stream*. You'll find a ton of outdoor skills in this book–but there's always more to learn. Check out Fieldandstream.com for more great outdoor content.

CREDITS

Photography

All photos courtesy of Shutterstock unless otherwise noted.

Alexander Ivanov: 136 row 1 left, 136 row 1 right, 136 row 2 left, 136 row 3 left, 136 row 3 right, 136 row 4 left, 136 row 4 right; **Bahco:** 085 Pruning saw; **Bark River Knives:** 079 Trailing Point; **Benchmade Knife Company:** 079 Spear Point; **Big Agnes/Backbone Media:** TOC page 2, 011 bottom left, 011 bottom right, 014, 015, 041 top, 048, 051, 090, 096 097, 101, 114, 126, 170; **Böker:** 079 Hawkbill; **Browning:** 069 Bird-and-Trout knife; **Bryce Robinson:** Author's Note top right; **Camp Chef:** 060, 061 right; **Colby Lysne:** Author's Note bottom right; **Council Tool:** 082 American felling ax; **Courtesy of @lawsonhammock:** 043; **Courtesy of Eureka!:** 037 left page bottom right; **Courtesy of Gorilla:** 089; **Courtesy of Grayl:** 094 Bottle filter; **Courtesy of Henkel:** 064; **Courtesy of HEST:** 054; **Courtesy of Katadyn:** 094 Pump Filter; **Courtesy of Outdoor Edge:** 069 Everyday Carry; **Courtesy of Ozark Trail:** 037 right page middle; **Courtesy of Platypus:** 094 Gravity-Fed filter; **Courtesy of Sawyer:** 094 Squeeze filter; **Courtesy of Steripen:** 094 UV Purifier; **Courtesy of T. Edward Nickens:** Author's Note bottom left; **Courtesy of The North Face:** 044 right; **Courtesy of WhiteDuck:** 037 right page bottom; **CRKT:** 069 fillet knife, 079 Wharncliffe; **Cutting Edge:** 079 Spey Point; **Estwing:** 082 Camping Hatchet; **Gerber Knives:** 079 Clip Point; **Global Cutlery USA:** 073 sharpening rod; **Grand Forest:** 082 Splitting Ax; **Industrial Revolution:** 069 Bushcraft knife; **Jim Golden Studio:** 127, 128, 129, 130, 131; **L.L. Bean:** 082 Hudson Bay Ax; **Nate Mattews:** 159; **Outdoor Edge:** 079 Drop Point; **Scott Wood:** Author's Note top left; **Seek Outside:** 037 right page top right; **SOG Specialty Knives & Tools:** 069 tactical knife, 079 Tanto; **Spyderco:** 074, 079 Leaf; **Steel Will:** 079 Straight Back; **Sven-Saw:** 085 Folding saw; **T. Edward Nickens:** TOC page 3, 011 top left, 016 bottom, 020 bottom, 029, 056, 086, 094 far right, 100, 103, 106, 107, 133, 144, 163, 171, 187, 191, 193, 195, 196, Ol' Taj, 204, 217, 218, 223, 226, 228, photo spread end of family camping, Acknowledgments; **USGS:** 122; **W.R. Case & Sons Cutlery Co:** 079 Sheepsfoot; **W.R. Case & Sons Cutlery Co.:** 069 Trapper knife; **Wabos:** 143; **Waterbury Publications:** 083)

Illustrations

Christine Meighan: 071, 072, 113; **Conor Buckley:** 077, 078, 084, 189, 220; **Dan Marsiglio:** 074, 188; **Hayden Foell:** 181; **Lauren Towner:** 104, 115, 116, 148, 152, 222; **Paul Williams:** 105; **Raymond Larette:** 040, 041, 112, 119, 232, 234; **Robert L. Prince:** 155, 158, 161, 164; **Vic Kulihin:** 145;

weldon**owen**

CEO Raoul Goff
VP Publisher Roger Shaw
Editorial Director Katie Killebrew
Associate Publisher Mariah Bear
VP Creative Chrissy Kwasnik
Art Director Allister Fein
Editor Ian Cannon
Project Editor John Taranto
VP Manufacturing Alix Nicholaeff

FIELD STREAM

2 Park Avenue
New York, NY 10016
www.fieldandstream.com

Waterbury Publications, Inc., Des Moines, IA
Creative Director Ken Carlson
Editorial Director Lisa Kingsley
Associate Design Director Doug Samuelson
Associate Editor Tricia Bergman
Associate Editor Maggie Glisan
Production Designer Mindy Samuelson
Proofreader Andrea Cooley
Indexer Mary Williams

© 2021 by Weldon Owen Inc.
P.O. Box 3088
San Rafael, CA 94912
www.weldonowen.com

ISBN 978-1-68188-749-4
Printed in China
First printed in 2021
2021 2022 2023 2024
10 9 8 7 6 5 4 3 2 1